# Conflict, Age & Power in North East Africa

# Eastern African Studies

\* forthcoming

# Conflict, Age & Power in North East Africa

## Age Systems in Transition

Edited by

**EISEI KURIMOTO &
SIMON SIMONSE**

James Currey
OXFORD

E.A.E.P.
NAIROBI

Fountain Publishers
KAMPALA

Ohio University Press
ATHENS

James Currey Ltd
73 Botley Road
Oxford OX2 0BS

East African Educational Publishing
P.O. Box 45314
Nairobi
Kenya

Ohio University Press
Scott Quadrangle
Athens
Ohio 45701, USA

Fountain Publishers
P.O. Box 488
Kampala
Uganda

**British Library Cataloguing in Publication Data**
Conflict, age & power in North East Africa : age systems in
transition. - (Eastern African studies)
  1. Age groups - Africa, Northeast  2. Political customs and
rites - Africa, Northeast  3. Age-structured populations -
Political aspects - Africa, Northeast
  I. Kurimoto, Eisei  II. Simonse, Simon
305.2'0961

ISBN    0-85255-252-1 (cased)
        0-85255-251-3 (paper)

**Library of Congress Cataloging-in-Publication Data available**
ISBN    0-8214-1240-x (cased)
        0-8214-1241-8 (paper)

Typeset in 10/12 pt Baskerville by
Long House, Cumbria, UK
Printed and bound in Great Britain
by Villiers Publications, London N4

# Contents

# Contents

# List of Maps

# List of Figures

# List of Tables

# List of Photographs

# Preface

The studies included in this volume were initially presented to the symposium on 'East African Age Systems in Transition: Contemporary Political and Military Contexts', held at the National Museum of Ethnology, in Osaka, 28 November–3 December 1995. It was sponsored by the Taniguchi Foundation and organized by the Senri Foundation and the National Museum of Ethnology. This was the nineteenth symposium under the same organizational framework. Two symposia in the past covered the same region, and topics related to this one. Both of them were convened by Katsuyoshi Fukui and the results were published, the first edited by Fukui and David Turton (*Warfare among East African Herders*, 1979) and the second edited by Fukui and John Markakis (*Ethnicity and Conflict in the Horn of Africa*, 1994).

The idea for this sort of symposium on North East African age systems originated in the early 1980s when Simon Simonse and I were both engaged in fieldwork in south-eastern Sudan based at the University of Juba. We were working among different but neighbouring ethnic groups, which share similar systems of graded age-sets: *monyomiji* systems. They seemed to us to be vital and central political institutions among those societies, and we soon observed that they were also playing a significant role in the present civil war in the Sudan. It brought to our attention that there was a need to evaluate and re-evaluate the *monyomiji* systems in a broader regional perspective. In 1986 we were forced to evacuate Juba, as the civil war was escalating, and our research had to be discontinued.

Simonse spent a year at the National Museum of Ethnology between 1992 and 1993 as visiting professor and this was the time when our joint interest in age-systems re-emerged. We discussed plans to hold an international symposium, and it finally took place in 1995.

When the idea of the symposium was proposed, some of my colleagues were rather surprised. For them East African age systems are already a settled case; they are an old-fashioned topic far from 'post-modern' matters. I had a totally different idea, of course, and during the symposium Simonse and I, as well as other participants, became firmly convinced that age systems are still a theme worth studying. Age systems are not dead, and indeed there are a number of fields, both ethnographic and theoretical, to be investigated and reinvestigated. Most importantly, age systems are still meaningful and relevant to the lives of many people in North East Africa. We hope that the readers of this volume will share our view.

Twelve scholars participated in the symposium and presented papers: six from Japan and six from abroad. Apart from John Lamphear, who is a historian, all of us were anthropologists. Katsuyoshi Fukui and Sharon Hutchinson were unfortunately unable to contribute to this volume, but all the rest have papers here. Half the contributions are by Japanese scholars. Together, with the fact that it was hosted in Osaka, the symposium testifies, in our view, to the growing academic interest in African studies in Japan. As Japanese scholars usually write in Japanese, we hope that this book will make part of the achievements in African studies in Japan accessible to a wider community of students and scholars.

The symposium and the publication of this volume became possible thanks to various sources of support and assistance. We would like to express our gratitude for the generous support of the Taniguchi Foundation. The staff of the National Museum of Ethnology and the Senri Foundation made tireless efforts to make the symposium possible and successful. We are grateful to, among others, Dr Komei Sasaki, then Director General of the Museum, and Dr Tadao Umesao, President of the Senri Foundation. Ms Yuko Matsumoto and Mr Tomoaki Hirakawa offered assistance with secretarial duties. We are also grateful to Dr Douglas H. Johnson, Editorial Director of James Currey Publishers, for his cooperation, and to Mrs Margaret Cornell who performed the work of copyediting.

Finally, we would like to express our appreciation of the Grant-in-Aid for Publication of Scientific Research Results of the Ministry of Education, Science, Sports and Culture of Japan.

*Eisei Kurimoto*
*Osaka*
*September 1997*

# Notes on Contributors

**Kaori Kawai** is associate professor at the Faculty of Humanities and Social Sciences, Shizuoka University. She has been conducting field research on ethno-medicine, sexuality and family among the Chamus.

**Toru Komma** is professor of cultural anthropology at Kanagawa University. He has carried out research among the Kipsigis and Tiriki and published numerous articles on the subject. His publications also include studies on Japanese folklore and rural society.

**Eisei Kurimoto** is associate professor at the National Museum of Ethnology, Osaka. He is a social anthropologist and has conducted research among the Pari in South Sudan and the Anuak in western Ethiopia. He has published *People Living through Ethnic Conflict* (in Japanese, 1996) and co-edited *Essays on Northeast African Studies* (1996).

**John Lamphear** is professor in the Department of History, University of Texas at Austin. He has carried out research on the history of the Jie and Turkana, and has numerous publications on this subject, including *The Traditional History of the Jie of Uganda* (1976) and *The Scattering Time: Turkana Responses to Colonial Rule* (1992).

**Nobuhiro Nagashima** is professor of social anthropology at the Faculty of Social Sciences, Hitotsubashi University. He started fieldwork among the Ugandan Iteso in 1968, and then among the Kenyan Iteso in 1977. He has published two ethnographies, *The Teso* (in Japanese, 1972) and *The Ethnography of Death and Sickness: The Ideology of Misfortunes among the Kenyan Iteso* (in Japanese, 1987) and a number of articles on the Iteso as well as on social anthropology and African studies.

**Shun Sato** is professor at the Department of History and Anthropology of Tsukuba University. He is an ecological anthropologist who has been conducting fieldwork on the Rendille since 1975. His publications include *The Rendille: Camel Pastoralists in Northern Kenya* (in Japanese, 1992), *Essays on Northeast African Studies* (co-edited with E. Kurimoto, 1996) and numerous articles on the Rendille and East African pastoralism.

**Günther Schlee** is professor of social anthropology at the University of Bielefeld. He has carried out research on various Cushitic peoples both in northern Kenya and southern Ethiopia and is the author of *Identities on the Move* (1989) and many articles.

**Simon Simonse** is professor of anthropology at the École Polytechnique in Paris and a research fellow attached to the Institute of Cultural and Social Studies at the University of Leiden. He has carried out research on the political structure and violence among various peoples in southeastern Sudan and is the author of *Kings of Disaster* (1992).

**Paul Spencer** is professor emeritus at the School of Oriental and African Studies, London University. He has done research on the Samburu and Maasai, and is the author of *The Samburu* (1965), *Nomads in Alliance* (1973), *The Maasai of Malapalo* (1988), and the editor of *Society and the Dance* (1985) and *Anthropology and the Riddle of the Sphinx* (1990), a volume on aging and life courses. He is currently working on *Models of the Maasai*.

**Serge Tornay** is professor at the Musée de l'Homme. He has carried out research on the Nyangatom in southwestern Ethiopia and has published a number of articles on social organization and warfare among them.

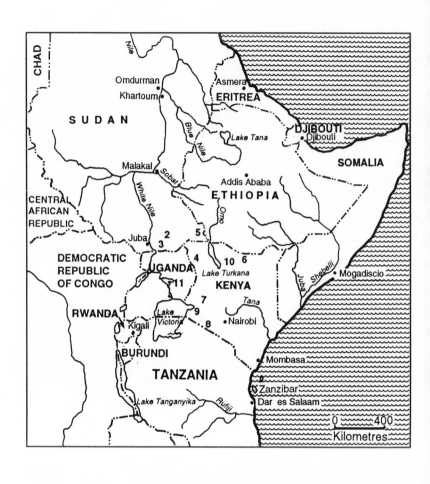

*Map 1 North East Africa*

# 1 Introduction

## SIMON SIMONSE & EISEI KURIMOTO

North East African age systems[1] have been the object of a variety of anthropological approaches. The first Western observers, impressed by the martial flamboyancy of the classes of young men, especially among groups such as the Maasai, generally understood the age systems as military organizations. Sets, in their view, corresponded to 'regiments', operational units of warfare, and age-grades to a hierarchy of command. The *moran* has become a classical image of a certain type of African, celebrated by travelogues and films, and exploited by the tourist industry.

By the middle of this century, with more detailed and scholarly ethnographic descriptions available, the exclusively military role of age-sets was put in doubt. Evans-Pritchard's observation, in 1936, that the Nuer age-sets did not play a military or political role of importance opened a whole range of new questions. If age-sets are irrelevant for defence and war, what are they good for? In the functionalist climate of the 1930s Evans-Pritchard's predictable answer was that they contributed to the integration of society by providing its male members with an identity and a structure of authority that cut across allegiances based on kinship (Evans-Pritchard, 1936: 254; 1940a: 260). Indeed, this point has been taken for granted by later anthropologists.

This integrative role of age-sets is ambiguous, however. In Evans-Pritchard's *The Nuer*, the chapter on the age-set system makes up the last part and is very short compared with the other chapters. It gives an impression to the reader that, unlike the political and lineage systems, the age-set system is not fundamental but something odd and supplementary to Nuer society. Evans-Pritchard himself argues that the former two systems and the latter are 'consistent', but not 'interdependent' (1940a: 257, 260). The integrative role is therefore not so important as in the case of political and lineage systems. Moreover, at the time of Evans-Pritchard's fieldwork the Nuer age-set system had already undergone 'rapid and great modification under European rule', while other systems had not (1940a: 257). The uneasiness and ambiguity in Evans-Pritchard's treatment of Nuer age-sets has certainly had an effect on studies of North East African age systems.

On the other hand, Evans-Pritchard leaves us with a significant question unanswered, namely, 'why does age become stratified into formal sets?' (1936: 268). Indeed, a system of age-grades without age-sets and with individual recruitment would have sufficed to create these unifying identities. And the Nuer do not have such a system of age-grades. One of the aims of this book is to offer an answer to Evans-Pritchard's question. In fact, in his 1940 book on the Nuer, Evans-Pritchard provides an important lead to finding an answer, a lead he did not exploit himself. He points to the structural homology between the lineage and the age-set systems:

> Likewise [to the segmentary lineage system] the institution based on age is highly segmentary, being stratified into sets which are opposed groups, and these sets are further stratified into successive sections (1940a: 255).

Evans-Pritchard's observation concerning the non-military and frequently non-political nature of age systems was soon endorsed by a number of other anthropologists working in Eastern Africa. Peristiany showed that the age-sets of the pastoral Pokot played only a marginal role in the conduct of war, the defence of the country being assured 'on the principle of the nation armée' (1951: 282). Only specifically prestigious military roles were reserved to full initiates. Gulliver in his description of the generation and age-set organization of the Jie went a step further, emphasizing the essentially ritual role of the age system and adding that the 'age organization had no significant connection with war-making and raiding' (1953: 167). He added that the powers derived from elderhood in the age system had no political consequences, nor did they offer any economic advantages. In the wake of Evans-Pritchard, Gulliver under-lined the 'vital integrative factor' of the system (1953: 165).

In fact, it was by building on these observations that significant theoretical progress was made in the field of studying age systems. Two books with contributions from various authors mark this progress. In *Age, Generation, and Time* (1978), edited by Paul Baxter and Uri Almagor, age systems are systematically analyzed as ideological formations, or as institutions to 'create cognitive and structural order', which regulate demography and long-term social stability (Baxter and Almagor, 1978: 5). *Age, pouvoir et société* (1985) by Marc Abélès and Chantal Collard can be seen as a French echo of the former book. While Baxter and Almagor emphasize the ideological potential of age-sets and generation-sets, the contributors to the latter book widen the scope by putting more emphasis on relations of seniority/juniority in the kinship system.

## Age Systems as the Arena for Political Drama

Both *Age, Generation and Time* and *Age, pouvoir et société*, in principle, argue for the non-military and non-political nature of age systems and regard their function as essentially ritual. One of the points the present book wants to make is that this is not the case, for two reasons. First, in many societies age systems do function as military and political organizations. In his introduction to Peristiany's study of the Kipsigis Evans-Pritchard himself fully endorses Peristiany's view of the age system as the agent of military and political action in Kipsigis society (1939). Besides, other studies have continued to appear in which age systems are shown to function as military organizations and systems of distribution of power as discussed below.[2] Secondly, in our view, it is difficult, and sometimes misleading, to draw a clear line between ritual and political (including military) spheres, especially where violence or antagonism is concerned, as demonstrated by Spencer in his study of the 'rituals of rebellion' among the Maasai of Matapato (Spencer, 1988). For instance, 'mock-fights' with sticks between age-sets and between a retiring and a new ruling age-grade, which are widely found among societies with age systems, are indeed a form of 'ritualized' violence. At the same time they are also occasions in which normally latent or implicit political rivalry is openly expressed, sometimes resulting in less ritualized and more politicized confrontation (e.g. Kurimoto, 1995a).[3] The *gada* systems among the Oromo, which have by far the most elaborate and intricate rituals (Legesse, 1973), offer us another significant case. Baxter and Almagor regard the function of *gada* as primarily ritual (Baxter and Almagor, 1978: 18; Baxter, 1979: 152–3). On the other hand, Legesse (1973) emphasised political function and other scholars have recently affirmed his point (e.g. Bassi, 1996).[4] In this volume, therefore, we shall try to take account of the political significance of age-system rituals by focusing on the antagonistic relations between various social actors – seniors and juniors, men and women, territorial units within an ethnic group, and ethnic groups.

Another question we would like to raise in this book is the appropriateness of the 'ethnic group' or 'society' as the unit of analysis in the study of North East African age systems. Age systems in this part of Africa have fascinated many anthropologists because of their enormous variety of forms, regulations, and structures, and because of their wide distribution across linguistic and ethnic boundaries. Naturally, it has been tempting to make systematic comparisons of these systems: general classification based on models (Prins, 1953; Eisenstadt, 1956; Stewart, 1977; Bernardi, 1985);

mathematical models to solve the 'generation paradox' – the issue of under-aging and over-aging (Spencer, 1978); typologies of demographic and adaptive strategies (Sato, 1984a and 1988; Peatrik, 1995). Those comparative studies are certainly useful and have deepened our understanding with regard to age systems. On the other hand, they are prone, and the general ones in particular, to be caught in pitfalls, just as comparative studies on kinship systems are. Here, two major problems can be discerned. One is, as argued by Leach many years ago, that they may be reduced to mere 'butterfly collection' (Leach, 1961). The other problem is, as argued by Schlee in this volume, that those comparative studies are based on the assumption that each age system is consistent and independent, being an integral part of a larger system, 'society' or 'ethnic group'.

In this book we shall try to take account of age systems at the 'meta-ethnic' level, setting them in regional and historical contexts. We find that North East African age systems are an essentially inter-societal phenomenon. They are instrumental not only in binding different kinship groups, village communities, and territorial sections of a region, but also in bringing together different ethnic groups as meaningful units of interaction, both antagonistic and peaceful. What this proposition tells us is that the 'cultural boundaries' of age systems are beyond those of individual societies or ethnic groups. This point seems to be obvious if we consider the fact that similar age systems are found in a region among different linguistic and ethnic groups. The point has never been fully explored, however, presumably because of the premise that the appropriate unit of anthropological/ ethnographic studies should be a 'society' or 'ethnic group'.

Our approach is partly inspired by *Identities on the Move*, Günther Schlee's pioneering work (1989) on the significance of clans at the meta-ethnic level among Cushitic-speaking peoples in the Ethiopian-Kenya borderlands. In this book Schlee demonstrates the relevance of this approach, not for clans this time, but for age systems. A recent study by Ichiro Majima on the '*Poro* cluster' in West Africa (1997) is highly suggestive and in line with this argument. Just like age systems in North East Africa, *Poro* secret societies are widely found among various Mande and related ethnic groups in the 'Central West Atlantic Region' of West Africa. On the one hand, these secret societies show a considerable variation in structure and function; on the other, they have wider membership and networks across ethnic boundaries. Like us, Majima has adopted a regional and historical approach, although he is more oriented to the reconstruction of cultural history. His study also makes us aware of the important fact that two institutions, which have been given quite different labels by anthropologists, i.e. age systems and secret societies, have more in common than one might presume. *Poro* societies have politico-judicial power, an

4

initiation ceremony including circumcision, songs and dances, a seniority order, and grades. There are female societies called *Sande* (like female age-sets), and notably some *Poro* societies played a significant role in the early resistance against colonial rule (Majima, 1997: 9–15).

The 'meta-ethnic' approach within regional and historical contexts is, we believe, a means of widening and deepening the scope of empirical ethnographic studies. What is required first, in order to achieve this, is to define the actual regional and historical contexts, appropriately and manageably, that we are dealing with. We propose to set up some regional 'arenas' in which age systems interact. In terms of time depth, we do not go back to a remote past, but restrict our discussion to the nineteenth century onwards, because that is the period when the entire region has shared social turmoils and changes – migration, epidemics, famine, advent of colonial powers, encroachment of state administration and the market economy, etc. – which have transformed age systems as well as societies. These arenas, as discussed below, are also relevant in analyzing politico-military relations within and between age systems.

An arena can be defined by a degree of shared respect for rules which prevent an all-out escalation of violence, by a shared age system, and by maintaining a number of shifting and mutually opposed but internally cohesive communal identities. Enemies are categorized according to the shared assumptions concerning the degree of violence that may be used in their mutual confrontations. On the basis of a shared understanding of these systems of categorization, the following arenas can be demarcated (Map 1, p. xiv). Our list is provisional and only covers the arenas the contributors to this volume are dealing with.[5] The contributions are arranged geographically according to these arenas.

Going from the northwest to the southeast we begin with the arena formed by the *monyomiji* systems, in the west almost touching on the Nile and stretching to the Kidepo river in the east (Map 2, p. 30). The politico-military units are normally large villages whose defence is in the hands of the *monyomiji*, the ruling generation. The core of this arena is formed by the Lotuho (Eastern Nilotic) speaking peoples but also includes Madi (Sudanic), Lwo (Western Nilotic) and Surma speakers. The contributions of Kurimoto and Simonse in this volume deal with this arena.

To the east of the Kidepo begins the vast arena of generational systems of the Karimojong type, the core being formed by speakers of the Karimojong (or 'Ateker' of the Eastern Nilotic) languages but also including Surma speakers such as the Didinga, the Narim and the Koegu (Kwegu), the Lwo-speaking Labwor, the Kuliak-speaking So, the Omotic-speaking Kara, and the Southern Nilotic Pokot. *Asapan* is a term used all over the area, in some dialects meaning initiation, in others referring to the transfer of power from the generation of fathers to that of sons. This *asapan* arena stretches from the Boma plateau in the north to the Pokot of the Kenya-Uganda border in the southeast, from the Iteso in the southwest to the Kara and Koegu in the northeast (Map 3, p. 80). The contributions of John Lamphear and Serge Tornay relate to this arena. The people of the *asapan* and *monyomiji* zones do not practise circumcision. Sacrifices of cattle by sons to their fathers play a pivotal role in the transfer of power, a circumstance that has led Abrahams to suggest that the two practices were substitutes for one another (Abrahams, 1978:46–47).

East and northeast of Lake Turkana, stretching into Ethiopia, lies '*das Land der Gada*'. Schlee's contribution studies the mode of inclusion of several peoples of Somaloid origin in this zone (Map 4, p. 122). South of the land of the *gada* lies the vast arena, stretching all the way into Tanzania, where varieties of the Samburu-Maasai (Maa speakers of Eastern Nilotic) graded age-set systems hold sway, dealt with in this volume by the contributions of Kaori Kawai and Paul Spencer (Map 5, p. 148).

The age systems of the Kalenjin peoples occupied a zone between the *asapan* zone to the north and the Maasai arena to the east and include speakers of Southern Nilotic languages as well as Bantu (Tiriki, the extinct system of the Bukusu) (Map 5). Toru Komma's contribution on historical changes undergone by the Kipsigis age systems deals with this area. Circumcision is an integral part of age systems of the *gada*, Maasai, and Kalenjin types.

Where different arenas border on one another, we find societies that are tuned to deal with different types of enemy age systems. This is the case with the Rendille, dealt with by Shun Sato in this volume, who have external relations with peoples of the *gada* and Maasai zones. The pastoral Pokot appear to adopt a similar position between the age systems of the Kalenjin peoples and those of the *asapan* group (Peristiany, 1951:188). Another marginal case is the Teso of Uganda, who are located in the periphery of the *asapan* arena bordering on the Kalenjin and Maa speakers' zones. The contribution by Nobuhiro Nagashima deals with the Teso.

An arena is the stage for political drama. In most studies of age systems the political is narrowly understood as 'a particular distribution of power': a more or less coherent, hierarchical, set of roles, dealing with the coordination of social action, usually, but not always, involving an actor, collective or individual, who has the capacity to act on behalf of the political unit as a whole (e.g. Bernardi, 1952: 331). Our primary focus, however, is not on the distribution of power, but on its enactment in situations where power differentials are established or where power is put to the test. Power ultimately, before being 'distributed', or parcelled out in a generally accepted way, always goes back to a situation of contest, of rivalry. Age systems, in the perspective pursued here, are as much arenas for power games as they are a mechanism for dealing with corporate tasks or a ceremonial facade for gerontocratic power. The oppositional dynamism embedded in age systems is widespread, as we shall argue. With few exceptions, it has been viewed as a side-effect in the analysis of age systems. In our field experience of age systems, the oppositional dynamic of age-based power relations is as fundamental as their distributional dimension.

While looking for antecedents to define our perspective, we found that our emphasis on antagonism, as opposed to a distributional, hierarchical perspective on power relations, largely reflects the distinction made by Gregory Bateson between symmetrical and asymmetrical or complementary interactions (1958: 171–97). In Bateson's terms, one could say that the study of age systems has favoured the asymmetrical structures to the detriment of the symmetrical dimension.

In the remainder of this introduction we shall first elaborate on the conceptual foundation of our approach, drawing inspiration from another, more recent, study of a Melanesian society. This will be followed by a presentation of the various contributions to the book. These have been grouped according to the principal actors in the power contest staged in the arena defined by the age systems: (i) the role of the age system in relations between societies or ethnic groups; (ii) the antagonism between generation-sets and age-sets; (iii) women's age-sets and gender antagonism; (iv) the role of age and generation systems in impeding or promoting political and social change.

## Sepik Model and its Relevance to North East Africa

Our Batesonian assumption is that, in principle, in all more or less stable relations there are two mechanisms at work: one generating increasing symmetry, the other tending to create cumulative asymmetry. In symmetrical interactions the partners to the interaction imitate one another's behaviour. If sustained, such interaction culminates in unresolvable conflict or in intolerable closeness. In asymmetrical interactions both partners seek accommodation: if one party leads, the other allows himself to be led; if one wants to show off, the other lets himself be impressed, etc. A relationship in which asymmetry prevails will be predominantly complementary with regard to the roles played by the partners. Too much complementarity, however, imposes increasing restrictions on the spontaneous initiatives and response, and will be experienced as oppressive. If the asymmetry in one sphere of interaction is not balanced by symmetry in another, the oppression will spark resistance.

Bateson's treatment of these concepts in his analysis of the *Naven* ceremony of the Iatmul of the Sepik river valley in New Guinea has rightly become classical. Yet few anthropologists have introduced Bateson's analysis to their own field material. Bateson's distinction allows us to make a distinction between power as a dimension of a scenario based on complementarity between social actors and power as the stake in a contest between social actors. In the first case we are speaking of a hierarchy based on age, distribution of power according to age-grade, the allocation of tasks on the basis of age-grade membership. In the second case we are dealing not only with confrontations between senior and junior sets, the struggle for promotion to the next senior age-grade, but also with the attempts of the elders to keep the juniors down by bullying, haranguing, or scheming.

To get a more concrete idea of the implications of symmetrical political interactions, as opposed to arrangements based on complementarity, we leave Bateson's Iatmul, and follow the Sepik river upstream till we reach the Manabu people of Avatip, traditional enemies of the Iatmul. The anthropologist Simon Harrison conducted a study on warfare among this group. In *The Masks of War* he argues that political action in Melanesia in general was not concerned 'with the maintenance of peace and order, but, much more basically, with the generation of specific kinds of conflicts and divisions' (1993: 25), nor 'with creating bridges between groups conceived as pre-existing entities, but with constituting political groups through opposing them antagonistically to one another'. Hence 'groups bring themselves into existence in counterpoised pairs by constructing an opposition between them' (1993:17).

In Harrison's analysis groups are created by engaging in conflict and not as the result of processes of networking between existing descent groups. Unity and community are created by confrontations with enemies. Clans in Avatip do not form clearly bounded units, they are rather anchoring points in a network of exchange and marriage. The conflicts between village communities are at right angles with the solidarities and complementarities established by clanship and affinity. Community is established, not by adding a cross-cutting identification to potentially hostile groups, but by aggressively imposing a fusion of identity and interests by carrying out attacks that cut across and negate the routine loyalties based on descent and exchange.

Along the Sepik river the agent promoting this massive sense of communal identity was the 'men's cult'. The men's cult was the organization responsible for warfare, and identified with the assertion of the values of community over those of clanship. Political action coincided with the provocation of conflicts that generated and regenerated this sense of community. The conflictual symmetry in relations with the outside was mirrored by a conflictual symmetry inside the men's cult. In fact, the men's cult was organized on the basis of age-grades. Relations between age-grades were marked by the same aggressive symmetry: stick-fights, arbitrary bullying of junior grades by the senior ones, mock-raids, frequently leading to serious injuries (1993: 81).

Harrison's analysis contains various lessons. It clearly demonstrates the irrelevance of functionalist explanations of war that necessarily favour defence rather than aggression and the maintenance of the cosmic and social order rather than wanton destruction. In most ethnographic studies, the enemy belongs to a society different from the one studied by the anthropologist. Harrison's approach allows us to study aggression, attacks and predatory expansionism as an integral part of the reality of war, and not as a side-effect of the search for security. Harrison shows that the Avatip waged war with utter disregard for existing peaceful ties. And yet, war also served the construction of community:

> The Melanesian men's cults were not simply cultural responses to a violent world, but attempts, specifically by men, to prescribe such a world whether or not it actually existed at the level of behaviour. The cults were not simply functional adaptations to war but were male organisations for 'producing' war and for producing the bounded groups to wage it (1993: 149).

The role of war in the construction of communities is Harrison's second lesson. He is open to the powerful consensual effects of violent confrontation, an aspect largely overlooked in Bateson's *Naven*. Communities along the Sepik are maintained as bounded units by a dynamic of 'collusion in conflict'. By opposing one another they continue to exist as discreet units. Elsewhere we have called this mechanism 'consensual antagonism' (Simonse, 1993). The third lesson is the view that war is not necessarily an interaction between strangers as members of industrial societies might assume. Harrison's study shows that enemies have a close knowledge of one another and, when they are not at war, engage in a variety of friendly exchanges. It presents us with a new image of enemies, very different from that in common understanding. Enemies are not something to be totally alienated, negated or destroyed. In the concluding part of the book he argues:

> They fought and fostered war in their cult, not because they lacked normative ties beyond the village but, quite the opposite, precisely because they had such ties and could only define themselves as a polity by acting collectively to overcome and transcend them (1993:150).

We believe that all three lessons are relevant to our study of North East African age systems, in particular to the two major emphases in this volume discussed above: the political aspect of rituals and the 'meta-ethnic' approach. The applicability of Harrison's model of warfare to the East African situation was first perceived by David Turton in an analysis of the motivation for warfare among the Mursi. According to Turton, war between the Mursi and their 'closest enemies' always implied an abrupt and violent denial of the existing normative ties. As with the Avatip, the world of peaceful exchange is the normal situation, while war is about the cultural construction of communal identities. The model is also applicable to intra-societal antagonism: stick-fights ('ceremonial duelling' in Turton's words) between territorial segments of the Mursi (Turton, 1993: 174–7).

Harrison's most profound contribution, which is insightful not only for Melanesian or North East African contexts, but also for the study of human society in general, seems above all to be that his study of the Avatip may free us from the premise that warfare, or violent relations resulting from antagonism, is an abnormal and vicious situation to be got rid of. This is a deeply rooted ethical view, partly based on the Hobbesian notion of human nature, and partly on universal humanism, both Occidental and Oriental, and has overshadowed academic studies of war and aggression (Harrison, 1993: chap.1; Kurimoto, 1997). In our view, the standpoint of regarding the antagonistic relations embedded in age systems as primarily ritualized ones is also overshadowed. However, as Harrison has argued, and we shall argue in this volume, war and antagonistic relations are sometimes constructive and creative. We do not, needless to say, admire violence. But it is true that we should be free from the above premise, at least for the time being, in order to study war and violent relations.

In this volume we may try to go a little further than the point that Harrison has reached. In North East Africa, significantly, among societies of the same arena, and within a single society, both antagonistic and peaceful relations do co-exist at the same time, or rotate in accordance with the age-system cycle. Therefore, 'normative ties' are not something to 'overcome and transcend', as is the case in Avatip. In our case, these normative ties refer to the shared age system, and we take into consideration both of the opposite relations – antagonistic and peaceful – although more emphasis is put on antagonism. In other words, we shall argue that symmetrical and asymmetrical relations can be compatible, and, if not, conditions leading to incompatiblity will be analyzed.

It is striking that, whereas in North East African age systems it is the hierarchical, complementary aspect that has above all retained the attention of anthropological observers, in Melanesian societies, at least in the material presented here, the oppositional structure of men's organizations has apparently made the greatest impact. This raises the question whether this reflects a relatively greater preponderance of symmetrical interaction in the Melanesian social systems as compared with the East African ones.

## Inter-societal Antagonism

One of the central themes of this volume is that, like the men's cults of the Sepik river, the East African age systems provide the framework for generating communal identities from enmity and belligerence. Ethnicity, as one of the more embracing identities, is shaped in confrontations which take place on a stage prepared by the interlocking age systems of the groups concerned. While the possibility of violence is a premise of these confrontations, this does not imply that the age system is a specialized military organization. In the societies we are dealing with warfare is not (yet) a specialized social activity, though – as Lamphear shows in his contribution – little was needed to effectuate a change in that direction. The early observers who equated the age systems with a military organization were, before anything else, guilty of anachronism.

The age-organization is part of the institutionalization of the confrontational scenario between enemies. The ordered confrontations allow the different segments of the system to promote, define or redefine, and publish their identity. Confrontations may be violent, ritual (curses) or theatrical (mock-battles). Where the age-sets do not operate militarily, the age system will normally be an important ethnic marker and will function as an ideological, if not the political, springboard for launching and repelling attacks. As in the segmentary lineage system the age system provides the different sections of the community with a pre-established course of action in case of an attack, according to the structural position of the aggressor.

Because of an implicit recognition of the dual nature of warfare – promoting identity and reinforcing internal unity by organizing violence towards outsiders – historians have spoken of 'ritual battle' in opposition to 'true warfare'. Of 'true warfare' one can only speak after a well-defined evolutionary threshold has been passed (Keegan, 1993: 98, 100). The distinction – on which Lamphear will elaborate in this volume – coincides with a functional differentiation between warfare as an instrumental activity and warfare as a socially unifying and edifying activity.

In our view the distinction is acceptable on two conditions, which we believe those who forged the notion did not always have clearly in mind. One should, first of all, avoid the suggestion, implicit in this notion of 'ritual warfare', that contemporary, 'total' warfare is devoid of ritual or sacrificial meaning. Secondly, one should refrain from considering the instrumentalization of warfare as a unequivocal sign of social progress. Bringing a war to a ritually acceptable end, containing its potential of violent escalation, is, from a social perspective, an achievement rather than a sign of evolutionary primitiveness. There are no indications that would justify the assumption that societies at a lower level of technology are more inhibited about killing their fellow human beings than we are. If numbers of casualties remain low, it is the result of the successful application of cultural devices. Normally, these only work between societies sharing the same military organization, between partners who share the same regional war-culture. Between societies with different military organizations, a balance of power in the battlefield would be more difficult to achieve. The weaker party is bound to suffer repeated defeat and become marginalized, extinct, or, alternatively, may adopt the military organization of the enemy.

The North East African region offers various examples of such militarily marginalized peoples: the Okiek (Ndorobo) of central Kenya, the Kuliak speakers of Northeastern Uganda, the Sonjo among the Maasai (Jacobs, 1979: 48–49; Gray, 1963), the Koegu (Kwegu) of southwestern Ethiopia (Matsuda, 1994), etc. One of such peoples, the So, has adopted the Karimojong age system (Laughlin and Laughlin, 1974). It is interesting to observe that the relationships of these weaker groups – symmetrically speaking – with the peoples surrounding them tend to be compensated by a complementary relationship. The Kuliak speakers, for example, are being attributed with special powers over rain by the surrounding Karimojong speakers, the Ndorobo provide the circumcision specialist for the Kisongo Maasai (Jacobs, 1965:287).

Military confrontations between enemies are timed in relation to the ceremonies of initiation and transfer of power. Most societies expect their newly initiated to prove their bravery in a raid on the enemy – whichever groups may be selected for the purpose. In the *gada* area, generation-sets circumcised at the same time into the *raaba* grade were expected to bring home the genitals of the enemies they had slain, as trophies. While, among the Boran nowadays, the generation-sets (*luba*) fulfill a largely ritual role, the newly formed age-sets (*hariya*) are still under the customary obligation to prove themselves on the battlefield, though the practice has now been forbidden (Baxter, 1977:84–89). Among the *monyomiji* societies the periods preceding and following the ceremony in which power was transferred from the senior to a junior generation, were the occasion for heightened confrontational activity. The military feats of the junior sets were taken as proof of their competence to take over from the rulers. Among most peoples initiation was the sign for a show of bravery in the face of the enemy. Spencer discusses the raids of the Maasai *moran* after the *eunoto* ceremony, which were held to establish the reputation of the set. Even among the societies where the generation-set system had largely become a ritual affair, as among the Boran, the same scenario prevailed – although the elders did not agree (Baxter, 1979: 93).

Four of the contributions to this volume explore the role of age systems in interethnic relations. Schlee analyses the traditions that account for the adoption of the Boran *gada* system by the Gabbra and Garre, both groups of proto-Rendille-Somali origin. The adoption is characterized as an imitation with a difference. The Gabbra and Garre emulated the Boran system in order to be able to compete better with the Boran, but, at the same time, they introduced their own set of succession rules independent of those of the Boran, thereby underlining their separate identity. A similar ambivalence is observed in the attitude of the Gabbra to the Boran during the Gabbra promotion ceremonies. On the one hand, the Boran are chased away from the water-holes around the Gabbra temporary ceremonial capital, but on the other hand, they are allowed to exercise a measure of control over the Gabbra promotions. They, and only they, have the privilege of providing the sacrificial animal that launches the series of *gada* rituals. Boran and Gabbra identities are reproduced in inter-actions that alternate between symmetrical and complementary sequences. It would appear that both are a necessary part in an inter-ethnic scenario that underpins the continued separateness of the identity of the Gabbra.

Kurimoto examines the interrelations between the age systems of different ethnic groups in the *monyomiji* area. On the one hand, the age-set systems in the area are described as symmetrically opposed units in an arena consisting of multiple levels of more or less controlled confrontation (dance, sports, stick-fights, war); on the other hand, the age systems in the *monyomiji* area appear as a single hierarchical system with a shared code of con-viviality, cutting across territorial and ethnic segmentation, and facilitating cooperation in trade and hunting between culturally diverse people.

Within the *monyomiji* arena several sub-arenas can be distinguished, each with its own rhythm and rules of generational succession. The *monyomiji* systems seem to have expanded in a process in which culturally different communities (Lulubo, Pari, Bari groups, Tenet), bordering on the *monyomiji* zone, inserted themselves in the symmetrical power game of their already established opposites by adopting the confrontational style and convivial obligations of the age organization, the age organization of the newcomers mirroring that of their closest partners/rivals. There are indications that, in this process, the junior age-sets took the initiative. They seem to have adopted the *monyomiji* identity in rebellion against the elders in power, whether these were lineage elders (Madi, Lwo groups) or generational gerontocrats (Surma speakers). The speed with which the system has been adopted by some communities is amazing; in Kurimoto's words, 'age systems are good to be copied'. In the case of the Acholi of Parajok it took only a few years.

The other issue in interethnic relations with which this book deals is expansion. Spencer focuses on the expansion of the Maasai and compares it with that of the Nuer and the Oromo. Lamphear makes a comparison between the Turkana, Jie and Maasai. While Spencer is concerned with the socio-economic factors that pushed the Maasai to adopt an aggressive stance towards their neighbours, Lamphear's interest focuses on new structures of leadership that gave the societies he studied a comparative advantage over their neighbours. Spencer points to the antagonism between juniors and elders in Maasai society as a factor pushing young men to the raiding of their neighbours, Lamphear shows how, towards the end of the nineteenth century, a new type of leader emerged who made military use of the disgruntled juniors, and introduced a new, more instrumental, type of warfare.

## Antagonism Between Segments of the Age System

Two main issues will be treated under this heading: the complementary opposition[6] between segments based on age or generational membership, and the question of sovereignty in societies where the age system functions as the political system. We have already noted that Evans-Pritchard was the first to comment on the structural homology between age systems and lineage systems based on 'complementary opposition'. Jacobs (1965:294), Gulliver (1963:59) and, later, Spencer (1975) showed the fruitfulness of this point of view in their analyses of the age systems of the Maasai, where the age-sets occupying alternating age-grades formed alternating antagonistic pairs.

The model of complementary opposition has two premises: (i) that the relations determine the units they disconnect and (ii) that, when hostilities occur, the more encompassing relations determine the relations between the groups encompassed. The prototypical antagonistic relationship is that between enemies. While this is intrinsically violent, non-violent relationships between sections of the society are also structured according to the same model, the violence being ritualized or enacted in controlled competition or mock confrontations. The important social spin-off of the enemy model is its positive effect on the cohesiveness of the opposing groups. Relations between the units of age systems are structured according to the enemy model and, though in principle non-violent, they have the potential to lapse into violence.

Harrison, in his study of the Avatip, emphasized the overtly aggressive character of the 'institutional antagonism' between the different age-grades of the men's cult. The Avatip considered it detrimental to a man's life-force if he were to eat with members of junior age-grades. Age-grade antagonism was further expressed in aggressive pride, stick-fights and arbitrary bullying of juniors by the seniors (1993: 81). Relations between age-sets and generation-sets in East Africa follow a similar scenario. Stick-fights between age-sets and generation-sets are common in the societies of the Karimojong and *monyomiji* clusters (Kurimoto, 1995a; Tornay in this volume).

Tornay, Komma and Simonse deal at length with the antagonism inherent in age systems. The core of Tornay's contribution is an impressive case-study of a prolonged inter-generational conflict between the generation of the Elephants and that of the Ostriches. When the Elephants refused to hand over power to the Ostriches, the latter 'hit them with sticks' which hardened the attitude of the Elephants. At this show of disrespect the Elephants solemnly declared that they would never hand over power to the Ostriches. Then the leading age-set among the Ostriches, suspecting that the Elephants would transfer power to one of their junior age-sets and skip them, pronounced a curse on their juniors if they were ever to agree to take power from the Elephants.

In the early 1990s when Tornay last visited the Nyangatom the system was still in a state of stalemate. The Ostriches, who were looking for ways of forcing a breakthrough, encountered resistance from the clan that traditionally provided the human victim for the succession ceremony. The discussion now focused on the kind of substitute that would be acceptable for the transfer. At stake was the unity of the Nyangatom as a society.

At the end of the nineteenth century, a similar conflict had split their neighbours, the Toposa, into two concurrent father generations. According to the standard explanation junior and senior members of the generation-set about to succeed their fathers fought over the apportioning of meat (Müller, 1991: 561) and formed two competing generation-set lines – a situation which could easily have led to a split of the Toposa as a people and political unit. Recent developments indicate that the two concurrent generation-sets are considering giving their sons the same name. While the name-giving *per se* is without doubt a ritual process, the decision to use the same name for both groups is a political act, the result of lobbying between conflicting views of the future of the Toposa nation.

In his contribution on the *monyomiji* systems Simonse discerns a swing of the pendulum in the developmental cycle of the generational system. The years preceding and immediately following the transfer of power are marked by an intensification of antagonism, both in external relations and in internal, inter-generational conflict. In the period preceding the transfer of power the junior, candidate generation goes on raids, often against the wish of the ruling generation. In the years following the change-over the new rulers are expected to prove themselves, now in 'legitimate' warfare. As time goes by hierarchy and complementarity take over from antagonistic symmetry as the principal scenario governing the interactions between successive age-sets. The relative calm is only to be broken by the maturation and insertion of new age-sets. Hierarchy and conflict are equally important dimensions of the age system. Each of them prevails during a particular phase of the maturation cycle of age-sets and generations.

**15**

Spencer's interest focuses on the economic realities behind the antagonism between young and old among the Maasai. He argues that the antagonism between juniors and seniors goes back to a contradiction between two modes of enlarging one's herds: a violent predatory mode and a non-violent domestic mode in which the herd expands through natural reproduction. The *moran* are the champions of the predatory mode and try to undercut the power of their elders with the cattle stolen in raids. The seniors try to keep their juniors in place by controlling marriage transactions where the cattle of their self-reproducing herds are the principal asset. Spencer shows how, within the Maasai area, the power balance between elders and *moran* results in varying degrees of gerontocracy. The elders' degree of control decreases as we pass from the Samburu in the north to the Arusha Maasai in the south. Among the Samburu the relationship between elders and *moran* is full of frustration for the latter whereas in the south, with the institution of the warrior villages (*manyata*), the power game between the two is more open.

Economic and social aspects of gerontocracy are also a main theme of Shun Sato's contribution to this volume. He analyses the Rendille, camel pastoralists in northern Kenya, as a rigid gerontocratic society with a strict rule of primogeniture. From a socio-ecological point of view, it is argued, the power of the elders rests on control of the flow of two major resources: women and camels. Although antagonistic relations between dominating elders and oppressed young men, and between eldest sons and junior ones, do not usually take the form of open confrontation, yet there are means for the weak to manipulate for their benefit. Camel transactions, which Sato analyses in detail, are one of these means. As many of the North East African societies with age systems are predominantly pastoral, his contribution is valuable.

Sovereignty refers to the recognition of a person or group as the ultimate power over a territory or a group of people. Despite the charisma that is usually an attribute of sovereignty, the recognition of the political actor who will be the sovereign is, in the last analysis, the result of a power contest – between persons, dynasties, clans, generations, etc. – and is always open to renewed challenge, by rivals, by enemies, or by rebellious subjects. While sovereignty is culturally elaborated as a deeply complementary relationship between the incumbent of power and his subjects, its social roots are in the sphere of symmetrical conflict. Sovereignty has both internal and external aspects: recognition is demanded both from the subjects of the sovereign as well as from those of neighbouring polities, from friends and enemies alike.

In our Melanesian model sovereignty is clearly in the hands of the institution labelled 'the men's cult'. In Harrison's analysis power is the ability not so much to influence others as to resist and ignore the routine claims that others constantly make upon oneself. The more powerful one is, the less answerable one is to others. The sovereignty of the senior grade in the men's cult was displayed in a whole array of more or less arbitrary acts of aggression, against enemies, against juniors, against women, in order to prove its utter unanswerableness to others. Sovereignty was the 'religious hypostatisation of a collective posture of aggression to outsiders' (Harrison, 1993:148).[7]

In the North East African societies where age systems are the 'primary model' of political organization, we find a variety of configurations with regard to who are the incumbent(s) of sovereignty. The most straight-forward situation is that described by Tornay where the generation of the 'fathers' has political and ritual sovereignty over the generation of the sons. Tornay's account of the blocking of the succession of the Ostriches by the Elephants has all the elements that we associate with dynastic intrigue: intransigence because of a dispute of long ago, conspiracies – and suspicions of conspiracy – to overthrow the set in power, lobbying for the acceptance of a new principle of legitimacy, etc.

The expression of rebelliousness by the junior generation may take other forms. Among the Dassanetch and Samburu the members of the sets aspiring to power suffer outbursts of anomic behaviour, uncontrolled violence, verbal abuse, hooliganism, violence among peers, and, among the Samburu, psychosomatic fits of 'goat-madness' (Spencer, 1965: 162). Dassanetch interpret this behaviour as a direct affront, as a subversion of the norms that regulate the interaction between the gerontocrats and the junior generation. After resisting the impetuousness of the junior generation for a number of years, Dassanetch elders will concede that their generational charisma has lost its appeal. They will step down and hand over sovereignty to the new generation (Almagor, 1983: 635–48).

In most other societies with age systems the situation is more complex. Sovereignty is vested in a number of competing offices. Among the Oromo three different institutions may be considered as the agents of sovereignty: the *gada*, the *gumi gaayo*, and the *qallu*. To assert its invinci-bility, a set that had acceded to the *gada* grade was expected to raid, kill, and bring home the severed genitals of members of a, preferably new, group of enemies. Seen from the enemy's point of view, *gada* had real political consequences and was not to be played down as inconsequential ritual. While relations with enemies were mercilessly antagonistic, internal antagonism was curtailed by the rigorous formalism of *gada* succession, though mock-battles between the sets of fathers and sons were part of the *gada* ceremonies of some groups (Stanley and Karsten, 1968: 101–2). Despite the heavy ritualization of the power of the *qallu*, the alternative source of supreme authority among the Oromo, some sequences in the ceremonial blessing of the leaders of a new set occupying the *gada* rank (among others, a mock confrontation) betray a deeper level of antagonism between the two principles of sovereignty (Hinnant, 1978: 233–8). More powerful than the *gada* and the *qallu*, the assembly organization of the Oromo, the *gumi gaayo*, held every eight years with the participation of all segments of Boran society, overrules decisions taken by *gada* councils (Schlee, 1994a; Shongolo, 1994; Bassi, 1996).

Among the peoples of the *monyomiji* group antagonism between alternative agents of sovereignty – the *monyomiji*, as the ruling generation, and the king/rainmaker – was quite open. Since both carried responsibility for the cosmic and social well-being of the society, the king blamed the *monyomiji* if things went wrong (defeat by enemies, drought, pestilence), while the *monyomiji* held the king to account for all kinds of disasters, especially for drought. Death was the fate of the king if he was unable to shift the blame on to the *monyomiji* or some other agent of evil (Kurimoto, 1986, 1995; Simonse, 1992).

In the contributions dealing with political change the central issue is the emergence of new political actors encroaching on, and replacing, the sovereignty of the elders. The greater freedom of the *moran* vis-à-vis the elders is linked, by John Lamphear, to the rise of the prophets (*laibons*) during the nineteenth century. The prophets pulled the *moran* away from the control of their elders and reorganized them, in the *manyatas* away from the village, as the fighting force that enabled the Maasai to expand over wide areas.

A parallel development is described by Komma for the Kipsigis. Prophets emerged as a rival power to the elders. The prophet led the *moran* in raids and consolidated their power by redistributing the wealth thus acquired. The power of the prophets, however, was short-lived. Against the will of the prophets, a new generation of warriors was initiated and enrolled in the King's African Rifles. When they reached elderhood many of them were appointed as government chiefs. The era of the prophets was brought to an end by a combined exercise of chiefly and elderly power. The chiefs exiled the prophets' clan to an island in Lake Victoria, while the elders stopped the recruitment to the Maina warrior age-set. Among the Maasai as well as the Kipsigis, prophets imposed themselves by contesting the control of the elders over the initiation of the warrior-set.

The more recent encroachment of the power of prophets on that of the elders may provide a clue regarding the position of the rainmaker-kings in the *monyomiji* area and of the *kallu* among the Oromo. With respect to the role of the rainmaker-kings, it is striking that there is a wide range in the scope of their influence over ceremonies of transfer of power. While in some polities the Rainmaker does not intervene at all, we see that, in the more centralized kingdoms of the Lotuho, the king is heavily involved in the transfer of power from one generation to the next.

In most cases the ruling generation exercises its power in competition with a prophet, rainmaker or sacred king. In the division of responsibilities it is normally the single office-holder who is vested with the sacral dimension of power, while the ruling generation or age-set deals with more mundane concerns, though never exclusively.

Where no prophets or kings have encroached upon the sovereignty of the ruling generation, the full burden of sacral power remains with the fathers. Among the Nyangatom the fathers are the recipients of sacrifices brought by the generation of their sons. In this respect their position is equivalent to that of gods or divine kings. The transfer of sovereignty from the generation of Divine Fathers to that of the sons has deeply sacral significance. Among the Nyangatom it involves an act of parricide. A member of the defunct generation of fathers is bought by the sons. Before wandering off into the bush, the man engaged in the transfer of power (*asapan*) acts as a sacrificer for the benefit of the generation of sons, thus reversing the normal direction of sacrifice.[8]

## Gender Antagonism and Women's Age-Sets

Though descriptions are rare and thin, women's age-sets have been recorded for a large number of East African peoples: the Lotuho and Maa peoples and some of the peoples of the Karimojong group, for the Kalenjin, the Gikuyu and the Meru. What are these women's age-sets good for? How do they relate to the male-centred, enemy-focused age systems, if they fit at all? As with the male systems, the little that has been written on female age-setting emphasizes the use of age-grades for the allocation of tasks.

We wish to argue in this study that women's age-sets have the same origin and obey the same mechanisms as their male counterparts. The antagonism in which women's age-sets are involved is not with the enemy outside the group boundary, but with the men. In societies made up of antagonistically structured groups, women have not overlooked the opportunity the system offered them: to unite in opposition to the men.

Women's age-sets do not form a coherent system in themselves. They do not have the neatly balanced pairs that can unite people and split them according to a mechanism of complementary opposition. Their principal reference is the male system. Though their rhythm of formation does not coincide with that of the male sets – girls often begin forming sets at an earlier age than boys – the succession of female sets tends to mirror that of the men, both in frequency and time-span, as shown by the comparative analysis of Kertzer and Madison (1981: 124).

There is no lack of evidence of concerted group action by women.

Lulubo women call the ruling generation to account when drought or pests threaten the crops. They call a meeting and make their grievances known. Depending on their view of the situation, the *monyomiji* will take action or defuse and discredit the initiative of the women. Typically, the men consider the women unnecessarily alarmist, while the men are considered irresponsible by the women (Simonse, 1992: 359). The role of women as custodians of the ripening harvest is common to most societies practising the *monyomiji* system. The typical duty of female age-sets, after they have been formed, is to weed the field of the King/Rainmaker.

In much of the Lotuho area girls' age-sets are formed when a group of girls is considered old enough to bring firewood or water to the meeting place of the *monyomiji*. During the first years after the formation of their age-set girls are involved in competitive activities: coeval age-sets from different villages hold sports matches (running and wrestling), and try to capture one another's flags in nightly expeditions. The girls' age-sets have their own organization and leadership. Among the Lulubo these were copied from the colonial and national military and administrative organization. The girls' age-sets act as a school in competitive skills in which a sense of solidarity and cooperativeness is developed, largely outside and in opposition to the male domain.

Father Maconi (1973) has described the female age-sets (*akiworeta*) of the Karimojong. Once every 10 to 15 years Karimojong teenage girls who inhabit the same territorial unit form a new age-set. Led by a matron who is a member of the grandmothers' generation, they celebrate *akiwor* – literally 'elopement', running away from home with a lover against the will of one's parents. They choose a name and an emblem and conclude the ceremony with a sacrifice analogous to that performed at the initiation of male age-sets. The only objective of the formation of female age-sets is, according to Maconi, to give a boost to the solidarity of young women, similar to the solidarity in male age-sets. No new rights are acquired as a result of the initiation and, apart from some songs relating to the group's emblem, nothing new is learnt.

Maconi expressly places the formation of the girls' age-sets in the context of the antagonism existing between the sexes and compares it to the antagonism between fathers and sons (1973: 350). Courting visits by a prospective husband are one of the occasions when the gender antagonism finds most dramatic expression. Another interesting point made by Maconi is that the female age-set system had only a limited time-depth, the first remembered set coinciding with the youngest age-set of the generation of Zebras which retired in October 1956 (Dyson-Hudson, 1966: 159). Maconi suggests a historical explanation in conclusion:

> In a state of social crisis, as a result of economic difficulties or because of the conflicts between men and women, the women organize themselves by creating

internally cohesive groups to actively assert their presence and underline their importance in a society dominated by men, and to protect themselves against the power of men. This aspect is obvious throughout with the female age-sets [our translation] (1973: 358).

In this respect it is interesting to observe the wide range of variation in the way communities institutionalize the antagonism between the sexes. In the different Lotuho-speaking polities that are located along the Lopit range we observe a neat gradation, going from north to south, in the degree to which competition between the sexes is openly expressed. (i) In the north among the Dorik and Ngotira the women follow their own cycle of recruitment, independent of that of the men. They have their own changeover (*nefira*) ceremony. The initiates pay a bull to the female generation in power who are known as 'women *monyomiji*', or 'the female fathers of the land' (*monyomiji enongorwo*). In order to qualify for the initiation a woman normally has one or more sons who are *monyomiji*. (ii) Among the Lomiya and Lohutok, further south, the 'women *monyomiji*' take over power after the *nefira* of the men. Their cycle runs in synchrony with that of the men. Female age-sets have the same designations, according to the portion of the sacrificial animals to which the members of the set are entitled: head, neck, etc. (iii) In the Lotuho villages at the southern tip of the Lopit range, female age-sets gradually lose their meaning once a woman has married. At marriage a woman belongs to the age-set and generation of her husband and women are called the 'wives of the *monyomiji*' (*angorwo monyomiji*), not female *monyomiji*.

As we go from north to south, the autonomy of women gradually fades. Women in north Lopit form a collective body that is independent in its recruitment, and are identified as 'mothers of the *monyomiji*', while the organization of the women who are in the middle of the range mirrors that of the *monyomiji* and depends on it for its rhythm of recruitment. Among the Lotuho in the south, a married woman is a member of the *angorwo monyomiji* simply by individual title, because she is married to a *monyemiji*. After having borne their first child their original age-sets become irrelevant. What counts is the age and generational position of their husbands.

The case of the Chamus, a Maa-speaking group, is even more extreme. In this volume Kaori Kawai argues that among the Chamus girls do not form sets of their own. They pass through a number of stages marked by clitoridectomy, marriage, birth of the first child and menopause. Since attainment of each of these stages is on a strictly individual basis, Kawai speaks of 'physical aging categories', not of grades. When a woman marries she is considered to be affiliated to the age-set of her husband. Wives of male age-mates are considered as co-wives and are expected to show respect to the wives of men of senior age-sets and to take action if

**21**

wives of junior age-sets are seen to misbehave. Kawai produces some interesting case studies of disciplinary action by wives of seniors against wives of juniors. What these cases prove is that the 'groups of co-wives', called female age-sets by Kawai, mainly function as an extension of a male interest in the orderly behaviour of women, especially of the young wives of elderly men. The female age-set only acts as a corporate unit when collective punishments are imposed on it. It is clear that the situation among the Chamus has moved a long way from the defiant antagonism of the Karimojong women.

In the second part of her contribution Kawai shows the continued importance of clitoridectomy to the Chamus. While unmarried mothers find ready acceptance, uncircumcised mothers do not. For girls, educated and uneducated alike, to be circumcised remains a promotion, a crucial means of attaining adulthood.

## Age Systems and Political Change

There is a general assumption that age systems are incompatible with modernization. They are seen as linked to a warrior past, and as having no relevance once modern state power is firmly established. Evans-Pritchard argued, based on his observations up to the 1930s, that age-set systems among the Nuer and other East African peoples were 'the first to undergo rapid and great modifications under European rule' (1940a: 257). It is true that North East African age systems have undergone profound changes since the nineteenth century, and indeed many of them became extinct (see Nagashima's paper in this volume). It is also true, on the other hand, that quite a number of age systems have persisted and are surviving, sometimes assuming new significance in the modern political environment. The Nuer are no exception. After more than half a century since Evans-Pritchard's fieldwork, the anthropologist Sharon Hutchinson has found that, for Nuer men, initiation into an age-set or, more precisely, the initiation itself, which consists of the ordeal of scarring the forehead, is still a crucial social marker of adulthood. This practice and ideology became a focus of controversy in the early 1980s as the number of young men not undergoing initiation was increasing (Hutchinson, 1996: chap.6).

The contributions in this volume link age systems to political change in three different ways: as organizations of military and political expansion, as a cultural complex promoting a disposition towards oppositional politics, and as a repository of cultural identity.

Age systems were an integral element in the political and military transformation that affected large parts of North East Africa during the nineteenth century. Lamphear's and Spencer's contributions deal with this transformation. Lamphear places it in a general evolutionary perspective. While before the nineteenth century most armed conflicts in North East Africa conformed to the model of 'ritual warfare' – a confrontation in which the use of violence is limited as a result of a mutually respected war-code – during the nineteenth century a new type of expansive warfare appeared. Leaders with a more instrumental concept of war strategy emerged and pushed their societies above 'the military horizon', a term used by Turney-High to indicate the type of warfare characterized by a clear group objective, the use of tactical operations, a definite command structure, the ability to conduct campaigns to reduce enemy resistance, and a structure for supplying the troops with food (Turney-High, 1991: 30).

In the societies studied by Lamphear, it was the warrior-grade that provided the manpower for this revolution in warfare; among the Maasai, the Turkana and the Jie, leaders with vision – prophets in the case of the Maasai and Turkana, and war leaders among the Jie – seem to have been well aware of the military potential of the age-organization. They built up followings from among the warriors. They successfully competed with the elders for control over the warriors and turned them into effective 'regiments' that brought back the spoils of their raids to their leaders for redistribution, thus adding power to their position.

In contrast to Lamphear, Spencer emphasizes, on the one hand, the martial charisma of the *moran* – reminiscent of the 'religious hypostatisation of a collective posture of aggression towards outsiders' of the Avatip (Harrison, 1993: 148) – and, on the other, the antagonism between elders and *moran* as the motor behind the warfare and expansion of the Maasai. Warfare and raiding were the answers of the oppressed junior generation to the protracted minority imposed on them by the elders. They offered an opportunity to acquire bridewealth that was used in asserting their independence in relation to their elders.

Among the Turkana and Maasai the historical process of military expansion ended in internal rivalry among the heirs to the power amassed.

Age systems, in the second place, are the embodiment of a disposition towards oppositional political strategies. In his contribution Simonse shows that resistance to colonial rule in the *monyomiji* area came, principally, from age-sets of young men who had not yet taken over power. The early armed opposition on the part of southern Sudanese to the new independent Sudanese government started with the Torit Mutiny in 1955. The town of Torit is located in Lotuholand and the year coincided with the taking over of power by a new generation of *monyomiji*. King Lomiluk of the Lotuho Kingdom of Tirangore was one of the organizers of a series of ambushes and attacks on government targets between 1955 and 1959. His group, some 400 strong, consisted of muti-neers and new *monyomiji* who had just taken over (Simonse, 1992: 312–14). Thus generational antagonism in the area seems to have been one of the factors in mobilizing people in the early years of the civil war.

It is remarkable that the same pattern was repeated in the current civil war started in 1983. Kurimoto analysed the mobilization of the Pari juniors into the Sudan People's Liberation Army (SPLA). Out of more than 2500 Pari men who joined the SPLA, only about ten were *monyomiji* when they enrolled. An important motive for joining the guerrilla army was the opposition of the junior generation to the rule of the age-sets in power (1994: 106–9).

Generational antagonism was also a factor in the Mau Mau uprising. According to testimonies collected from elders by Githige (1978), the aspiring Maina generation – who were blocked from taking over power – were bitterly opposed to the Mwangi, their predecessors whom they blamed for selling the white highlands to the British.

Finally, even if the age systems have stopped operating as a military, political or ritual system, they remain an important element in the construction of ethnic and national identities. According to Komma in this volume, for instance, reference to the largely defunct age systems of the peoples now united under the Kalenjin label still plays a role in the construction of ethnic identity. The traditions the Mau Mau used in its ideological struggle against foreign rule were taken from the Gikuyu age system. It appealed to the young people to form a new generation of *Iregi* ('rebels', the name of the mythical first generation that took over power from the tyranny of women) and to carry out a new *itwika* (ceremony of the transfer of power) that would restore the land to its rightful owners. Names of previous generations were employed to refer to sub-divisions of the movement, while one of the base-camps of the Mau Mau was called *Thingira*, the name of the hut where the newly circumcised spent their first period away from home (Kenyatta, 1938: 186–230; Lonsdale, 1992: 345).

*Gada* is a crucial element in the construction of the new Oromo identity. Interestingly, in a recent book, *Being and Becoming Oromo*, the result of a workshop convened to 'identify elements from which an Oromo ethnic consciousness and a sense of national identity have been, and are being, moulded' (Baxter, Hultin and Triulzi, 1996: 7), nearly half the papers referred to the Boran of northern Kenya, partly because they are one of the few Oromo groups that maintain the *gada*, which many Oromo nationalists like to consider as the prototypical Oromo institution, despite the fact that only a minority of Oromo still practise it. As the Mau Mau movement drew imagery from the age system, the Oromo Liberation Front adopted *gada* terminology in naming its institutions and officials. In his contribution to this volume, Schlee points to some of the paradoxes in

24

the use of *gada* as the central marker of Oromo identity. Because of these paradoxes Marco Bassi, in his paper in the above book, pleaded for a shift from *gada* to the *gumi gaayo*, the 'assembly of multitudes' remarkable for its democratic procedure, as the central symbol of a pan-Oromo identity (Bassi, 1996). Schlee (1994a) and Shongolo (1994) also favour the *gumi gaayo* as a marker of national identity because of the connotation of violence that still clings to *gada* in the memory of many Oromo sections that were forcefully incorporated. A parallel self-consciousness is manifested by a Lokoya intellectual and SPLA officer, Lomodong Lako, in his recent monograph on his own people, the Lokoya; he calls *monyomiji* an 'ethnic government' (1995).

Age systems, and the image of militant warriors in particular, may be manipulated on the stage of national politics. During the 'Rift Valley conflict' in Kenya (1991), Kalenjin attackers, who were allegedly mobilized by the ruling KANU (Kenya African National Union) government, were usually armed with traditional weapons and painted their faces with clay, as they do during the initiation ceremony to warriorhood (Human Rights Watch Africa/Africa Watch, 1993: 15–16). Although we do not know the extent to which the existing age-set system was actually utilized for mobilization, it is significant that, in the conflict which was not only about local or 'tribal' affairs but was concerned with a critical national issue, the image of Kalenjin warriors was still very powerful and effective for both parties to the conflict. In the contemporary national politics of Kenya, the image of 'Maasai *moran*' is also manipulated for the benefit of the Maasai, particularly for Maasai politicians who are strong KANU supporters. There is ample evidence for this in the Kenyan newspapers and magazines.

Three major factors may account for the demise of age systems: modern education which offers an alternative system of grading and progress in life, the spread of capitalism which generates new relations of power that undermine the authority of elders, and state interventions which ban the performance of functions essential to the continuation of the system.[9]

One of the alternatives for a society to adopt is a sort of 'defensive stance'. This is the case of the Rendille as argued by Sato in this volume. They intentionally adhere to camel pastoralism which is the basis of their society. They do not sell camels to the local market, and when in need of cash they sell only cattle. By putting up a barrier to the encroaching capitalism, they have succeeded in preserving gerontocracy and the age system. They have been able to do this because the Rendille are located in a remote and arid region where the Kenyan government sees little point in intervening.

Nagashima argues in his contribution that among the Ugandan Iteso each of the three factors played a role in the demise of the age system, although he puts the emphasis on state intervention. The Baganda, who established colonial rule in Iteso, stopped the ceremonies of transfer of power. Later, in the 1950s, educated Teso on the Sub-County Council delivered the final blow by condemning the practice as leading to violence and as a waste of resources. Nagashima tells us how, during Christmas 1969, he participated in what was probably the last Iteso *asapan*.

The Iteso case is interesting because, even in the pre-colonial period, their age system seems to have played a very limited politico-military role. Nagashima's case study offers a counterbalance to the rest of this volume, because its argument moves in the opposite direction.

The age systems of the Kipsigis and the Gikuyu came to a similar end. In this volume Komma describes how the Kipsigis government chiefs, with the full collaboration of the elders, punished the Maina warrior-set by prematurely closing their recruitment, in response to their unruliness. When the next age-set, the Chuma, proved to be no better and set fire to the houses of the elders, the old system was definitively abolished.

The new Gikuyu generation of Maina was meant to take over from Mwangi power around 1930. Because of a conflict between different sections of the Gikuyu over the location of the *itwika* (ceremony of the transfer of power) the colonial government postponed the ceremonies. In view of the intensification of nationalist political activity in Kenya the ban was extended. The special conditions of World War II caused the postponement to become indefinite and the Maina were never confirmed in their power (Leakey, 1977: 1278–84; Ville, 1985).

Extrapolating from current trends of social change among the Chamus, as analysed by Little (1992), Spencer expects the Maasai age system eventually to give way to the predatory encroachment of capitalism. By taking advantage of opportunities offered by the market, Chamus young men free themselves from the control of their elders, set up small enterprises, and employ their impoverished tribesmen who were too late to make use of the new economic opportunities. The overall result is the breakup of age stratification and peer solidarity, and their replacement by the new mechanisms of social exclusion/inclusion generated by capitalism.

******

We are now in a position to give an answer to the question of Evans-Pritchard with which we started this introduction: '*why does age become stratified into formal sets?*' We have shown that in order to answer this question, a preliminary distinction needs to be made between the dimension of symmetrical, antagonistic, relations and that of asymmetrical, hierarchical, relations. While 'stratification' is an ordering of social groups according to a hierarchical principle, 'sets' are units generated in the arena of age antagonism. While stratification accounts for the formation of grades, it cannot account for the formation of sets.

With the possible exception of the strictly regulated *gada* systems, age-sets comply with being stratified only after a struggle for promotion/resignation. 'Sets' then are mutually antagonistic groups, based on age or generational affiliation, engaged in the competition for positions in the age-grade system. Sets reach their peak of relevance in the period surrounding the promotion, succession or handing over of power. Later, when they have nothing more to win, their names may merge with those of adjacent sets, under a more comprehensive label.

We hope this volume will mean a partial rehabilitation of the view that age systems have military and political relevance. Though not military organizations *per se*, age systems are part of an institutional complex that makes societies fit to wage war. The contributions of Lamphear and Spencer show convincingly that, given certain conditions, age-sets are easily transformed into military units. Against those who deny the political dimension of age systems because of a lack of formal decision-making processes that could be labelled 'government', our answer is that politics does not start with government, but with competition for power. We hope to have shown that there is plenty of that in age systems.

# Notes

1  In making general references to systems of age-grades, age-sets and generation-sets, as distinct from kinship systems etc., we shall use 'age system' as the encompassing term. For convenience and simplicity we prefer the term age-sets to age-classes and age-groups.
2  Bernardi made an attempt to accommodate both approaches by making a distinction between, on the one hand, polities in which the age or generation system structures political relations and provides the framework for military organization, and, on the other hand, polities where it plays a secondary, more ideological, role. The former category he calls 'primary models', in the latter they are 'secondary models' (Bernardi, 1985: 42).
3  Even in the strictly formalized *gada* systems, we find more or less ritualized or theatricalized antagonism. For instance, mock fights between sets of fathers and sons were part of the *gada* ceremonies among the Gabricco Sidamo (Stanley and Karsten, 1968).
4  Baxter himself is quite aware that the conflicting views on the political function of the *gada* system may be attributed to the difference in the circumstances of fieldwork; while Legesse conducted fieldwork in the populous homelands during the period when the activities of generation-sets were at their height, Baxter did it in the much more arid periphery when generation-sets' activities were dormant (Baxter, 1978: 153). This suggests the need for long-term field research, as the cycle of age systems is often very long. What an anthropologist can observe is only a part of the full cycle.
5  Excluded are the various age systems of the Bantu peoples of Kenya and Tanzania, those of Western Nilotic peoples of South Sudan (Nuer, Dinka, Shilluk, Anuak, etc.), and those of the Omotic and Surmic peoples of southwestern Ethiopia. This is also because we are not able to find enough evidence that those age systems constitute 'arenas' for political drama comparable to those discussed in this volume. It is possible that future research

may reveal the existence of such arenas. Occasional references to them are made, however, when they offer us cases relevant to our discussion.

6  Because of its familiarity we have decided to stick to the term 'complementary opposition'. It will be clear that 'complementary' in this compound term has a different value from its usage derived from Bateson. In fact, 'complementary opposition' is a relationship manifesting itself in symmetrical interactions.

7  Spencer's observation that Maasai expansion and regional dominance were based, not so much on actual battles, but on martial display and on the charismatic, self-fulfilling, assumption of superiority over others, seems to be an echo of the Avatip posture.

8  Abrahams comments on *ameto*, the killing of an ox, for the fathers among the Labwor: 'We seem then to be partly operating here with a sort of sacrifice analogous to tribute to a divine king in a more centralised political context' (Abrahams, 1978: 46). Among the main recipients are those whom Dyson-Hudson has interestingly characterized as an authoritative corporate aggregate of elders (Dyson-Hudson, 1966: 227).

9  In modern Japan as well, these three factors worked for the demise of age-sets, which were widely found in peasant and fishing communities. They were in principle groups for unmarried young men, and sometimes female age-sets existed alongside male ones. They were banned by the Meiji government because of their incompatibility with school education and also because of 'immoral' activities such as courtship. Interestingly, many age-sets were transformed into youth associations which were instrumental in the government administration.

# 2 Resonance of Age-Systems in Southeastern Sudan

## EISEI KURIMOTO

### Prologue: Age Systems Across Ethnic Boundaries

In December 1985 I visited Liria, a Lokoya village, to attend the *Odhurak*, the New Year hunting ritual. The purpose was to compare it with the *Nyalam*,[1] the equivalent of the *Odhurak* among the Pari where I had been undertaking fieldwork. At Liria I was greeted by several Pari men, who were with their fellow Lokoya, all fully dressed for the ritual. I wondered why they were there and asked, 'Do you have any relatives here?' They said, 'No'. I then asked, 'With whom are you staying?' and they replied, 'We are with our age-mates.' They were with the members of the age-set whose age range was approximately the same as their own. It was well known to both sides which age-set of one people corresponded to that of the other. The Pari men were behaving as if they were real members of the age-set in Liria: they went to the ritual hunt, and danced and drank with their age-mates. They looked quite at home, and if they had not talked to me, I would not even have been aware of their presence.

By 1985, seven years after I had begun my fieldwork among the Pari, I was about to extend my anthropological interests, originally oriented to the 'ethnographic present' of Pari society, beyond it in both time and space. In the process, the age systems among the Pari and neighbouring peoples became one of the major issues. I had been informed that the Pari system had been adopted from the Lopit presumably about a century ago, and that the Lokoya regard the Pari system as a model for their own system and the interrelation is further extended to the Lulubo, who have synchronized their system to that of the Lokoya.[2] The episode in Liria attracted my attention and sparked off the idea that age systems provide a shared framework of codes of behaviour across ethnic boundaries. This paper is the outcome of efforts to account for the age system of a people in

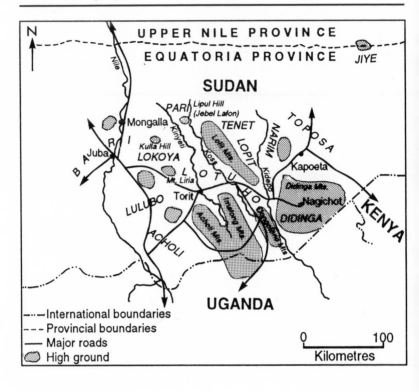

*Map 2* The Monyomiji *Arena, Southeastern Sudan*

terms of interethnic relations, or on the meta-ethnic level, both in regional and historical perspectives. It will be argued that, in a highly synchronized state, the graded age-set systems in the region play the role of an interethnic system in which territorial units, most of them smaller than ethnic groups, have emerged as equal partners for emulation.

## The *Monyomiji* Systems in Southeastern Sudan

In southeastern Sudan, a specific type of graded age-set systems, which we call *monyomiji* systems, developed among various peoples. Successive foreign authorities, which first encroached on this region during the latter half of the nineteenth century, government administration, and civil wars have failed to weaken the systems, which still persist and play a prominent role in social life. *Monyomiji* is the name of the ruling middle-aged grade in Lotuho, and means 'fathers' or 'owners' (*monye*) of the village (*amiji*). It is located between the grades of elders and young people. The linguistic and ethnic diversity of the peoples possessing these systems is remarkable. They are: the Lotuho-speaking peoples or the 'Lotuho cluster' (Eastern Nilotic of Eastern Sudanic), including the Lotuho proper or plains Lotuho, the Lokoya, the Lopit, the Ohoriok, the Lango (not to be confused with the Lango in Uganda), the Dongotono, the Logir and so on);[3] the Lulubo (Moru-Madi of Central Sudanic); the Pari and a part of the Acholi (Western Nilotic); and the Tenet (Surmic of Eastern Sudanic)[4] (Simonse, 1992: 46–7, 165–71; 1993: 67; Nalder, 1937). The Pari call the ruling age grade *mojomiji*, a term borrowed from the Lotuho cluster (see Table 2.1). The Bari (Eastern Nilotic) age system may deserve special consideration. Although it is not the *monyomiji* system,[5] it has had interrelations with the *monyomiji* systems of the Lokoya, Lulubo and Pari, as will be discussed later.

The *monyomiji*, which is basically composed of four age-sets, constitutes a sort of collective government, of which all men of the grade are members. It is, in fact, a highly cohesive political body. Its members are in power and are endowed with political, military and legal functions (see also Simonse's paper in this volume). It is interesting that in a recent monograph on the Lokoya, a Lokoya intellectual goes on to call it a 'ethnic government' (Lomodong, 1995). Indeed the *monyomiji* members take responsibility for maintaining law and order and assuring the security and welfare of the community. To achieve this they have to deal with the enemies of the community, both internal and external, and both real and imaginary (see Kurimoto, 1995a, for the Pari case).

The *monyomiji* system is a form of indigenous democracy. Although elders, young people, and most notably women are excluded, all men of

Table 2.1 Comparative Age System Terminology

| | Pari | Lotuho | Lokoya | Lopit | Lulubo | Bari |
|---|---|---|---|---|---|---|
| Elders | cidonge | amarwak | ohobolok | | | temejik |
| Middle-aged | mojomiji | monyomiji | monyomiji | monyomiji | monyomiji (juru ate) | kasarak |
| Youngsters | awope | aduri horwong, nyarhalu | nyarhalo | aduri holwang | teto | teton |
| Age set | lange | | operi | hilahaji | oku | toberon |
| Platform for age-set | bali | obele | bali | obele | bali | bali |
| The strongest wrestler | lithir | otir | otir | | | |
| The fastest runner | dwero | ofeja | ofeja | | otir | ngutu lo ringit |
| Drum house | dwondi-bul | nadupa | apipira | nadupa | | i kupe (lotir) |
| Drum posts | balacar | alore | odhiler | afalacar | | kadi na lori |
| Initiation of new monyomiji | mak paac | nonggopira, efira | abongoro, eviraru | efira | gbwilli ruli | wore, gbilili ('bilili) |

The data for this table (except for the Lopit) are mainly based on 'Cultural Vocabulary of Peoples in Eastern Equatoria (Bari, Madi, Lokoiya, Lotuho, Acholi, Pari)', a joint research project by Simon Simonse, Torben Anderson and Eisei Kurimoto, which was discontinued in 1986 without being completed.

the middle-aged grade have the right to participate in the discussion of communal affairs and in the decision-making process. I am tempted to regard the community with a *monyomiji* system, whatever its population size may be, as being endowed with 'sovereignty' and thus constituting a state (see also Tornay's discussion of sovereignty in this book).

The *monyomiji* system is neither a type of gerontocracy nor a type of juventocracy. For instance, among the Pari, when the four age-sets took over power in 1977, they were aged approximately between 45 and 31. They stayed in power for eleven years. At the time of power being transferred, the members of the sitting *monyomiji* are quite old. But elders are not 'retired' from social and economic activities. They have no executive power in the system but they may exercise influence over the *monyomiji* through their 'mouth', i.e. advice, invocation, curse or blessing. Youngsters have no say in the *monyomiji*'s decision-making and are the target of bullying. As they are the embodiment of 'the warrior ethos', they are often punished and fined by the *monyomiji* for their misbehaviour.

The community or territorial unit covered by a *monyomiji* system overlaps in principle with the 'rain area' under a hereditary rain king or chief, who is believed to possess supernatural powers to control rain. It should be noted that a territorial unit of the *monyomiji* system is usually smaller than an ethnic group (the Pari are an exception); there may be several systems in an ethnic group. A territorial unit consists of from one to more than ten villages (Simonse, 1992). For instance, in the case of the Pari, there are six villages with a total population of about 11,000. In this region, homesteads in a village are not dispersed but densely built-up, and the population size of a village is quite large, usually more than a thousand. A village is composed of several clan-based sections. Therefore, a *monyomiji* system has a segmentary structure with villages and village-sections as territorial segments.

The initiation of a new *monyomiji*, when the sitting members retire to the elderhood and the new ones take over, is one of the most spectacular ceremonial occasions. It also marks the beginning of a new world under a new administration, and this is symbolized by lighting a new fire after all domestic fires have been extinguished (reminiscent of the fire-making ceremony among the Maasai and Samburu). It takes place about every twenty years. (The Lotuho say it should be twenty-two.) In the Pari system, the succession is 'gradual'. The four age-sets hold power for about ten years. After that, the senior two sets retire and the junior two, joined by the two most senior age-sets of the young people, remain as *mojomiji* for another ten years. The second phase is considered a sort of transitional period (Kurimoto, 1995a). Nevertheless, the full cycle amounts to twenty years, which makes the Pari system coincide with the others. Some parts of the Lopit, and possibly the Lotuho of Loudo (Simonse, personal communication), have a similar gradual succession system.

Circumcision is not practised at all by these peoples. It is not therefore an integral part of the initiation into the age system or into *monyomiji*hood. In fact, the Pari have no initiation when boys are enrolled in the system. The Pari system also has nothing to do with marriage regulations. A young man, not yet initiated as a *monyomiji*, is free to marry, so long as his father can afford to pay at least a part of the bridewealth (12–15 head of cattle). Control of the flow of essential resources, i.e., cattle and women, which is regarded as a prerequisite for many of the East African age systems, therefore has little significance among the Pari (for comparison, see Sato's paper in this book). This should be seen in the light of the relatively smaller economic and ideological importance of cattle (they have no 'favourite' or 'personal' ox) and the lower polygyny rate among the Pari, compared with other East African pastoralists and agropastoralists (again, see Sato's paper). The Pari may be an extreme case, since it is known that the plains Lotuho do have a series of initiation ceremonies when an age-set is formed, and the marriage of young people is prohibited (Grüb, 1992: 102, 133–7; see also Simonse's paper in this volume). But it is not known how strict is the control of cattle and women, or to what extent the control is an integrated and essential part of the age system.

Another notable characteristic of the systems is that, unlike many other age systems in East Africa, no generational principle is in operation. Among the Lotuho the two successive *monyomiji* belong either to Tome ('Elephants') or Jifia ('Followers'). This may seem to resemble 'alternate generation-sets', but no relation by descent is recognized between Tome and Jifia. They are not referred to as 'fathers and sons', and two successive Tomes or Jifias are not recognized as 'grandfathers and grandsons'. It is not therefore easy to find evidence in the Tome-Jifia that a generational principle was at one time in operation among the Lotuho. The lack of generational principle implies that there is little discrepancy between the ideal and the real in the *monyomiji* system. Age variation among age-mates of an age-set is relatively limited, and is free from the intricacies caused by the 'generation paradox' (Spencer, 1986). It is a practical system based on biological age.

## Resonance of Age Systems: the Pari Perspective

*Origin*

As I have argued elsewhere (Kurimoto, 1995a), the Pari claim that they adopted the *mojomiji* system from the Lopit. The process of adoption seems to have been gradual and developed into the present form towards the

1  Pucwa, a Pari village. Note the densely built-up homesteads and the central dancing ground (*thworo*) left below  (Eisei Kurimoto, 1985)

2 Yegivegi, a Lopit village
(Eisei Kurimoto 1984)

3  A Pari *monyomiji* in full
dress for dance, standing
in front of the drum
house. He wears a hat
with ostrich feathers,
leaopord skin on back,
giraffe tail on left upper
arm, bead necklaces,
black and white colobus
skin on chest, and skirt.
He has a spear and club
in his right hand and
horns in his left. Sun
glasses and military boots
are a modern fashion.
(Eisei Kurimoto, 1979)

end of the last century. The external origin of the Pari *mojomiji* system seems probable because other linguistically (and historically and culturally) related peoples in the Southern Sudan – Western Nilotic peoples in general and Luo peoples in particular – do not have a similar graded age system. Many of them do have age-set systems such as the Anywaa (Anuak) (Evans-Pritchard, 1940b), Shilluk (Howell, 1941), Nuer (Evans-Pritchard, 1936, 1940a), and Dinka (Lienhardt, 1958; Deng, 1971), but these age-sets are not graded in a hierarchy and there is no 'ruling' age grade endowed with political power.

A comparison between the Pari and Anywaa age systems would seem to be of interest here, because the two peoples have a close linguistic affinity and claim to share a common ancestry. Evans-Pritchard reports that the Anywaa have kinds of age groups which are named either by village headmen or nobles, and which act as armed bodyguards for them. He regards these groups as directly associated with and organized for the benefit of political leaders, and refrains from calling them age-sets in an age-set system (1940b: 42, 69–70). This system seems to be quite different from the Pari age system, and rather similar to the Dinka age-set in its relations with the leadership; it is opened and closed by the religious chief, the master of the fishing spear (Lienhardt, 1958: 103). The Shilluk age-set system described by Howell has a certain similarity with the Pari system in the sense that it has age-grades. An age-set is essentially a military organization and when those in the junior grade are promoted to the senior, those in the senior retire from the warriorhood. However, unlike the Pari, the Shilluk age-set system seems to have little politico-judicial sugnificance (Howell, 1941: 56–60).

The folk terms for an age-set in Pari and Anywaa are respectively *lange* and *lwak*. Although the two languages are almost identical and share most of the basic vocabulary, they are different. The term *lange* is not found in Anywaa, while in Pari *lwak* means a group of people. This may also suggest that the Pari age system is not a developed form of the Anywaa system, but rather a new invention. It is noteworthy that the word *lange* or any similar word meaning an age-set is not found among other peoples with *monyomiji* systems (Table 2.1). A linguistic connection might be traced to the Bari or Murle. Among the Bari the word *langet* means 'a voluntary association around a chief or a rich and influential man whose war-band they would have been in the old days' (Nalder, 1937: 128) or a group of guests at a meat feast composed of individuals of approximately the same age (Spagnolo, 1932: 402). Among the Murle, who occupy the territory between Anywaaland and Pariland, *lango* (sing. *langdhet*) means 'best friends' (Lewis, 1972: 91). It is quite plausible to assume that the present age system of the Pari should have been formed under influences from different sources, and not simply copied from the Lopit, as oral traditions

**35**

*Table 2.2  Age-set names of the successive* mojomiji

| Liborceri | |
| --- | --- |
| *(jowic)* | |
| Marik | (right) |
| Mathaor | (left) |
| Akara | |
| Lidukaara | |
| Korodo | |
| Kwe | |
| Thomme | |
| Ithada | |
| (Ibou) | |
| *(jo-wic, jo-geedo)* | *(jo-tengo)* |
| Akem | Amukwonyin |
| Muura | Merithigo |
| (c.1887-c.1897) | (c.1897-c.1907) |
| Bongcut | Limojo |
| Corogo | Amerkolong |
| (c.1907-c.1917) | (c.1917-c.1927) |
| Alangore | Kalang |
| Igari | Wanditio |
| (c.1927-c.1937) | (c.1937-47) |
| Ukwer | Kwara |
| Lilalo | Bondipala |
| (1947-58) | (1958-67) |
| Kilang | Anywaa |
| Thangakwo | Akeo |
| (1967-77) | (1977-88) |
| Madan | Madir |
| Morumaafi | Lidit |
| (1988- ) | |

*Note:* Names of the two junior age-sets of *jo-tengo* are omitted.

claim. It is difficult to draw a concrete conclusion about this issue of origin because reliable data on the Lopit age systems are very scarce; moreover, there are several systems working independently.

However, what is available from the Logotok and Iboni sections of the Lopit indicates that there are very few age-set names in common between the two peoples (Tables 2.2 and 2.3), to say nothing of the correspondence

*Table 2.3  Ruling age-grades and age-sets in Logotok and Iboni (Lopit)*

| LOGOTOK (LOHUTOK) | | IBONI | |
|---|---|---|---|
| Ruling age-grade | Age-set | Ruling age-grade | Age-set |
| Immou (1770–90) | | | |
| Obeleng Beleng (1790-1810) | | | |
| Otulihiria (1810-30) | | | |
| Hahuli (1830-50) | | | |
| Imeri (1850-70) | | Tuhet | |
| Hurajak (1870-90) | | ? | |
| Hadi Hifyong (1890-1910) | | Iboyo | |
| Aharanya (1910-1930) | | Nasara | |
| Akara (1930-50) | Okidik Holong Odinok | Shalin | |
| Miriyang (1950-70) | Omojok Yaya Ewoho Ferika Krito Imotok | Ohomorok (1956-78) | Bela Irenge Bula Ohilok |
| Balu (1970-) | Lohilok Bola Ongililu Tabaho | Tuhet (1978-) | Fara Ajona Kanyaru Mulek |

Sources: LOGOTOK: Jurey 1981: 30, 37. IBONI: Interviews with Luke Ipotu Ojok and Remijo Lohide.

in chronological sequence which we find among the Pari-Lokoya-Lulubo systems. We have to be careful, however, as the data on the Lopit age systems are limited. The Logotok (Lohutok) and Iboni are located on the southeastern side of the Lopit mountains. Data on other villages, especially those in the northern parts with whom the Pari have had closer relations, are not available.

*Correspondence and borrowing of age system vocabulary*

Many of the Pari age-set names do not make sense in the Pari language. They were originally age-set names or ruling age-grade names of neigh-bouring peoples. (Note that, in the case of the Pari, the *mojomiji* are referred to by the name of the most senior age-set. But among the Lotuho cluster, they take a specific name, apart from age-set names.) Let us examine some of the oldest ones (Table 2.2). As for Marik and Mathaor, they are not Pari names. They should therefore be of foreign origin, but I have not yet found from whom they were adopted. Some of the early age-set names during the latter half of the nineteenth century are of Lotuho origin. They are Akara, Lidukaaro, Korodo, Thomme, Ibou and Muura. *Akara* means the Toposa in various Lotuho languages (*Akaro* in Pari) and the name of the *monyomiji* in Hiyala village during 1853–73 (Table 2.4) (Grüb, 1992: 144). Dukaaro (Lidukaaro) is the name of the *monyomiji* in Loronyo village during 1867–89 (Hino, 1980: 144). Korodo is the name of *monyomiji* during the Mahdist period (Hatulang: personal communication). Tome (Thomme), which means 'elephant' in many Eastern Nilotic languages, is one of the 'alternations' of the Lotuho *monyomiji*. Ibou and Mura (Muura) are Lotuho, but may not be age-set names. They mean respectively a 'hyena' and a

*Table 2.4   Ruling age-grades in four Lotuho villages and in Imatari*

| HIYALA | TIRANGORE | CALAMINI | LOBIRA | Period of rule |
|---|---|---|---|---|
| Lemio | Lemio | Ohonyemorok | Lemio | 1793–1813 |
| Awalang | ? | ? | Ihare | 1813–33 |
| Ollongo | Boro | Ogoloma | Hiliama | 1833–53 |
| Akara | Logugu | Hihaya | Ofonik | 1853–73 |
| Nganyanio | Ojetuk | Tibong | Turuk | 1873–93 |
| Domoro | Ngafat | Segelle | Tifinak | 1893–1913 |
| Imatari | Murahatiha | Tuhutuhu | Tehata | 1913–33 |
| Boro | Ngohe | Gala | Ogugu | 1933–57 |
| Nganyanio | Balu | Tibong | Ohuru | 1957–77 |
| Akara | Oahuruk | Hiyaya | Ofonik | 1977– |

| IMATARI | Period of rule |
|---|---|
| Offuruk | 1669–91 |
| Mirriyang | 1691–1713 |
| Jiffia | 1713–35 |
| Tome | 1735–57 |
| Lemio | 1757–79 |

*Source:* Grüb, 1992: 144: Imatari. Hino, 1980: 45.
*Note:* Imatari is the village where all Lotuho lived together before dispersion in the eighteenth century.

'destroyed place' in Lotuho. Mura could be a Bari age-set name meaning 'the unripe' (Beaton, 1936: 139). It is also the name of a Lopit village. After these age-set names, only Kalang and Kilang are of Lotuho origin.

*Table 2.5  Pari age-set names of Bari origin.*

| PARI | BARI | Meaning in Bari |
|---|---|---|
| Kwe[a] | Lokwe | 'Those who stick feathers in their hair'. |
| Akem | Akim[b] | 'The overturners'. |
| (Muura | Mura | 'The unripe'.) |
| Amukwonyin | Mukkonyen | 'Those with closed eyes, because they fear nothing'. |
| Mirithigo | Mertiko[b] | 'The intoxicated'. |
| Bongcut | Bonswot | 'The earshakers' |
| Corogo | Soroko | 'The stabbers'. |
| Limojo | Limojong | 'Those who stay in their places'. |
| Amerkolong | Merkolong | 'Sun drunk'. |
| Alangore | Longure | 'The bright-eyed who turn amorous glances on all women'. |

a) It may be a Bari word meaning 'head' (kwe) (Muratori, 1948: 105).
b) According to Spagnolo (1932: 395), they were borrowed from the Lokoya.
*Source:* Beaton, 1936.

*Table 2.6  Age-classes in Bilinian villages, Bari.*

| BILINIAN | 'DOMADAN | BIRINDI |
|---|---|---|
| – | – | Mulure |
| | | Kiman |
| A Kupir | A Kupir | Akupir |
| Shuroko | – | – |
| Amukonyen | Mukkonyen | Mukkolong |
| – | Akim | Akim |
| Bonshua | Bonswot | Bonswot |
| – | Soroko | Soroko |
| Limojong | Limojong | Limojong |
| Merkolong | Merkolong | Merkolong |
| Amunga | Amunga | Amunga |
| Longure | Longure | Longure |
| Luberi | Lubere | Lubere |
| – | Umbira | Umbira |
| Kelang[a] | Lumadak-Konyen | Lumadak-Konyen |
| Losiwa | Losiwa | Losiwa |
| Amoron(Swodo[a]) | Naringa | Naringa |

a) Oxoriok age-class names.
*Note:* The list of Bilinian names comes from Seligman and Seligman (1932: 263–4). But the name Bilinian is not a village but a district name. It comprises 8 villages including 'Domodan and Birindi (Beaton, 1932: 144).

*Table 2.7   Age-classes in the five villages of Sindiru, Bari.*

| KWORIJIK | JABUR | MORSAK | MEJI | WOROGOR |
|----------|-------|--------|------|---------|
| Lomurie | – | – | – | – |
| Lomeran | Mulusuk | – | – | Launtwan |
| Pitundyan | Monoja | Rujakiding | – | Losegga |
| Pajutwan[a] | Lubere[a] | Lubere[a] | Lubere[a] | Mukkolong[a] |
| Nongkure | Limojong | Rombur | Mukkolong | Nongga |
| Wanyan | Sirimba | Renyaka | Longure | Pajutwan |
| Losiwa | Losiwa | Monoja | Lo'dumun | Wanyang |
| – | – | Loringa | Nerkulya | Nongkure |
| – | – | – | Loringa | Losiwa |
| – | – | – | Losiwa | – |
| – | – | – | Naruja | – |

a) These were the oldest men on the Tax Lists in 1932.(Beaton 1932: 145)

*Table 2.8   Age-sets and ruling age-grades in Liria (Lokoya)*

| Age-sets | Ruling age-grades |
|----------|-------------------|
| Kalang | |
| Ocwada | Amukonyen |
| Okwer | ( ? –1956) |
| Otila | |
| Kalang | |
| | |
| Kwara | |
| Bondipala | |
| Itiyo | Thome |
| Yulu | (1956–72) |
| Tangakwo | |
| | |
| Tangakwo | |
| Iticok | Mura |
| Akiu | (1972–) |
| Maridi | |

*Source:* Interview with Adriano Jacob Ohirek, June 1986, Juba.

Most of the Pari age-set names around the turn of the century seem to have been Bari (age-class) names, which are found in the lists by Beaton (1936: 134–42) (Table 2.5). It is significant that many of these Pari names also correspond well in chronological sequence with age-set names in Bilinian villages (but not with those in Sindiru) (Tables 2.6 and 2.7). They are Amukwonyin (Pari)-Mukkonyen (Bari), Bongcut-Bonswot, Corogo-Soroko, Limojo-Limojong, Amerkolong-Merkolong and Alangore-Longure. The members of Longure were possibly about 50–55 years old in 1932 (Beaton, 1932: 144). It had been named some 35–40 years before. At the time those of Alangore, who took over power in c.1927, would have been about 41–45 years old. This gap in age is consistent with the argument that the Bari age system was adopted as a model by the Pari.

Alangore is also the name of *monyomiji* among some parts of the Acholi, at Pajok (Parajwok) village in particular, and their age is identical with

*Table 2.9  Lulubo ruling age-grades*

| | |
|---|---|
| Mokido | |
| Mirtiko | |
| Dukaru | |
| Taruka | |
| Limojo | |
| Langure | |
| Muruli | |
| Obongoro | |
| Kalang | |
| Wandicho | ( ? –1948) |
| Okwer | (1948–58) |
| Kwara | (1958–75) |
| Lomini | (1975–) |

(Lado 1981; Simonse 1984)

*Table 2.10  'Age-grades' in Ngangala*

| 1. Wala Kara | The old men who walk about with nothing to do. |
|---|---|
| 2. Lukwong | Those shading their eyes with their hands and looking for enemies. |
| 3. Kurjuman (Turjuman) | Brave like the foreigners. |
| 4. Mukonyen | Those who shut their eyes and rush to war. |
| 5. Bonswot | Those who shake their ears. |
| 6. Merkolong | Hard and full of fire (sun drunk). (oldest on Tax Lists) |
| 7. Longure | The bright-eyed. |
| 8. Igari | Vide Oxoriok. |
| 9. Kalang | ditto |
| 10. Wanditio | ditto |
| 11. Osoda | ditto |
| 12. Ukwer | ditto |
| 13. Otela | ditto |

those of the Pari. It would have been adopted by the Acholi from the Pari, not directly from the Bari (see below).

It is remarkable that after Alangore there is no Pari age-set name which seems to have been adopted from the Bari. On the other hand, starting from Kalang, we find a high degree of correspondence with the Lokoya (Liria village) and the Lulubo, both in age-set names (in the case of the Lulubo, names of successive *monyomiji*) and in their chronological sequences (Tables 2.8 and 2.9). Because all of these Pari age-set names, except Kalang, are in Pari, and because the Lokoya in Liria and the Lulubo admit that they have adopted them from the Pari, we assume that the Pari system has been working as a model for at least the past sixty years.

Apart from the word *mojomiji*, there are other terms concerning the age system which have been adopted from the peoples of the Lotuho cluster (see Table 2.1). The *mojomiji* is also called *weegi-paac*, 'fathers of the village', which is apparently a direct translation of *monyomiji*. The senior two age-sets of the *mojomoji* are called *jo-wic*, 'the head people'. When an animal is sacrificed, they take the head, while the next two age-sets take the neck. (The idea would appear to have originated from the Lotuho cluster who call the most senior age-set 'head' and the next one 'neck'.)[6]

Other examples are *bali* (*obele* in the Lotuho cluster) which means a gathering place or a club house for an age-set, and *lithir* (*otir*), the strongest wrestler in an age-set. The Pari word for the drum posts in the central dancing ground, *balacar*, is also found among the Acholi and Lango. For them it is not drum posts but branched poles on which trophies of killed animals are hung (Seligman and Seligman, 1932: 116 and Plate XXXIII). Pari informants told me that the word had been derived from the Lopit word *afalacar*, meaning drum posts.

## Directions of Mutual Relations and their Background

Let us now expand the scope of our examination to mutual relations between age systems. First, between the Lulubo and the Bari, many of the older names of the Lulubo *monyomiji* seem to have been of Bari origin, namely Mokido (Mokkido), Miritido (Mertiko), Limojong (Limojong), Langure (Longure) and Muluri (Muruli?) (names in brackets are Bari names) (Beaton, 1936) (see also Table 2.9). The relations between the two age systems may be considered in the context of the close cultural affinities between the two peoples (Simonse, 1992: 52), irrespective of their linguistic difference. There are also names borrowed from the Lotuho cluster. Dukaru is adopted from the Lotuho proper (Dukaaro). Taruka is an age-set name of the Lokoya meaning vulture, and Obongoro should be derived from *abongoro*, the Lokoya word for the taking over by a new *monyomiji*).[7] After Obongoro, the names of the four following Lulubo *monyomiji* were borrowed from the Pari by way of the Lokoya of Liria, as discussed above. Then the present *monyomiji*, Lomini, is a Bari age-set name meaning 'the brave' (Beaton, 1936: 138).

It seems that interethnic relations between the Bari, especially those at Bilinian village, and the Pari were much stronger during the last century than at present. Trade was a major aspect of this. As recorded by the first European travellers and missionaries who started to visit Bariland in the 1840s after the opening of the White Nile trade route, indigenous trade relations had already been established between the western Ethiopian highlands and present-day eastern Equatoria, with the Pari acting as middlemen. Copper, brass, glass beads, cloth, and salt, most of which came originally from northern Sudan, were brought in through the Pari. Not only the Bari, but other peoples like the Lokoya and the Lotuho also obtained these materials from the Pari. In exchange, the Bari traded iron, for the production of which they were renowned in the region (Kurimoto, 1995b).

During the last two decades of the nineteenth century, Bari society, which had once enjoyed prosperity, became totally devastated because of looting by armed invaders from northern Sudan and also because of the outbreak of rinderpest and smallpox. Many Bari took refuge among neighbouring peoples including the Pari (Simonse, 1992: 101–4). They seem to have stayed with the Pari for more than ten years, because their return home at the beginning of this century was reported in the colonial archives.[8]

Two Bilinian village names, Boyi and Bura, are interesting for our argument. Boi is the name of the dominant section of the Pari, including five villages apart from Kor (see below). In Anywaa (Anuak) it means the Pari. And Bura is one of the Boi villages (in Lwo languages *bura* is the place where the elders sit in a village). This may be evidence of a Bari-Pari connection in the past, which could go beyond the time scope of this paper. However, the presence of the 'Bori', now assimilated to the Mandari, on the east bank of the Nile to the immediate north of Bilinian (Buxton, 1963: 36) may suggest that in the past the Pari population had a wider distribution and the ethnic boundaries were more blurred than they are today.

At the time of my fieldwork among the Pari, they had little direct contact with the Bari or with the 'Bori' of Mandari. I did not observe cases of intermarriage, trade or visiting. But historical relations in the past would explain the correspondence in age-set names between the Bari and Pari.

The *monyomiji* system among the Acholi of Pajok (Parajwok) village merits attention. During the 1890s, the entire population of Kor village, one of the two sections of Pari society, took refuge at Pajok, after a series of serious stick fights with the Boi section. They stayed there for some years and it was the time when Pajok adopted the system from the Pari refugees (Kurimoto, n.d.; Simonse, 1992: 46), which explains why the age-set name of Alangore is shared by both peoples. The members were youngsters when they stayed at Pajok. The *monyoniji* system had originally come from the Lopit to the Pari, and was thus adopted by the Acholi.

The Pari have enjoyed friendly relations with the Lokoya of Liria. There has been no warfare between them in remembered history. The high degree of synchronization between the two *monyomiji* can be seen as an outcome and condition of this peaceful co-existence.

In contrast, the Lopit are looked down upon by the Pari as 'cowards' (*lwar*), who cannot match the Pari in warfare. They are, however, important partners in trade, bond-friendship and intermarriage. The Pari trade domestic animals, grain and dried fish and meat for large pots, grain and domestic animals from the Lopit. Trade relations become crucial for their survival, when either side is stricken by hunger. In addition, the Pari depend on the Lopit for the supply of bamboos which are needed for house construction and are not available in Pariland. In any event, the low esteem in which the Pari hold the Lopit may be the reason why they share few age-set names, whereas the Pari *mojomiji* system is said to have been adopted from the Lopit and the two systems have organizational similarities in the gradual transfer of power to the new *monyomiji*.[9]

It should also be noted that, as far as the Lopit age-set names available to us are concerned, there are few names shared not only with the Pari but with other peoples such as the Lokoya, Lulubo, Bari and Lotuho. This could be a reflection of their marginal politico-military position in the network of interethnic relations.

However, just as the Pari adopted the *monyomiji* system from them, there is another interesting case of Lopit influence, namely the Surmic-speaking Tenet, a small group of people surrounded by and intermingled with the Lopit, who live in the northeastern part of the Lopit mountains. They have the *monyomiji*, but the term refers to the young people whose power is very limited and who are under the authority of the elders. The adoption was not completed because of 'the gerontocratic bias' (Simonse, 1992: 46-7).

Unlike the Lopit, the Lotuho are considered formidable enemies (*jur*) by the Pari, while, like the Lopit, they are partners in trade and inter-marriage. I shall argue that the ambiguous relations of hostility and peace serve as a major condition for the resonance of age systems.

Hostility between the Pari, on the one hand, and the Lopit and Lotuho on the other, has deepened in the present situation of ongoing civil war. In 1986, the Lotuho village of Loronyo, one of the centres of 'the twin kingdoms' (Simonse, 1992) of the Lotuho, was attacked by the *mojomiji* and Pari young men who had joined the Sudan People's Liberation Army

(SPLA). A part of the village was burned and looted. In 1990 three Lopit villages were attacked and destroyed in the same way. The military role of the *monyomiji* system has been revitalized (Kurimoto, 1994: 102-4). Since the Lopit did not counterattack, the interethnic conflict has reinforced the derogatory view held of them.

## Emergence of an Interethnic System

*Peace, warfare and resonance*

Interrelations among age systems are complex. Although it is likely that the *monyomiji* systems spread originally from the Lotuho proper to other peoples, the interrelations as a whole cannot be explained as a matter of cultural diffusion from one centre to the periphery. The systems reacted to one another, in a process which is called 'resonance' in this chapter. This is particularly true, as we have seen, among the Pari, Lokoya, Lulubo, and Bari. The reason may be partly that we have richer data on these peoples. In my view future studies will reveal other phenomena of resonance among other peoples with *monyomiji* systems.

It is my hypothesis that the *monyomiji* systems developed into their present synchronized form as a result of the resonance in the historical process of interethnic relations, which have been of both peaceful co-existence and hostility. There should presumably have been the phenomenon that, in the repetitive cycle of peace and warfare, each social unit of the *monyomiji* system developed as the equivalent unit appropriate for meaningful interactions: as equal partners in peace and warfare. Thus the systems emerged as an interethnic system, providing a framework for shared codes of behaviour across linguistic and ethnic boundaries.[10]

For this interethnic system to be operational, members of the corresponding age-sets among the various peoples should preferably occupy the same status. In fact, there is a high degree of synchronization in the date of the initiation of new *monyomiji* among various peoples. Between 1955 and 1958, it took place among the Pari (1958), the Lokoya of Liria (1956), the Lulubo (1958), the Lopit (Iboni and Mura) (1956), and the Lotuho (1957), and again between 1975 and 1978, among the Lulubo (1975), the Lotuho (1976), the Lopit (1977–8), and the Pari (1977), with the Lokoya of Liria having performed it a little earlier in 1972. This synchronization is an indispensable aspect of the resonance. It enables corresponding age-sets always to share the same position in the *monyomiji* system, making them meaningful units for interaction.

The argument invites us to reconsider what we mean by an 'ethnic group' as an appropriate unit for ethnographic studies. A case in point is the age system of Ngangala village on the Juba-Torit road, reported by Beaton. It is located in the Bari-Lokoya-Lulubo border lands and, although its present inhabitants are generally considered to be Bari, their ethnic identity is complex. Oral tradition tells us that the founder of the village was a Lulubo man who married a Bari and an Ohoriok (Lokoya) wife. The inhabitants intermarry and are multilingual. The names of their 'age-grades' (possibly confused with age-sets) correspond well with those of the Pari-Lokoya (Liria)-Lulubo. In particular, later age-set names are almost identical with those of Liria (see Table 2.10) (Beaton, 1932).

The 'multi-ethnic' composition of Ngangala may be highly evocative of other peoples dealt with in this chapter, whom I have represented as concrete and distinct 'ethnic groups'. What matters is not whether the people of Ngangala are Lokoya, Bari, or Lulubo, but that, as a territorial unit, they do have a *monyomiji* system, which enables them to interact with other units.

As argued by Ehret (1982) and Simonse (1992), eastern Equatoria is a 'melting pot', where groups with different cultural and linguistic affinities, such as Cushitic, Nilotic (Southern, Eastern, and Western), Surmic, Central Sudanic, Kuliak, and possibly even Khoisan, have been interacting for thousands of years. The *monyomiji* systems hold the key to deepening and enriching ethnographic studies in the region.

The resonant nature of the *monyomiji* systems seems to have further theoretical implications. David Turton has recently argued, based on the work of Simon Harrison on Melanesian warfare and aggression (1993), that for the Mursi and their neighbours in southwestern Ethiopia 'war is a common ritual language by which they make themselves significant to each other and to themselves as independent political entities' (Turton, 1993: 32). His primary concern is to challenge the common-sense view that warfare is something abnormal to be eradicated. Although my emphasis is on both peace and war, Turton's argument is highly relevant to the *monyomiji* systems; they also provide the same sort of 'common language' to different political entities.

In the concluding part of his book Harrison argues as follows:

> They fought and fostered war in their cult, not because they lacked normative ties beyond the village but, quite the opposite, *precisely because they had such ties* and could only define themselves as a polity by acting collectively to overcome and transcend them (Harrison, 1993: 150).

Here 'normative ties beyond the village' refer to peaceful relations, i.e. trade and intermarriage. Significantly the role of war and peace in inter-village community relations in the Sepik basin of Papua New Guinea is parallel to that in interethnic relations in southeastern Sudan. A notable difference is that, for the *monyomiji* systems, there is no need to 'overcome and transcend' normative ties beyond the territorial unit of the systems. They are the commonly shared framework which assures interactions of both warfare and peace, and thus the autonomy and independence of each polity (territorial unit).

### 'Resonance' in the wider regional setting

The phenomenon of resonance or synchronization of the age systems between different peoples is widely found in other parts of East Africa. There are many cases of resonance between Bantu-speaking and 'Nilo-Hamitic' (Eastern and Southern Nilotic) peoples. For instance, the Sonjo, sedentary agriculturalists in Tanzania, are said to have borrowed graded age-set systems from the neighbouring Maasai, who used to be their enemies. In particular, military traits of the Maasai *moran* including their costumes are adopted by the Sonjo. The interethnic relations are not only of warfare and hostility, because Maasai also attend Sonjo rituals (Gray, 1963: 23–4, 83). Although it is not known whether, on those ritual occasions, people of both sides attend and intermingle on an age-set basis, and to what extent the two age systems are synchronized, it seems probable that the age system provides a common ground for interaction both of warfare and of peace.

A similar example is found in western Kenya between the Bantu-speaking Tiriki and the Kalenjin-speaking Tirik. LeVine and Sangree (1962) argue that the Kalenjin and Maasai have enjoyed military supremacy because of their age systems, and that some Bantu neighbours such as the Tiriki adopted the age system in order to defend themselves. Although the argument is based on the alleged 'military supremacy', which is later criticized by de Wolf (1980), the fact remains that the Tiriki adopted the Tirik way of initiation (male circumcision) and hence their age-set system. De Wolf himself also reports that the age-set system of the Bantu-speaking Bukusu is very similar to that of the Southern Nilotic speaking Sebei, although the two systems lack political, legal, or military functions (1980: 307–8). Recurrence of age-set names between the Bantu-speaking Kuria and the Southern Nilotic-speaking Kipsigis is pointed out by Ruel (1962: 18). This may also have extended to the Gikuyu and the Mbeere. They each have a pair of 'generation classes', and two of the four class names are age-set names shared by the Kuria and Kipsigis (Ruel, 1962: 36; Glazier, 1976).

It is not only Bantu peoples who have adopted age systems. An interesting case is the So of Uganda who were originally mountain-dwelling hunters and agriculturalists. As economic and social relations were established with the neighbouring Karimojong, the So adopted many of their sociocultural elements: not only the language and traits of a 'cattle complex', but also an age system which is a combination of generation-sets and age-sets. The borrowing of the Karimojong age system seems to have started around 1900 and was completed in the 1920s. In the process of adoption the So modified the Karimojong system to accommodate existing social institutions (Laughlin and Laughlin, 1974).

The relationship between the Koegu, Kara, and Nyangatom in the lower Omo valley of southwestern Ethiopia is comparable to the above case. The pastoral Nyangatom, who belong to the 'Karimojong cluster', have been expanding their territory from the Sudan side to the Omo valley. In the process they started to have contacts with the Kara, Omotic-speaking agriculturalists, who adopted the Nyangatom age-set names (Tornay, 1981: 168; see also his chapter in this volume on the Nyangatom age system). The Koegu, a minority group of hunter-gatherers and agriculturalists, who have their own language (Surmic) and ethnic identity but form a sort of subordinate class in Kara society, also adopted the Nyangatom age-set system, presumably via the Kara, and not directly from the Nyangatom. As the Nyangatom acquired automatic weapons from Sudan, and continued their territorial expansion, the Koegu switched their alliance from the Kara to the Nyangatom in the late 1980s. For the Koegu age-sets now have little political and ritual significance among themselves, but they are very useful when they and the Nyangatom exchange visits, since they can stay and eat with age mates of the corresponding age-set. In other words Koegu age-sets are meaningful in interethnic relations (Matsuda, 1992 and personal communication).

### Age systems: 'good to be copied'

As regards the *monyomiji* systems, emphasis is put on their political, military and judicial functions. Each system is essential to the social structure of its territorial unit. Some cases discussed above, however, show that an age system may be borrowed in a very casual way. It plays little role in the society which has adopted it, as, for instance, with the Bukusu, Sebei and Koegu. This leads us to question why the systems are so widely spread across ethnic and linguistic boundaries.

In principle age systems have universalistic characteristics. They provide a social framework for institutionalizing both stratified relations between seniors and juniors and egalitarian relations among peers. There is no doubt that these general characteristics are fundamental in the wide distribution of age systems. Another reason could be the visibility and the spectacularly splendid features of the ceremonies and activities of an age system. This is particularly the case for young people or warriors. These ceremonial occasions related to the age system are often accompanied by dances and singing, which offer the people opportunities of courtship and of expressing themselves in magnificent costumes.

Oral traditions narrating the origin of the Pari age system illustrate this. When a group of Pari men went hunting and came to a Lopit village, they saw Lopit dancing by age-sets. This was very attractive and beautiful and is why they adopted the system. A similar story is found among the Mandari. During this century their young men adopted the Atuot initiation ceremonies and started to form 'bead sets'. They have virtually no politico-military function, but helped Mandari youths to associate with Atuot and Aliab Dinka youths who have corresponding sets in cattle camps where they stay together (Buxton, 1963: 125–6). It is known that for young people cattle camps are the places of dances and courtship, and the Mandari's adoption of the bead set enabled them to participate in an multi-ethnic setting.

The songs and dances of one people are easily adopted by another, as long as they sound good and are fashionable. It does not really matter for those who adopt them what the original meaning of the songs and dances is. Nor does it matter whether they are adopted from friends or enemies. Thus *karuma*, a Murle dance, is very popular among the Pari. They also have many Lotuho songs. Among the Lulubo, Pari and Lokoya songs are commonly sung. Since the 1980s, however, Bari songs have become increasingly popular, as Bari became the language of literacy (Simonse, personal communication). Among the Koegu, a Nyangatom-style dance is popular and they dance to songs sung not only in Koegu, Kara and Nyangatom, but also in four other languages of neighbouring peoples (Matsuda, 1992).

Just as songs and dances are 'good to be copied', so is the age system. To use a metaphorical expression, the age system is like the institutions of the modern nation state. Every state has legislative, judicial, administrative, and military institutions, which guarantee its sovereignty and international recognition as a state. They are also 'good to be copied' and thus have become universal.

Significantly, as regards this aspect, age systems appear to have some common features with modern military organizations. The modern army, be it a national or guerrilla army, also has a well organized hierarchy, visible and spectacular ceremonies, songs and flags. Put in other words, age systems, the warrior ethos of young people, and the modern army have interacted and overlapped, forming a new, but tradition-based, politico-military culture. Taking the argument a little further in this direction, we can understand why most of the Pari young men joined the rank and file of the Sudan People's Liberation Army (SPLA) in the mid-1980s and have been actively engaged in military operations (Kurimoto, 1994).

In any event, how each state institution is operated differs from one state to another. In some states certain institutions are only nominal, while in others they are politically significant. In relations between two societies, such as the Nyangatom and the Koegu, or the Karimojong and the So, in which one society with an age system dominates the other in terms of population as well as cultural and political influences, the adoption of the age system may remain at the superficial level. In southeastern Sudan, however, owing to certain historical and social conditions, the *monyomiji* system developed and spread among societies which have no clear hierarchy or domination-subordination relations among them (with the exceptions of the Tenet and the Acholi of Pajok who are situated on the peripheries). The *monyomiji* systems ensure that those polities, i.e. the territorial units of the systems, are equal partners and provide a commonly shared framework of interactions of both peace and war.

# Notes

1 For *Nyalam*, see Kurimoto, 'New Year Hunting Ritual of the Pari: Elements of Hunting Culture among the Nilotes' (1996). It is performed at the beginning of the dry season and the first game is obtained and sacrificed in a ritual hunt. Similar rituals are found among the peoples discussed in this paper: *Odhurak* (Lokoya), *Naalam* (Lotuho), *Kajuwaya* (Lulubo) and *Lori* (Bari). This is another aspect of the cultural 'resonance' found in the region.

2 It was through personal communication with Simon Simonse and his Lulubo and Lokoya research assistants that I came to realize the issue.

3 The linguistic, cultural and historical configuration of the Lotuho cluster is a topic awaiting future study. The relationship between the plains Lotuho and the others, who may be called mountain or hill Lotoho, might be an interesting issue to compare with the ·Maasai-Dorobo, Kalenjin-Okiek, and mountain Pokot-plains Pokot relationships.

4 It has been reported that the Lango and Didinga age-set names have 'a large measure of correspondence' (Nalder, 1937: 20). However, as the Didinga age system is of the Ateker type (Simonse, personal communication), the resonance of the two systems apparently remains at the level of age-set name correspondence.

5 The Bari do have age-grades, but the middle-aged grade has little politico-military function.

6 Note that the Shilluk call sub-sets of an age-set 'head', 'neck' and 'middle' according to the order of seniority (Howell, 1941: 60).

7 *Obongoro* in Lokoya also means 'apology' or 'atonement' because taking over power implies apologizing to the sitting *monyomiji* (Simonse, personal communication).

8 'Report on Nile province' by Macallister, 16 June 1902, 'Shuli Correspondence' Inward vol.II, A/16/2, Uganda National Archives, Entebbe.

9 The duration of the Pari's present low esteem of the Lopit should be questioned. It may be misleading to assume that it is permanent and unchangeable. Otherwise it is difficult to explain why the Pari copied the age system of a despised people.

10 I am indebted to suggestions from Professor K. Fukui for this argument.

# 3 Age, Conflict & Power in the *Monyomiji* Age Systems

## SIMON SIMONSE[1]

In the debate on the structure of East African age systems the *monyomiji* systems of southeastern Sudan have so far played no role. This is regrettable not only because they present some unique features worthy of study in themselves, but also because they are an important link in the chain of East African age systems which makes them valuable for regional comparison.

Early observers completely overlooked the age system. Neither Baker nor Emin Pasha, both of whom spent time among the Lotuho and Lokoya, made any mention of the *monyomiji*. The first district administrators of the area after it was taken over by the Anglo-Egyptian Sudan, Lord Raglan and J. H. Driberg, make no mention of it. The Seligmans, who spent part of the winter of 1920–21 among the Lotuho, make only brief mention of the *monyomiji*: three pages on age-grades, age-sets and generational succession (1926:14-17) as compared with ten on kingship.

In 1937, a longer account, written by two administrators of Torit District, appears as part of Nalder's ethnographic survey (1937:91–8) and in 1940/42 *Anthropos* published a general ethnographic article by the missionary Molinaro (1940/41:173–5). Other ethnographic material left by the missionaries Pazzaglia and Muratori was later brought together in two doctoral theses written by students of the Catholic University of the Sacred Heart in Milano (Paolucci, 1970; Novelli, 1970).

The Lotuho were included in the list of locations to which the first batch of trained British post-war anthropologists was sent[2] but it so happened that Elinor MacHatton, after spending two years in Ilyeu, Eastern Lotuho, during 1951–52 and 1953–54, did not pursue her career as an anthropologist after she married the last British District Commissioner of Torit. Only after the Addis Ababa agreement did anthropologists appear again in the *monyomiji* area which had been one of the main battlefields of the Civil War: Grüb among the plains Lotuho of the kingdom of Loronyo (1992), Kurimoto among the Pari (a dozen articles in Japanese and English) and myself, based among the Lulubo but studying kingship among the Lotuho and Lokoya (1992).

The limited interest must be attributable to the obsession of the early observers with kingship as an indication of evolutionary progress. Seligman himself was deeply involved in the debate on divine kingship after he had provided Frazer with the core empirical material for *The Golden Bough*, on Shilluk regicide. Grüb, in his monograph on the Lotuho, criticizes the early ethnographers of the area like Seligman because of their Eurocentric focus on kingship: 'The observer sees what he is accustomed to see in Europe: individual dominance' (Grüb, 1992:128).

On the other hand, since travellers were usually the guests of kings they were ill-placed to make observations on age organization. 1995 saw the publication of the first monograph written by a *monyemiji, Lokoya of Sudan, Culture and Ethnic Government* by the Lokoya Philip Lomodong Lako. Significantly, the cover shows a drawing of a *monyemiji* in full dancing gear.

The *monyomiji* age systems are, with some variations, practised by all the Lotuho-speaking peoples: Lokoya, Lopit (comprising the Ngaboli, Dorik, Ngotira and Lomiya), Lango, Imatong, Dongotono, Logir, Plains Lotuho and Highland Lotuho or Ohoriok. The system has also been adopted by communities bordering on the Lotuho speakers: the Lwo-speaking Pari and Acholi of Parajok, the Madi-speaking Lulubo, and the Surma-speaking Tenet, the Bari of Ngangala.

The Lotuho proper have the largest political units among the communities sharing the *monyomiji* age system. Since the middle of the nineteenth century the Lotuho have been divided into three kingdoms: Loudo, the smallest and for a long time a separate unit, and two kingdoms which are successors to the historical kingdom of Imatari: Tirangore, comprising five villages under the dynasty of Hujang, and Loronyo with 14 villages under the Mayya dynasty. The current queen Ihure, who succeeded to the throne of Mayya after the death of her husband in 1959, has not been recognized by a number of sections in Loronyo itself; a dynastic rival has set himself up as a rainmaker/king. In the other societies of the Lotuho group of kingdoms may vary from eight villages to a single, large, village.

The Lotuho live in large compact villages, often numbering more than a thousand inhabitants and consisting of a number of sections (*amangatim*). Each section has its own ritual infrastructure: drum-house, pylon-shrine, dancing-ground, meeting-points for *monyomiji* and *aduri horwong*, etc. A number of villages are united under a king or rainmaker.

According to the typology proposed by Bernardi (1985:42) the Lotuho and related peoples qualify to rank among the societies where the age system is a 'primary model' of political organization. Applying the more restrictive criteria proposed by Tornay (1988:285) who criticizes Bernardi for including societies where the role of the age system is subordinated to the central authority of the king or chief, as is the case with the Nyakyusa age villages and the Zulu age-based regiments, the Lotuho still qualify as a 'primary model'.

In the Lotuho area the *monyomiji*, the ruling generation, are not subordinate to the king. They are his principal interlocutors and, frequently, his opponents. Their opposition can lead to deposing or even to killing the king.[3] The king and the *monyomiji* are engaged in a political game in which either can be loser or winner.

In historical times when the Lotuho or Lokoya kings wanted to strengthen their position they did not rely on the *monyomiji*. They formed their own armies consisting of clients whose loyalty was bought by the gift of firearms. Kings and *monyomiji* often pursued opposing interests. At the turn of the century, a few years after a series of spectacular victories by his *Awusu* or royal army, king Lomoro of Tirangore was expelled from his village by the *monyomiji*, accused of causing drought. Had the *monyomiji* identified with their king's victories, this should, at least in his own village, have given him enough credit politically to survive a season of drought.

## The *monyomiji*: age-grade, generation-set and alternation

The term *monyomiji* (sing. *monyemiji*), the 'fathers' or 'owners' (*monye*) of the village (*amiji*), may refer to different categories of men depending on the context in which it is used. In the first place it refers to the age-grade of men who have completed the initiation at the level of the village-section (*amangat*). It follows the grade of *eito horwong* (pl. *aduri horwong*) in which a boy stays for about five years. To become an *eito horwong* a boy simply digs a hole in front of his mother's house. As an *eito horwong* he is bullied to perform all sorts of menial duties for the *monyomiji* of his section.

Initiation at the sectional level is presided over by the *amonye mangat*, the Master of the Section, while the initiative for it is taken by the father of the initiand. It is a straightforward purificatory sacrifice, performed at around the age of 18 either individually or for a small group of coevals from the same *amangat*. The Master of the Section applies the rumen of a white he-goat, provided by the father, to the initiand's body to purify him before he is introduced to the section's drum house.[4]

At the end of the ritual year, all members of the section who have been initiated in the course of the year are given a group name. The occasion is called *najingana* ('entering') and qualifies a man to marry and to take part in war. During his first years as an initiate he should only play a supportive role in war, taking food supplies to the warring *monyomiji* (Novelli, 1973:600) and being responsible for the protection of the herds.

*Figure 3.1 Age-set formation and generational succession among the Lotuho over a period of 25 years*

| Name of Age-set | Year 4 of *nefira* | Year 9 of *nefira* | Year 14 of *nefira* | Year 19 of *nefira* | Year 2 of new *nefira* |
|---|---|---|---|---|---|
| A | After 4 years retired elders who entered age-grade of *amarwak* as *efirat* of the previous *monyomiji*, continue to play an advisory role | Retired advisory elders | Retired elders | Retired elders | Retired elders |
| B | *ahou* (head) of *monyomiji* | Leaders of ruling generation | *ahou* | *monyomiji ahou* | Retired elders |
| C | *amurut* (neck) of *monyomiji* | *amurut* | *amurut* | *monyomiji amurut* | Retired |
| D | *monyomiji etahunihi/nasuhe* (breast) or *nehiji* (middle) | *etahunihi* | *etahunihi* | *monyomiji etahunihi* | Retired |
| E | *efirat* of *monyomiji* | *efirat* | *efirat* | *monyomiji efirat* | Retired; as *efirat* of retired *monyomiji* advisers to F |
| F | *adhuri horwon* | Most have passed *najinganga* and are in age-grade of *monyomiji* | *olojingat* (*monyomiji* of the initiation, but not of *nefira*) | *olojingat* | After 3 years: *monyomiji ahou*; seniors of F have waited for 15 years for *nefira* |
| G | Not yet formed | *ahduri-horwon* | Most have passed *najinganga* and are now in the age-grade of *monyomiji* | *olojingat* | *monyomiji amurut* seniors of G waited for more than 10 years to take over |

*Figure 3.1 cont.*

| Age-set | Year 4 of *nefira* | Year 9 of *nefira* | Year 14 of *nefira* | Year 19 of *nefira* | Year 2 of new *nefira* |
|---|---|---|---|---|---|
| H | Not yet formed | not yet formed | *aduri-horwon* | Recently undergone *najingana* | *monyomiji asuhe* seniors of H waited for over 5 years as *olojingat* |
| I | Not yet formed | not yet formed | not yet formed | *aduri-horwon* | *monyomiji efirat* became *monyomiji* straight from *aduri-horwon* |
| J | Not yet formed | not yet formed | not yet formed | not yet formed | *aduri-horwon* |

Every four or five years these newly admitted *monyomiji* are united in one village age-set in a ceremony presided over by the Master of the Village (*amonyemiji*). When four successive age-sets have been formed in this way it is time to unite and push for the retirement of the age-sets making up the generation in power. The word *monyomiji* is also used to refer to the four age-sets who rule the village and the country for a period of 22 years. After this they hand over power to a new generation. English-speaking informants normally refer to them as 'the ruling generation'.

About a year after the changeover in the village, power is handed over at the level of the kingdom, a ceremony presided over by the king. This royal *nefira*, which is supposed to take place every 22 years, is considered the most spectacular they have, by the Lotuho.

At the level of the kingdom, those who have undergone only the sectional and village ceremonies are called *olojingat* ('those of the initiation'), as distinct from those who have been handed power in the *nefira*. For the *efirat* the *olojingat* are still apprentices.

As noted above, the meaning of the term *monyomiji* depends on the context: the same man, who claims services from *aduri horwong* as a *monyemiji*, may be ridiculed by the *monyomiji*, members of the ruling generation, as a mere initiate (*olojingat*).

At the *nefira* – the ceremony at which the fire is kindled from which all individual hearths will be ignited – the age-sets of the various villages are united into a single 'generation' with a name given by the king. They will

*Figure 3.2 Succession of alternations, using the same age-sets in Figure 3.1. The situation is depicted in the period that B, C, D, and E form the* monyomiji.

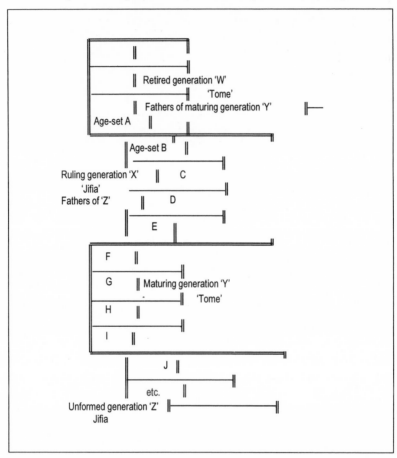

be responsible for the well-being of the country for a period of 22 years. Since admission to this group does not depend on age or achievement the term 'generation' is appropriate, although the idea that successive political generations should coincide with generations in the family and at the level of descent is absent.[5]

The idea of a filial link between alternating generations exists. Partly this is a corollary of the antagonism between adjacent generations. 'Fathers' are expected to help their 'sons' in their quest for power. In Lotuho this fundamental logic has resulted in the idea of two parallel 'set-lines', named after the generation whose succession to power caused the downfall of Imatari ('Tome') and who spread from the old centre to the various, still existing villages. The Jifia were their successors.

*Asik* (pl. *nahasik*), 'house', is the term used both for age-set and for the alternating generation. Members of the same 'house' should assist one another. The novices who are bullied by the *monyomiji* can expect help from the retired *amarwak* (elders). The retired elders are expected to use their influence to facilitate the rise to power of their 'sons', and to protect them against excessive demands imposed by the ruling generation. According to information collected by Pazzaglia, each *asik* has its own songs. From the age of *eito-horwong* a boy knows which alternation he will belong to and will learn its songs. Most of the songs give expression to the rivalry between the alternations.

Next to this filial rhetoric applied to alternations, the relationship between the *monyomiji* − 'fathers of the village' − and the rest of society is expressed as an adult-child relationship. The retired elders are equated with mere children under the care of the *monyomiji*. While the mechanism behind the solidarity between alternating generations is compelling, we should not make too much of the different idioms in which awareness of it is expressed. When I asked the *monyomiji* of Loming which of their generations was Tome and which Jifia, the question rang no bell.

To underline the organic unity of the generation, its age-sets are put in a hierarchical order. The oldest, the 'head' (*ahou*), and the second, the *amurut* (the neck), play a leading role in village affairs. The last two, the breast (*asuhe*) or the 'middle' (*nehiji*), and the *efirat* (those who have joined in the year of the *nefira*[6]) are assigned responsibilities of a more executive character. Each age-set is entitled to particular portions of meat at sacrificial meals, partly reflecting the body parts after which they have been labelled.

We need therefore to distinguish between the *monyomiji* as an age-grade and the *monyomiji* as a generation or alternation succeeding to power. A man who enters the *monyomiji* age-grade at the age of 20 may have to wait until he is 40 before he is allowed to speak in assemblies of the 'ruling generation' of his village. However, those who wait longest will have the most senior positions among the *monyomiji* when they finally take over power. A man who has waited for 20 years must be a senior *ahou*.

Among the Lulubo, Lokoya and Pari, who have cycles of relatively short duration (12–16 years), there is no explicit idea of a filial link between alternating sets of *monyomiji*. However, they do have a cyclical conception of succession and retirement. The retired elders are equated with children and the *monyomiji* should provide them with the same kind of attention and protection.

While the basic structure of the *monyomiji* system is the same among the different societies practising it, there is considerable variation in the concrete elaboration of the age system: in the procedures of recruitment, in the length of the period of rule, in the presence or absence of an overlap between successive generations, and in the synchronization of the transfer of power between different territorial levels (section, village, kingdom). The Lulubo, Lokoya, Pari and northern Lopit (Dorik and Ngaboli) do not have initiation rituals into the *monyomiji* age-grade at the sectional level. Only men who have participated in the changeover ceremony are *monyomiji*.

Among *monyomiji* societies the longest interval between handing over ceremonies is that among the Lotuho. Among the Lulubo and Lokoya the political situation and demographic pressures seem to play a more important role in determining the moment of handing over power. Power is transferred when the young ones are 'strong enough' or when the *monyomiji* are failing in strength. Strength is relative and is measured in the matching of numbers.

The Lokoya and Lulubo are more accommodating with regard to the individual preferences of the candidate *monyomiji*: by paying a fine and a goat for purification, elder members of the age-sets immediately following those of the new generation may be incorporated in the junior age-set of the new *monyomiji* set. Sometimes members of a junior age-set, entitled to *monyomiji* membership, prefer to wait till the next handover ceremony, in order to be among the leading age-set, the *ahou* (Lokoya: *nahu*) of the *monyomiji*. All in all, some of the peripheral systems, though less elaborate, give the impression of a greater flexibility.

The age system of the Pari is characterized by a period of overlap between the rule of successive generations. A full cycle consists of six age-sets. The cycle begins with the transfer of power to four age-sets, the two senior ones forming the 'head' (*wic*). After a period of about ten years the two senior sets retire, leaving power in the hands of the two remaining sets, aptly named the 'rethatchers' or 'followers' (*tengo*) and to two newly recruited ones (Kurimoto, 1995a: 306). In compensation for the short duration and the relative insignificance of their role as *monyomiji*, the two most junior sets are expected to play an enhanced role as elders-advisers to the 'head' of the next *monyomiji*. New initiatives, a change in the style of government, are expected only from the 'head'.

In the timing of the transfer ceremony there is an attempt at synchronization between neighbouring political units. In the west the Pari normally take the lead followed by the Lokoya of Liria and the Lulubo. Among the Lotuho, the Loudo are the first to celebrate the *nefira*. As a result, *monyomiji* who travel to the villages of other ethnic groups will normally find approximate age-mates in their meat-group (see Kurimoto in this volume).

The Lotuho stand out in the length of the cycle. Most of the other societies practising the *monyomiji* system have shorter cycles or, like the Pari and the Lopit, break it up in two sequences. Among the Lulubo and

*Figure 3.3 Age-set formation and generational succession among the Pari over a period of 20 years. The shaded blocks are the sets forming the ruling generation.*

| Name of age-set | 4 years after change-over | 14 years after change-over | 24 years after change-over |
|---|---|---|---|
| A | After 4 years retired elders (*cidonge*) | Retired | Retired |
| B | *Wic* (head) *monyomiji*, or *geedo* ('builders') to new *monyomiji* right-hand set; | *wic* have retired, but now act in capacity of advisers to new *monyomiji* | Fully retired (*cidonge*) |
| C | Head *mononiji*: left-hand set | Retired advisers | Fully retired |
| D | *tengo* ('rethatchers') | After ca. 8 years the political leaders | Fully retired after 2 years |
| E | *tengo* | After ca. 8 years the political leaders | Fully retired |
| F | Age-set of young men in *awope* grade | Together with G, F has been added to *monyomiji* | Fully retired |
| G | Age-set of young men in *awope* grade | Age-set of youngsters with high aspirations since they will one day be *wie* | A new *wie* has taken over control of the country |
| H | Age-set in *awope* | *awope* | *wic* (left-hand) |
| I | Age-set in *awope* | *awope* | I and J age-set were added to the *wic*, one year after G & H had taken over power |
| | | | J: right-hand section of *tengo* |
| K | In formation | *awope* | K: left-hand section of *tengo* |

*Figure 3.4 Age-grades, age-sets and* monyomiji-*sets among the Lokoya and Lulubo. Age-set blocks of* monyomiji *are shaded.*

| Name of age-set | 4 years after change-over | 14 years after change-over | 24 years after change-over |
|---|---|---|---|
| A | After 4 years retired elders | Retired: *ohobolok* (Lok.):*temeji* (Lulubo) | Retired |
| B | *nahu* (head) *monyomiji* | Retired | Retired |
| C | *omurut* (neck) | Retired | Retired |
| D | *asuhe* (breast) | Retired | Retired |
| E | *alisang* | Retired | Retired |
| F | Age-set in grade of *otwat* (Lokoya); *teto* (Lulubo) | *nahu* (Lok.) or Lul. *gole* (hindquarters; royal part) of *monyomiji* took over recently | Will soon retire or already retired |
| G | Age-set in *otwat/ teto* grade | *omurut* (Lok.); *juju* (Lul.) | Will soon retire or already retired from control of country |
| H | Age-set in *otwat/ teto* grade | *asuhe* (Lok.); *'di* (head) (Lul.) | Will soon retire or already retired |
| I | Age-set in *otwat/ teto* grade | *alisang* (Lok.); *tuku* (Lul.) or *gele* (shoulder) | Will soon retire or already retired |
| J | Age-set in *otwat/ teto* grade | Age-set in *otwat/ teto* | Are about to succeed or have already succeeded |
| K | Age-set in formation | Age-set in *otwat/ teto* | Are about to succeed or have already succeeded |

*Figure 3.5 Relationship of Lotuho age-sets, age-grades and generation-sets to cohorts based on biological age and the changes over a period of 25 years. The table shows the youthfulness of the* monyomiji *in comparison with the leading generations of other age systems.*

| Age-cohort | Year 4–9 | Year 9–14 | Year 14–19 | Year 19–24 |
|---|---|---|---|---|
| 55–60 years | | | | A: retired elders |
| 50–55 years | | | in A: retired | B are now retired |
| 45–50 years | | In age-set A: retired elders of X, *efirat* elders | In B: still head of the *monyomiji* X | C now retired |
| 40–45 years | This cohort are mostly in age-set A, the most junior elders of retired generation X | In age-set B of Y: 'head' | C: still in neck position | D: now retired |
| 35–40 years | This cohort are in set B, the 'head' of the *monyomiji* of generation Y | In age-set C of Y: neck | D: *monyomiji etahunihi* | E: as *efirat* of Y now coaching the new *'ahou'* of *monyomiji* |
| 30–35 years | This cohort in set C, the 'neck' of the *monyomiji* | In age-set D of Y 'middle' | E. *monyomiji efirat* | F: *monyomiji ahou*, the leaders of generation-set Z |
| 25–30 years | This cohort mostly in age-set D, *etahunihi* | Age-set E: *efirat* | This cohort in F: leaders of *olojingat* | G: *monyomiji amurut* of Z |
| 20–25 years | In age-set E of Y, *efirat* of *monyomiji* | Majority of *adhuri-horwon* of F are now initiated in the age-grade of *monyomiji* | This cohort in G who are *olojingat* | H: middle *monyomiji* of Z |

*Figure 3.5 cont.*

| Age-cohort | Year 4–9 | Year 9–14 | Year 14–19 | Year 19–24 |
|---|---|---|---|---|
| 15–20 years | Mostly in age-grade *aduri-horwon* they have given themselves name 'F' | New set (G) of boys occupies the age-grade *aduri-horwon* | This cohort in age-set 'I' in *aduri-horwon* grade; currently being initiated | 'I' age-set have joined the *monyomiji* of Z at the *nefira*, as *efirat* |
| 10–15 years | Some boys start to join age-grade of *aduri-horwon* | Members of this cohort join *aduri-horwon* | Members of this cohort start joining *aduri-horwon* | Some boys of this cohort start to come out as *aduri-horwon* |

Lokoya the cycle is usually shorter: between 12 and 18 years, for four age-sets, as compared with the Pari cycle of 20 years and six age-sets. Half-way the head ('*wic*') age-sets are retired to make place for the 'rethatchers' '*tengo*') and two more junior age-sets who are admitted to *monyomiji*-hood when the followers take over (Kurimoto, 1995a:306). From the point of view of the Lotuho *monyomiji* their western counterparts give in too easily to the pressure of their juniors. The secret of the longer cycle of the Lotuho is the fact that they run their system on two different levels: the initiation into the *monyomiji* age-grade at the sectional level, on the one hand, and the succession to generational power at the village and kingdom levels, on the other. Neither the Pari nor the Lulubo and Lokoya have an initiation into *monyomiji*-hood preceding the ceremony of the transfer of power.

As a result, it seems that the average age of the *monyemiji* in the western systems is somewhat lower, even if the juniors take power at a later age. Extrapolating from data collected by Kurimoto (1995a: 266) the age-range of the Anyua *monyomiji* of Lafon at their accession to power was between 44 and 30, and at their retirement in 1988 between 55 and 41. Basing ourselves on informants' statements, comparable figures for the Lotuho – which are not available – would show a range of 20–45 at the *nefira* and 40–65 at retirement.

## *The functions of the* monyomiji

The *monyomiji* form the core institutional framework of the village. They are responsible for the welfare of the community, for its security, peace, moral integrity, and also its harmony with cosmic forces. The word 'responsible' here is used in a strong sense: when things go wrong, when enemies are not kept at bay, when there is drought, the *monyomiji* are blamed and have to account for their policies. They may be called to account by the King, by the juniors aspiring to power, and, especially in the case of disasters affecting the food situation (drought, crop pests, crop-eating animals), by an emergency assembly of the women. A poor performance on the part of a particular generation may lead to reshuffles of its officials or to its premature retirement.

Intellectuals from *monyomiji* societies enjoy drawing parallels between the structure of modern democratic republican systems and government by the *monyomiji*. The following equations are made by Philip Lomodong from Liria in his 1995 monograph on Lokoya culture. While the assembly of all *monyomiji* is defined as the legislative power, the two most senior age-sets of the *monyomiji* (including the 'head') form the executive power. The two junior age-sets form the army. The rainmaker/king is the President of the State. He also chairs an inner cabinet consisting of seven ritual specialists (Master of Grain, Master of War, Master of Winds, etc.). Information between the cabinet and the *monyomiji* of the different sections is passed through the *ololongolier* ('emissaries', 'messengers') called the Information Ministry by Lomodong. The *monyomiji nahu* of each section represent the central authority at the local level (Lomodong, 1995: 25–8).

Lomodong also refers to an unwritten 'constitution' of the *monyomiji*, the *Oiring lo Monyomiji*. Since I never heard of it during my fieldwork in the early 1980s I assume that it is a newly established 'code'. Lomodong explicitly adds that the text refers to present conditions and can be further adapted to modern developments. Since it gives a vivid impression of the duties of the *monyomiji* and of the style in which these are promulgated I reproduce Lomodong's translation:

1    Every 12 or 20 years the *Monyomiji* shall change the government.

2    The *Monyomiji* shall nominate two of their members from each camp[7] to the *Monyomiji* Inner Council which comprises the *Monyomiji* and the Chief Priests.[8]

3    The *Monyomiji* shall beat an alarm drum if an enemy or wild beasts attack people or goats.

4    The *Monyomiji* shall whistle if an enemy or a lion attacks. A drum is beaten to alert the people.

5    Anyone who kills somebody shall compensate by giving a daughter or cows.

6    The *Monyomiji* shall punish the people who violate the laws of the state.[9]

7    Accidental killing of a person shall be paid for by a sincere apology in addition to handing over some goats or cows for 'cooling' the heart of the deceased person.

8 The *Monyomiji* shall declare war on an enemy when they deem fit. The case shall first be forwarded to the Chief of Defence for consultation and blessing.[10]

9 The *Monyomiji* shall arrange to dig a field belonging to the Chief of Rain.

10 The *Monyomiji* shall supervise the function of the Chiefs throughout the year.

11 The *Monyomiji* shall oppose the elopement of the wife of the Chief or of his son. This is because of the fear of 'adufio', the withholding of rain, the 'pouring' of epidemics on to the village or the loss of crops or animals.

12 The *Monyomiji* shall make sure that their hunting grounds are not infiltrated by others, rivers not fished in and fruit trees not harvested from.

13 The *Monyomiji* shall respond to the alarm of *'ohiribo'*[11] which advises chiefs to perform their duties.

14 The *Monyomiji* shall stage the funeral dance (*'otuhe'*) for Chiefs, important elders[12] and the Monyomiji.

15 The *Monyomiji* shall pay homage to the family of a deceased colleague.

16 When the Chief dies, the *Monyomiji* shall stage the funeral rites and dance to mourn him or her.

17 The *Monyomiji* shall cooperate in communal projects like digging water reservoirs for animals and wells for people, as well as in fighting fire.

18 The Chief of Rain shall be the President of the *Monyomiji* cabinet or council. He shall be appointed or removed whenever the *Monyomiji* deem fit.

19 When there is a grain harvest, the camps shall contribute grain to the Rain Chief.

20 The *Monyomiji* shall question, arrest and fine those who do not obey the orders and conventions of the village.

The document illustrates the duality in the source of legitimate power: on the one hand, the authority of the *monyomiji* in the age system, on the other, the authority of the various *ohobu* of whom the *ohobu lohuju*, the Rainmaker,[13] is the most important. Each power keeps the other in check: Three articles (9, 16, 19) deal with the duties of the *monyomiji* vis-à-vis their king, while three others (10, 13, 18) deal with the supervisory powers of the *monyomiji* over the king, including the power to remove him. While he cannot remove the *monyomiji*, the king can punish them by his power of *adufio*, sending disasters such as drought, epidemics, etc. The fear of *adufio* is the main lever of respect for the king (11). The other Masters also have the power of *adufio* within the limits of their domain (poor crops, barrenness, missing arrows, storms, etc.) Other commandments deal with war (3,4,12), internal peacekeeping and settlement of disputes (5,6,7,20), as well as with communal labour (17) and respect for the dead (14, 15).

4  Mock-charge by *monyomiji*, Liria village, Lokoya (Eisei Kurimoto 1985)

5 The village of Loronyo and the plains, the heartland of the Lotuho
(Eisei Kurimoto 1984)

6 Stick-fight… Members of an age-set in the young men's grade sitting in the
central dancing ground (*thworo*) before the fight. Pari. Note the spectators
(Eisei Kurimoto 1984)

Rain is a primary public concern and the king is feared, blamed or idolized according to the weather. Rain is the central issue in an annually repeated moral drama lasting from the onset of the rain till the end, in which the king and the *monyomiji* are the main actors. If he is 'good', the rains are timely and plentiful. His displeasure, however, has immediate meteorological effects. If it is triggered by the misdeeds of his subjects, the prime duty of the *monyomiji* is to remedy the situation. The king may also be 'evil'. That is when the *monyomiji* have to take drastic action.

There is a fair degree of overlap between the public duties of the king and the *monyomiji*. Both are responsible for maintaining unity and peace in the village. Both play a role in settling conflicts, both are expected to be above sectional and clan interests. The glory of a particular king's reign is tied up with the fortunes of the *monyomiji* set with which his name is associated. Oral history indicates that new *monyomiji*-sets have installed a new king, of their own choice.

*Age-set antagonism and generational succession*

The word choice of informants immediately betrays the antagonistic character of the changeover ceremony. The older generation is 'pushed out', power is 'taken away' from the elders, the village is 'seized', a 'new era' begins. Educated informants repeatedly described the ceremony of the transfer of power as a 'revolution'. Junior generations of certain villages enjoyed repeating their claim that they were more 'revolutionary' than anybody else.

The names of age-sets aspiring to power are often chosen to express defiance of the ruling generation, of authority in general, and of the powers of elderly men. The *monyomiji* who took over power in Lowe (Lokoya) in 1959 called themselves *Thimomonye* ('Those who ignore their fathers'). Those in Ngulere in the same year called themselves '*Lofohitu*' ('Immune to sorcery').

The larger the junior generation, the more intense the antagonism. When during the last years of a generation's rule the numbers of its successor-generation equal or surpass its own, reciprocal challenges and clashes will become more frequent. The importance of numbers is reflected in age-set and generation names: *Naboro* (Lotuho: sand), *Ama* (Lotuho: locusts), *Dotiti* (Lotuho: a long line of people), *Iru* (Lotuho: swarm of birds).

New age-sets are formed in opposition to the sets adjacent to them. Among the Lulubo and Lokoya where the first steps towards age-set formation are quite informal, groups of age-mates of the same section join in herding small livestock. While out in the field they engage in sports and

**65**

goat fights. When the group is getting large there will be a tendency for its senior members to exclude the juniors from certain activities, or for the juniors to show their independence and proclaim their own identity.

Stick fights between adjacent age-sets of juniors are common (see Kurimoto, 1995a:286 for a case-history). Stick fights between sets of the same age of neighbouring sections may be even more frequent (Kurimoto, 1995: 288–90). The size of rival age-sets is an important factor in determining the break-off point for the formation of new junior age-sets. The consequence of a split in an existing age-set is a weaker position in stick fights and competitive sports.

When the average age is around 18 the sectional age-sets unite at the level of the village under a new, more inclusive, name and flag. By assuming communal duties – cleaning and repair of the village infrastructure – they present themselves to the community as aspiring to *monyomiji*-hood.

The Lotuho system is more formalized on this point: after a boy has reached the age-grade of *aduri horwon* and has been included in an age-set he is the legitimate target for bullying by the *monyomiji* of the *amangat*. Juniors are sent on all sorts of errands. Apart from known prohibitions (not eating groundnut-paste in public, not entering the drum-house and the place where the *monyomiji* sit), they may at any moment be faced with new prohibitions issued by the *monyomiji* and be punished for non-compliance. Punishments consist of beatings and fines varying from the simple provision of a bowl of beer to the forcible removal of small live-stock. If one member of the group misbehaves, punishment is preferably administered in such a way that the entire group suffers. Relations with girls are a special concern in this permanent supervision. Unmarried girls are said to belong to the *monyomiji*. Till the day of initiation the *monyomiji* exercise permanent pressure on the juniors. Before the day of his initiation can be fixed, the novice is presented with a bill of outstanding misdeeds for which he will have to apologize by paying fines (Grüb, 1992:135).

The model for the administration of punishments is the raid. In carrying out these punitive expeditions use is made of antagonism between adjacent age-sets. *Olojingat*, who are expected to be more intransigent than full *monyomiji*, are entrusted with the punishment of *aduri horwon* offenders. In turn, the *olojingat* are bullied by the *monyomiji efirat* (the most junior age-set of the *monyomiji*): the dance that concludes initiation at the sectional level is forcefully interrupted by the *monyomiji efirat*. The new *olojingat* are chased away from the dancing ground with the message that they still have a long way to go before their *nefira*. While the *olojingat* terrorize the *aduri horwon*, and the full-blown *monyomiji* continue to treat the *olojingat* as minors, the tension between the *monyomiji* and the future generation-set builds up as the numbers of the junior generation and the initiated age-sets increase.

There is, however, one notable exception, mentioned by Grüb (1992: 139), to this capitalization on the rivalry of adjacent age-sets. During the period immediately preceding the *nefira* the *efirat* of the new alternation practise, together with the *aduri horwong*, a dance mimicking the expulsion from power of the incumbent *monyomiji*. They also join in training in club fighting, running, and wrestling. Grüb does not comment, but we can assume that this will lay a basis for the later cooperation with the retired *efirat*, who will act as advisers to the *monyomiji* and the next *ahou*.

In the atmosphere of confrontation and vigilance created by this tension, age-sets grow into unified blocks with a strong sense of internal egalitarianism and with effective informal leadership patterns. During the years preceding the *nefira* the junior generation tries to make a name for itself by carrying out raids, often against the will of the ruling *monyomiji* and the king. During the same period, stick fights between alternations are frequent. This is the time when the forces of the ruling and the succeeding alternations match. Before the last *nefira*, which was scheduled for October 1976, the police had to intervene several times in clashes triggered by attempts of the ruling *monyomiji* to postpone the date of the transfer of power by one more year. In the end the old generation compromised and agreed to have the *nefira* in 1976.[14]

Normally such confrontations should only be mock battles. Frequently, however, the situation gets out of hand and men are injured, or even killed. Mock battles are part of the handing-over ceremony both at the village and kingdom level.

At the *nefira* presided over by the king there is a mock battle between *efirat* on one side and *olojingat* on the other, from which the *olojingat* are supposed to emerge victorious. This battle is fought with sticks and shields the day before the kindling of the new fire by the king. The fight is said to be very fierce, since the new alternation are expected to take their revenge for all the unfair treatment they have been subjected to during their minority as *olojingat* and *aduri horwon*. Injuries were common and fatal casualties did occur, sometimes leading to postponement of the transfer of power.[15] Grüb, without quoting dates and places, mentions a case of a *nefira* where the drum was grabbed by force, instead of being ceremonially rolled from the side of the retiring elders to the new *monyomiji*. He was also informed of instances where the *monyomiji* were simply chased from the village, and power was usurped without ceremony (1992:140).

The struggle for power between generations is not only fought in open confrontations. There is a lot of intrigue: curses, suspicions of curses, smear campaigns, etc. In the mid-1980s the Anyua *monyomiji* of Lafon were accused of deliberately withholding the rain to prevent the transfer of power to the younger generation. A good harvest is the condition for holding the ceremonies. In Lokiliri (Lulubo) the Limojo around 1910 did the opposite: they secretly caused drought to discredit the ruling *monyomiji*. The conspiracy was discovered and the rain-princes involved had to flee abroad (Simonse, 1992:176).

### Complementary opposition as a political achievement

Age systems constitute a political arena that has many features in common with the much better documented arena of competition between territorial units or lineage segments. Territorial organization among Lotuho speakers is structured as 'complementary opposition'. Village sections receive help from the sections of their own moiety if they are attacked by sections of opposite moieties. In conflicts between villages, all the village sections of both moieties will join together to face the common outsider (Simonse, 1992:143–64).

Similarly, conflicts between adjacent age-sets will receive no priority when there is confrontation with age-sets of the competing generation. The bond between the retired elders – whose younger age-sets are still virile – and the juniors who are *olojingat* or *aduri-horwon* establishes a power balance during the period when the rising generation is too small to face the *monyomiji* alone. In fact, the complementary opposition model provides a perfect explanation of the alliance between alternating sets, a feature of age systems called 'a mysterious phenomenon' by the formalistic Stewart (1977:125). Once we admit the competitiveness of age-set relations – a dimension that is completely overlooked by Stewart – it is one of the easiest aspects of the age system to account for.

The issue of the bond between alternations has been dealt with by Abrahams in a similar way. According to the principle that 'the enemies of my enemies should be my friends' alternate generation-sets cooperate in a context where relations between proximal sets are characterized by antagonism (Abrahams, 1978: 50-55). In contrast to the *monyomiji* systems, the Labwor prescribe that fathers and sons should not be members of proximal generations.

Earlier we used the term 'set-lines' to refer to the allied alternations of the Lotuho. It is the term used by Baxter to translate the Oromo word *gogesa*, the successive generation-sets (*luuba*) that are linked by paternal descent (Baxter, 1988:156–9). If the principle of complementary opposition accounts for the generation of alternating set-lines, it should also be able to explain set-lines with four intermediate sets as in the *gada* age-system.

By shortening the duration of the period that a generation-set occupies in one grade, the number of sets taking part in the system will be multiplied. Assuming that the relations between these more numerous sets are also structured by alliance and opposition – for example, opposition of both alliance partners to the two sets senior and the two sets junior to them – a larger number of set-lines, in our example five, will be created: the situation of the *gada* system. If we run the system with three set-lines we have the Dassanetch age system (Almagor, 1989).

This explanation of the emergence of age systems with multiple set-lines is more economical than that put forward by Müller-Dempf. Müller argued that the conflict between junior and senior age-sets that split the Ngitukoi generation of the Toposa in two, created two *de facto* generation-set lines. For generation-set lines to emerge Müller's model assumes (i) an unprogrammed conflict between age-sets of the same generation, (ii) a successful resolution of the conflict resulting in the decision that the power or Fatherhood of the country will henceforth rotate between the age-sets who are parties to the conflict, and (iii) a mutual agreement on the shortening of the period of rule or fatherhood. While it is possible that these conditions, after some time, will be fulfilled, it is not likely that this will happen very easily four times in a row. The current conflict in Toposa, dating from 1880, has still to be resolved (Müller-Dempf, 1991: 566). I therefore put forward my explanation of the origin of the system – as a systematic effect of complementary opposition – as a more economical one.

The interesting implication, not only of my explanatory model but also of that of Müller, is that the origin of the *gada* systems, which because of their apparent artificiality seem products of conscious social engineering, can be explained in terms of political process. Whatever they are now, in origin they were not 'cognitive systems'.

Similarly, there is no need to turn to binary cognition to account for the dualism in age systems, as structuralists may be inclined to do. A dual organization of sets emerges as the contingent result of a concrete social process, which binary symbolism may, of course, appropriate in such a way that the process that gave rise to the dualism is no longer immediately recognizable.

During the period immediately preceding the changeover, the forces of the junior generation and the *monyomiji* are matched. The moment power – the ultimate political prize – will be handed over depends on the numbers of the new generation and on the way the confrontations are managed. A *monyomiji*-set which is disgruntled with the poor style of its juniors, may decide to postpone the handing over of power, while a corrupt and weak *monyomiji* set may be expelled before its time is over.

In some polities of the Lotuho-speakers there is a remarkable correspondence between the segmentation of the age system and that of the territorial system. Both are three-tiered. The age-set corresponds to the section, the smaller units of both systems. While village sections are polarized in moieties age-sets are always in pairs, the senior age-set being associated with the right and the junior one with the left. Alternations correspond to villages. *Amiji*, the word for village, is also used to refer to the alternations.[16]

Strategies to express and control rivalry between groups are the same in the arena of territorial groups as in that of age-groups: the prohibition of spears in fights between age-sets and sections, the staging of mock fights, competition in sports and dances, etc. However, an important difference between territorial 'complementary opposition' and age-set antagonism is the regular oscillation of the age system between states of mutual competition and of hierarchical order. The periods preceding and immediately following ceremonies of initiation and transfer of power are marked by increased tension between age-sets and generation-sets. After the new set has made its political point, a period of relative calm follows in which relations between the two are regulated by the hierarchy of the grading system. Transition ceremonies have a similar effect on the general political climate to that of elections in a parliamentary democracy. As in modern democracies, domestic tensions spill over into foreign relations. But in inter-societal generational politics the younger generation always takes the role of the 'hawks', while the *monyomiji* who are due to be retired and the elders are the 'doves'. A typical conflict was the attack, in 1955, of the new *monyomiji* of the Tirangore kingdom on the men of the rival Lotuho kingdom while they were celebrating their *nefira*. The life-cycle of a 'set' is simultaneously marked by various stages of competition and a changing insertion in the successive grades of the system.

From an overall functional point of view, it could be stated that the social cohesion of Lotuho society is served in two ways by the organized opposition of age-sets and generation-sets. It serves the internal consensus of age-sets and generation-sets who are made to confront one another in a more or less orderly way. Secondly – as in the classical Nuer case – it creates bonds of solidarity which cross-cut territorial divisions. From the functionalist sociological angle, it would be interesting to find out whether periods of heightened inter-generational tension correspond to periods with a lower rate of conflict between territorial divisions, and vice versa.

Since Evans-Pritchard demonstrated in *The Nuer* that segmentary societies are able to create political stability over wide areas by a process in which conflicting groups control the scope of the conflict by matching the forces they bring into the field, segmentary systems have been the object of anthropological admiration. Here were people who did not give up their sovereignty to an agent monopolizing the use of physical force, in order to cope with conflict, but who used conflict creatively and with restraint. This admiration has been responsible for the disregard of the possibility that segmentary systems may not work when no balance is struck between the conflicting parties and the weaker party is annihilated.

Segmentary systems are extremely vulnerable. Whether a balance of forces is reached in a conflict, and whether the recognition of this balance will lead to a halt of the violence, necessarily depends on a number of factors including policy decisions by the participants in the conflict. A balance of forces can be easily broken when external allies, whose power is disproportional to the level on which the conflict is fought, want to intervene. This is what happened when in the nineteenth century the rival Bari kingdoms invited foreign armies to fight on their sides. Interestingly, in the Bari case, the balancing dynamic continued to work. Because of the rivalry, first between trading companies, and later between the Egyptian Government and the Mahdists, each party found its own foreign ally. The overall level of violence rose tremendously, because of the introduction of firearms, with disastrous effects for the Bari population (Simonse, 1992:306–11). More commonly, only one of the two protagonists was able to mobilize the support of a powerful ally, usually with disastrous consequences for the weaker side. The balance of power between generations can also be lost. According to historical tradition two large population centres of Lotuho-speakers, Segele and Imatari,[17] have disappeared because one of the generations called in a powerful ally, thus upsetting the usual balance: Segele was destroyed as the result of a conflict between the *monyomiji* and the *aduri horwon*. The *monyomiji* killed two *aduri horwon* ringleaders in an exemplary punishment. Both were princes, who had refused to carry out the orders of the *monyomiji*. The queen, their mother, requested king Ngalamitiho of Imatari, the traditional rival of Segele, to wreak a terrible revenge upon the *monyomiji* of Segele. She was not satisfied when *Ohonyemorok*, the ruling generation of Imatari at the time, offered to go on a punitive expedition; she asked for the successor generation to be added to the military force. All the gates of Segele were sealed off by the enemy, large numbers of the inhabitants were killed and the village was burnt down and never recovered.

In the case of Imatari the conflict was between the ruling generation *Miriyang* and their successors *Tome*. One day the young men challenged the authority of the *monyomiji* by dancing with girls of their own age in the dancing ground: an act strictly prohibited for non-*monyomiji*. When the boys were found out they fled with the girls to Dongotono where, according to one version of the story, they obtained wives by way of sister exchange. In this way they married, bypassing their fathers' bride-wealth and authority. The *monyomiji* wanted to take revenge for this insult by attacking the Dongotono who had offered them refuge, but king Ngalamitiho, who wanted to keep the peace, stopped them. The rebellious generation challenged Ngalamitiho's weak attitude and proclaimed his son Ohurak as king. When Ngalamitiho heard the song, he cursed his son and his people. Ohurak and the Tome succeeded in expelling Ngalamitiho from Imatari. He fled to the Toposa, the arch-enemies of the Lotuho. He returned later with a Toposa army and encircled Imatari. The people fled to the king's palace which was used as a fortress. Ngalamitiho ordered the walls of his palace to be pushed down. As the palace was overrun Ngala-mitiho disappeared – in lightning according to the story – and Ohurak was killed. The Lotuho then dispersed to the various villages they still occupy today.

To the extent that the stories reflect historical events, they show the precariousness of the inter-generational power balance, even under conditions that have not yet been marked by the introduction of firearms or the presence of foreign armies. To the extent that the stories are legendary, they show how the Lotuho conceive of generational conflict. It starts with a demonstrative takeover of the public facilities of Imatari: the village dancing ground which includes the village shrine and drumhouse. This is followed by an armed confrontation between the competing generations (which is stopped by the king at the last moment); on top of that there is the challenge of the *aduri horwon* to the monopoly of the *monyomiji* over the services of the *odwo*, the unmarried girls.

For the purposes of our argument there are two lessons to be drawn from these stories. In the first place, that the antagonism between 'sets' is not just a ritual or ceremonial drama but a political struggle that is fought with all available means. Secondly, that the political equilibrium between generation-sets is not given. It has to be achieved, as the outcome of political action or political restraint.

### The monyomiji *in the contemporary political context*

When the *monyomiji* systems make the headlines, it is usually because of the rebellious behaviour of the juniors, as in Imatari and Segele a century and a half ago. Colonial records indicate that most of the resistance to the imposition of colonial rule came, not so much from the *monyomiji*, but from the juniors. The colonial powers used to deal with the kings. Most kings in the *monyomiji* area welcomed the colonial powers because the new ally strengthened their position in relation to the *monyomiji* (Simonse, 1992: 246–8). Since the king and the *monyomiji* were normally on speaking terms, most disagreements were sorted out between them. Not so with the youngsters.

In Lokoya, for example, gangs of 'young bloods' continued to attack mail carriers, government patrols, and the team constructing the telegraph line from Mongalla to Torit. It later turned out that the gangs were led by the son of the King of Ilyangari (Simonse, 1992:177). When he was found out, the chief of Ilyangari, unlike Ngalamitiho in Imatari, chose to side with his rebel son, thus causing the British to have to dispatch one more Lokoya patrol.

The political radicalism generated by the *nefira* celebrations of the mid-1950s is likely to have contributed to the rebel activity which, during the late 1950s, was largely concentrated in Torit District, and more particularly in the Lotuho area. A number of attacks on government targets took place even before the Torit mutiny (18 August 1955) which is conventionally taken to mark the start of the civil war. The *nefira* of Torit and the villages in the immediate vicinity took place on 10 October 1954, the Royal *nefira* at Hoding on 5 May 1955, while the royal *nefira* of Tirangore had taken place in September 1953. In the months preceding the *nefira* at Hoding a series of arson attacks occurred in Torit and its surroundings: in January the Local Government Centre and the American Mission Hospital in Lohutok were set on fire, in February the houses of the District Commissioner and a high-ranking military officer in Torit were burnt down. The northern District Commissioner accused the Head Chief of Torit District, the highest 'native authority' among the Lotuho, of instigating the attack on the DC's house. The attacks were carried out by a group of around 500 men consisting of a core of mutineers assisted by a majority of local warriors. The latter, we may safely assume, were *monyomiji* of the 1954/5 levy (Simonse, 1997: 312–4).

During the second wave of fighting in the Civil War around 1965, the Lulubo and Lokoya men enrolling in the Anyanya belonged on the whole to age-sets which had not yet reached *monyomiji* status. This created a situation in which members of the junior age-grade were in a position to issue commands and requisition food from the Kwara 'in power' (1958–75). According to one member of the Kwara in Lokiliri (Lulubo) this was a humiliating experience. Many Kwara lost interest in being *monyomiji* and were ready to hand over power to their successors at the first opportunity that presented itself.

This scenario was repeated at the beginning of the current civil war. Kurimoto (1994:106–9) provides an analysis of the mobilization of the Pari juniors into the Sudan People's Liberation Army. Out of about 2,500 Pari men who joined the SPLA, only 10 were *monyomiji* when they enrolled. Dissatisfaction with the rule of Anywa (1977–88) was great among the junior generation. Anywa was blamed for the years of drought, which in 1984 had led to the murder of the rain queen. In 1985 the juniors felt that they were ready to take over, but their aspirations were typically ignored by the *monyomiji*. They were keen to find ways of impressing Anywa with their ability to take responsibility for village affairs. The recruitment by the SPLA was very timely. The activities of the Pari contingent in the SPLA were at their peak between 1985 and 1989. In 1988 Madan took over from Anywa. During the same period the juniors of the Lokoya and the Lulubo, largely for the same reasons, tried to enroll as government militias because their communities had been the first targets of attacks by the Pari SPLA.

**73**

The period of political radicalism on the part of the juniors normally extends to some years after the transfer of power. In the election campaign for the Regional Assemblies in 1982 young candidates generally appealed to the old-time generational antagonism by presenting themselves as supporters of a new generational style of rule.

## Conclusions

In summarizing I would like to underline the following points:

(i) The *monyomiji* age systems of the Equatorian east bank of the Nile are simultaneously structured by an oppositional and a hierarchical principle. The oppositional dynamic operates at several levels of inclusion, in such a way that, in the context of a provocation, lower-level divisions ('sets') are overruled by the more inclusive connections. The hierarchical principle provides a non-conflictual mode of interaction between sets and members of different sets. It gives rise to a linear progression of grades, in which juniors are expected to yield to their seniors. Concurrently, occupation of the next senior grade is the main stake in the competition between sets.

(ii) From a diachronic angle, the *monyomiji* system corresponds to a cycle in which, during a first phase, the amplification and exacerbation of antagonism between the maturing and retiring generation overrule the available possibilities for hierarchy. In a second phase, the antagonism discharges into an institutionalized crisis, in which the old incumbents of power are removed and a new hierarchical order is established.

This cycle is simultaneously political and ritual. At the political level it brings about a circulation of elites. Each new generation is full of idealism and is convinced it can do better than its predecessor. During the run-up to the transfer of power the juniors capitalize on the weaknesses of the rule of the sitting *monyomiji* in order to discredit them. Now, in their own time, they will implement a political programme that gives better guarantees for the security, peace, welfare, etc. of the community.

As a ritual cycle the *monyomiji* system achieves an exemplary transformation of potentially violent interaction into ordered hierarchy. The transmutation is operated through sacrifice, 'by passing through the ox' as the Maasai would say (Spencer, 1988:184). The most elementary hierarchical ranking is the allocation of age-sets to the various portions of the sacrificial animal, by turning them into 'meat groups'.

The various stages of the cycle are given theatrical expression in a wide variety of songs, dances, and mock fights. The provocative and sportsmanlike style of these cultural manifestations explains the appeal the *monyomiji* societies have for the Western observer.

(iii) The stability of the relationships established by the age system depends on a balance of oppositional and hierarchical interactions. When antagonism is no longer kept in check by a modicum of hierarchy, conflicts will get out of hand – as in the case of the fall of Imatari. On the other hand, when hierarchical relations rigidify and are no longer renewed in a ritual or political reversal, they will either become oppressive or become a formality incapable of providing a deeply felt sense of social order. The conception of social stability used here obviously derives from the intuitions of Gregory Bateson, who in his *Naven* analyzed social equilibrium as the combined result of 'symmetrical' social processes tending towards increased antagonism and 'asymmetrical', 'complementary' processes favouring mutual accommodation (Bateson, 1958:171–97). The importance of the contrast between a symmetrical and an asymmetrical dynamic in age systems has been highlighted both by Spencer in his distinction between the models of 'opposing streams' and the 'gerontocratic ladder' (1976) and by Abrahams when he distinguishes 'linear' from 'polar' qualities in the relations between successive generations (1978:52–3).

(iv) The *monyomiji* systems are striking in the scope they give to the free play of age antagonism. In this they betray their common cultural roots with the Maasai whose age system was the first to be analyzed in terms of complementary opposition (Gulliver, 1963:59; Jacobs, 1965:294). In the continuum between Maa systems with a 'geronto-cratic' (Samburu) and an 'oppositional' (Arusha) bias, they are certainly closer to the latter.

In contrast to the *monyomiji* systems where generational confronta-tion is generally concentrated in one major politico-ritual climax per cycle, open age-set confrontations in the Maasai system occur at four points during the cycle: in the opening of a new age-set of *murran*, in the establishment of their *manyata*, in the run-up to the *eunoto* sacrifice marking the transition to senior *murran* status, and finally in the nation-wide *olngesher* ceremony in which the *murran* are promoted to elderhood. While in the *monyomiji* area the promotion of one group means the simultaneous retirement of the other, the Maasai cycle allows for more overlap. Because of the double alliance between junior *murran* and firestick-elders and between senior *murran* and senior elders, the boundary between junior and senior age-sets is less sharply drawn.

In comparison with the peoples of the Karimojong cluster the *monyomiji* systems are striking in their relative youthfulness and organizational compactness. By dropping the requirement that successive generations should reflect paternity and filiation in the kinship system, the interlocking of age-sets, generations, and age-grades is as good as it could be. There is no discrepancy between the roles attributed on the basis of age and generation, and no loopholes for hidden gerontocratic agendas, as in the Karimojong cluster where the age-sets play a role in the social division of labour while the generation-sets have a *de facto* ritual role (Tornay, 1979). No age system retires its elders so completely from public life as the *monyomiji* systems.

The *monyomiji* systems offer no support to the thesis defended by Baxter and Almagor that age systems, by giving legitimacy to the exploitative interests of a privileged group, are a superstructural phenomenon. In Lotuho the family elders who control the cattle with which their sons marry and who receive the bride-service for their daughters will normally belong to the age-grade of the *amarwak* (retired elders). To effectuate their claims as household heads they rely on their agnatic kin, not on the *monyomiji*. Conflict between lineages or sub-clans will typically be settled by the king/rainmaker or by another ritual expert. The *monyomiji* system has no hidden interface with the lineage system or with economic organization. The *monyomiji* are what they say they are: enemies of interests and inclinations that may negatively affect the cohesion of the community. Problems are typically formulated in terms of hostile forces which need to be confronted. Typical solutions are the imposition of fines, bans on specified activities, curses, raids, ultimatums, executions. The bold radicalism of their style of intervention does not tally with the calculated protection of private interests (of elders, of lineages, of the king, of individuals).

(v) We have seen that the impact of the *monyomiji* age systems in the modern political and military context is attributable to their antagonistic structure, their political radicalism, and the powerful *esprit de corps* that is formed during years of confrontation between seniors and juniors. Because of their disadvantaged position in the age-organization the juniors who have not yet achieved *monyomiji*-hood are more likely to rally behind new political and military initiatives.

# Notes

1 In 1985 and 1986 I carried out fieldwork in East Bank Equatoria as a research officer of the Netherlands Foundation for Scientific Research of the Tropics (WOTRO).

2 Other members of this 'generation-set' of anthropologists who worked in societies with age systems are Godfrey Lienhardt (Dinka and Anuak), Jean Buxton (Mandari), P.H. Gulliver (Turkana). We can also include administrators turned anthropologists like P.P. Howell (Shilluk), and B.A. Lewis (Murle).

3 For studies of cases of regicide see Kurimoto, 1986 and Simonse, 1992:345–73.

4 Unlike the people of the Maa group, their nearest linguistic relatives, the Lotuho do not practise any form of circumcision. In this respect they are closer to the Ateker systems, where sacrifice and a collective transition from son status to father status, and not circumcision, marks the transition to full manhood.

5 A significant number of the members of alternating generation-sets do have fathers belonging to the same ascending generation, and sons belonging to the same descending generation. With an interval of 22 years and taking into account the relatively low rate of polygyny, and the young age at marriage, it is probable that a majority of the members of generation C, classified as *Tome*, will be children of A, also *Tome*, while most of their children will be in E. I have to leave it to others to make this calculation. It should be clear, however, that recruitment to the *monyomiji* is solely on the basis of membership of the previously formed village age-sets.

6 *Efirat*, as the term used for the age-set initiated immediately before the *nefira*, refers to a different group from *efirat* used in opposition to *olojingat*.

7 *Obali*, village section, the equivalent of the Lotuho *mangat*.

8 These are the 'compartmental kings' of the community: the Rainmaker, the Master of Grain, the Master of Winds, etc. in Liria collectively called the '*Ovalahojok*', the Fingers of God (Simonse, 1992:264–81).

9 *Hamiji*: village.

10 '*Ohobu latang*', the 'Master of Hardware' or 'Master of War', one of the Fingers of God.

11 The beginning of the rainy season.

12 *Ohoboloni*, elders with local, usually sectional, ritual responsibilities, not belonging to the Fingers of God.

13 Because of the power vested in the role of the various *ohobu* I favour the translation 'Master', analogous to the 'Spear Masters' of the Dinka. Since the Master of Rain is everywhere the most powerful master I reserve the title 'King' for him. In the *monyomiji* area the Lokoya stand by the variety of *ohobu* to whom they pay homage. Besides the King and a range of minor ritual practitioners, they have a Master of Grain, Master of the Land (fertility of the soil), Master of the Mountain (fertility of human beings), Master of Winds and a Master of War, each from a different clan.

14 Torit People's Rural Council, Monthly Report, January 1976, *Torit District Files*, Southern Records Office, Juba, .

15 Because of the occasional casualties the colonial government prohibited the practice of mock battles and replaced them with more choreographic alternatives (Nalder, 1937:101; Simonse, 1992:184). Such a mock battle was witnessed by Peter Molloy in Loguruny and described in his travelogue on South Sudan (1957: 182–4).

16 The social system of the Logir, who inhabit the East flank of the Dongotono mountain, is, in another way, a replica of the age-organization: two rain-kingdoms each headed by a Rainmaker/King and each consisting of four villages (Simonse, 1992:187).

17 Segele was the centre from where, according to a Lotuho tradition, the Lokoya and Lopit originated. It was located in the plains to the west of the Lopit range. Imatari, located in the plains between the Dongotono and Imatong mountains, was the village from which the Plains Lotuho are believed to have originated. According to calculations based on

**77**

inter-generational intervals of 22 years Imatari came to its end around the year 1830. Segele must have been destroyed some 30 years earlier. Possibly it was later, because in 1860 'Matari' was mentioned to the French explorer Peney as one of the districts of 'Lotouka' and 'Suguerle' appears on a map drawn by the MacDonald expedition in 1898.

# 4 Brothers in Arms: Military Aspects of East African Age-Class Systems in Historical Perspective

## JOHN LAMPHEAR

### Age-Class Systems and Ritual Warfare

It is clear that the age-class systems (which include both age-based and generation-based models) of East African pastoralists and semi-pastoralists historically served a wide variety of purposes and were closely intertwined with other areas of society. In an essential way, however, age-class systems must be regarded as a means of control and resolution. This stems in part from the basic dichotomy in pastoral society between the expression of individual autonomy, on the one hand, and the simultaneous need for cooperation, on the other. The pursuit of autonomy, conditioned by the inherent mobility of pastoral processes themselves, frequently results in small-scale, atomized family groups and weak kinship structures, and can lead ultimately to dangerous fissions within the broader community as a whole. At the same time, the ever-present danger of cattle rustling by rivals and the extreme vicissitudes of pastoral management require some wider mutual support. This institutional expression of control and resolution also stems, of course, from the basic need to regulate the distribution of livestock and women within the society itself.

Historically the mechanisms of age-class systems have provided the necessary solutions to these challenges. In East Africa, where pastoral and semi-pastoral groups often lack strong kinship structures or centralizing authority, they frequently cut across territory and lineage, widening social contacts and instilling a sense of corporate, even 'tribal', unity. They also provided a clear notion of status and rank which could facilitate the exercise of political authority, usually of a gerontocratic sort. At the same time, age-class systems – whether as an abstract 'folk political theory' (Baxter, 1978) or a veritable 'stage' on which various actions can be played out (Spencer, 1976) – could help construct a self-image, giving a

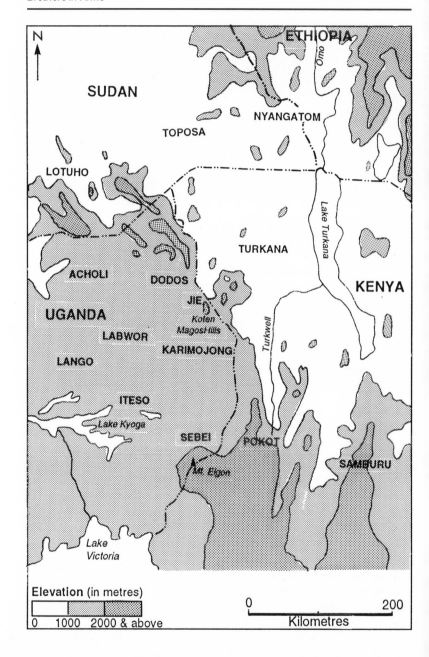

*Map 3  Sudan–Ethiopia–Uganda–Kenya Borderlands*

certain formality and pace to the process by which men matured from one social role to another. Similarly, they helped create corporate groupings of men who moved together through those roles, including one in which bands of armed 'brothers' stood solidly together to defend the society and its resources.

But herein was, of course, a powerful dilemma of a sort akin to 'setting the fox to guard the henhouse'. Its essence has been well captured by Paul Baxter:

> The maintenance of internal peace and harmony, simultaneously with a contin-uously aggressive front against their enemies has been ... an enduring problem [for pastoral societies]... If young men are kept in an almost continuous condition of physical and emotional readiness to fight in defense of [the society] how are they (i) restrained from going on the rampage or going on unwanted raids which provoke reprisals and (ii) restrained from utilizing their own ebullient force and energies to impose their will on the elders? (Baxter, 1979: 70).

Age-class systems provide the elders with the means to retain control and to limit the potential excesses of younger men in two different ways, the first religious and the second economic. The religious means entails the elders' control over major rituals, including those of the age-class systems, which often give the society its very definition. The spiritual wel-fare of the community rests securely in their hands. As the ultimate links with supernatural forces, the elders can threaten a curse which is much to be feared. The second means of control is derived from the simple fact that it is families, not age-sets or generation-sets, that own livestock, and so it is the family patriarchs who regulate the 'flow' of livestock through the community, ensuring by that very flow that the social order, in its broadest sense, is maintained. As individual fathers postpone the marriage, and thereby the independence, of their sons, so too do elders collectively control corporate bands of young 'warriors'. In this regard, the symbol-ism of the 'bell ox' or 'name ox', so commonly bestowed by fathers on sons in pastoral societies, becomes abundantly clear: the ox, a beast of immense potential power, is rendered docile through its castration by its owner. At the same time, the dynamics of the age-class systems often provide a 'queue discipline' which encourages young men to wait their turn, and play out a role entailing group solidarity, communal brotherhood, and obedient deference until such time as they enter a new role where individual acquisitiveness and differentiation are the norm. In many instances, then, age-class systems emerge as institutions to moderate and control the potential violence of the younger men, who, somewhat ironically, are entrusted with the security of the society. Typically, elders will stand in staunch opposition to any untoward escalation or expansion of hostilities which would allow younger men to break free of patriarchal religious or socio-economic regulation (Eisenstadt, 1956; Kipuri, 1989;

Spencer, 1976; Meeker, 1989; Almagor, 1979; Baxter and Almagor, 1978).

But there is another important dimension to all of this. From every indication, most East African societies prior to the early nineteenth century tended to be rather localized, segmentary and egalitarian, and they engaged in a decidedly stylized and limited form of conflict resolution. Fighting men often tended to be citizen militiamen, with the divisions between civilian and military aspects of society being quite indistinct. Battle formations, tactical and strategic concepts, and leadership structures were generally rudimentary. Armies were essentially armed mobs, aggregations of men whose motives for participation in warfare were usually personal ones and whose performance in combat was generally gauged in terms of individual bravery. The acquisition of trophies or 'spear raided cattle' was frequently a more powerful incentive for warfare than any larger economic or political motivation. When a specific personal goal had been obtained, a warrior might well decide to pack up and go home or even retire from further military activity altogether. Most of this activity took the form of intermittent raiding, rather than any large-scale or prolonged campaigning (Lamphear, 1994; Baxter, 1979; Peristiany, 1951; Welch, 1975).

Specific limitations on the conduct of war abounded, in some cases involving elaborate, almost chivalric military codes. Attitudes toward the killing of enemies in combat were highly ambivalent, the act being viewed simultaneously as a great achievement and a dangerous ritual pollution requiring lengthy purification. Often, the use of certain weapons was shunned, and those actually carried into battle had a religious significance that transcended any utilitarian purpose. Thus, Ateker war leaders were sometimes armed only with sticks whose lethality was derived almost entirely from supernatural associations, and fighting men of many communities guarded themselves with shields which afforded protection less from the thickness of the hide of their construction than from the mystical symbols painted on their surfaces. The calculated infliction of heavy casualties or the winning of a total, decisive victory was generally an alien concept. ('It is not good to exterminate a whole tribe', the Turkana used to say,[1] and in the later eighteenth century, the Maasai and Sonjo solemnly agreed never to strike at each others' bases of subsistence in their on-going military contests.) Truces could be called, even in the heat of battle, if one side began to lose too heavily. Above all, an essentially balanced condition of 'reciprocal raiding' was the goal. If the balance was threatened, various 'safety valves' such as migration, assimilation or boundary adjustment could effectively set things right. In many cases 'those who are raided' simply became 'those who raid'. (Lamphear, 1992; Gray, 1963; Turton, 1979; Meeker, 1989; Spring, 1993).

While the gerontocratic controls inherent in age-class systems certainly played their part in such limitations, they can be seen as emanating even more essentially from a wider condition which a generation ago H.H. Turney-High, in a truly iconoclastic study, somewhat ethnocentrically labelled as 'primitive war', a condition quite different from 'true' or 'civilized' war. While the precise threshold – the 'military horizon' – between the two can be elusive, the concepts have helped us to grasp essential differences between the mode of warfare traditionally practised by most human civilizations and that which was developed mainly, though by no means entirely, by the societies of the West, for the most part in relatively recent times. This 'true' warfare – the sort described by Karl von Clausewitz in the nineteenth century as 'total' war – is based on the application of just a few relatively simple principles or conditions. In Turney-High's view there are only five of these basic conditions that must be met before any society can rise above the military horizon to true war. They are:

• tactical operations, which involve the use of 'correct' formations;

• an adequate logistical system;

• group, rather than individual, motivations to undertake military activity;

• the ability to conduct protracted campaigns and not just isolated raids or battles;

• an effective system of command (Turney-High, 1991:30).[2]

Remarkably, Turney-High notes, most of the world's peoples were unable to apply these conditions or to devote themselves to the lethal shock tactics of 'face-to-face' combat that tend to stem from that application. This is because, he argues, human society is in its essence pacific: peace 'seems to be the normal situation in the minds of even warlike peoples' (Turney-High, 1991:226 and cf. Keegan, 1993:333). Without entering the morass of eternal debate among social and behavioural scientists about the 'nature or nurture' of human aggression, it can still be noted with some confidence that most societies traditionally have sought, in various ways and to various degrees, to restrain violence and to reduce conflict to a situation where 'feelings were more often hurt than bodies'; where war becomes 'more psychological than lethal' (Turney-High, 1991:186).

More recent observers have elaborated the same theme. Diane McGuinness, for instance, has noted that, unless they face some quite severe distress, egalitarian societies of the sort typical of East Africa will always adopt 'a more feminine solution' to conflict resolution, relying on negotiation rather than on the escalation of aggression (McGuinness, 1987: 306). Similarly, John Keegan, who has become perhaps the predominant figure in contemporary military history, argues that while 'ritual battle' (the equivalent of 'primitive war') is usually rather more than the harmless, quasi-athletic contest some have made it out to be, it is always fraught with an array of limiting devices which seek to avoid the escalation of combat and to subordinate the potential ferocity of fighting men to the 'constraints of law and custom' (Keegan, 1993:338). It is, in short, a type of conflict which, more than anything else, is marked by moderation. (In this paper it will be termed 'ritual war', a composite of Turney-High's and Keegan's terminology.) It is this controlled moderation, Keegan argues, that is its greatest distinguishing feature from 'true' warfare.

* * * * * *

While a controlled moderation certainly was an essential feature of traditional East African military systems, it should be noted that, by their very nature, the pastoral and semi-pastoral peoples, with their age-class systems, met some, if not most, of the criteria listed by Turney-High as marking the military horizon. To begin with, most of these systems traditionally had a strong, virtually inborn, sense of tactics and tactical organization. This may have been derived largely from the instinctive ability of herders to destroy the cohesion of a herd and break it up into manageable parts; to get around a 'flank'; to cut off a line of retreat. Age-sets or their component parts could easily play the role of constituent units in a coordinated battle line or column (what Turney-High described as 'correct' formations), and there is every reason to suppose they actually did so, even in the distant past. In terms of the second criterion, an adequate logistical system, pastoralists have another inherent advantage over peoples practising other forms of subsistence in that the livestock itself can be effectively converted into a mobile commissariat, even over long distances and for extended periods of time (Evans-Pritchard, 1940c; Baxter, 1979; Keegan, 1993; Meeker, 1989).

In terms of achieving a group, rather than individual, motivation for military activity, age-sets again could not only help to meet this criterion, but a good bit more as well. The emphasis on the egalitarian solidarity of age-sets in itself provided powerful collective motivations. In addition, the isolation and compartmentalization of young men in a period of 'warriorhood', so strong a feature of many age-class systems, bear a striking resemblance to key aspects of the regimental systems of European armies. As with the period of warriorhood, regiments were constructed so as to isolate and restrain a potentially aggressive and disruptive element of society. In so doing, however, both warrior age-sets and regiments developed a powerful sense of unique corporate identity, proclaimed by carefully prescribed costumes, jealously guarded emblems, private battle hymns and other hallowed traditions, all of which were regularly displayed, in the first instance on the ritual ground, in the latter on the parade ground. As Spencer (1993:141) has put it, 'warriorhood is a time

**84**

when young men are trapped in a regime imposed by the elders and yet at the same time are a law to themselves, a society within a society'. In Europe, military society became progressively differentiated from its larger cultures, and a fiercely unique sense of *esprit de corps*, vested in individual regiments, would be a crucial element in the emergence of 'true' warfare itself. With some East African societies, the individual age-sets, especially those based on biological rather than generational age, much more resembled an army of conscripts (where certain men are obligated to collective military service for a given period of time) than a 'nation in arms' militia-system more commonly associated with African military systems (Keegan, 1993; Welch, 1975). This system of long service, permanently available conscripts, together with the logistical advantages of a pastoral economy noted above, address the fourth of Turney-High's concerns: the ability to conduct protracted campaigns.

It was only in the last of Turney-High's categories, an effective system of command, that East African age-class systems were patently deficient. By their very nature, these systems provided an exceptionally poor basis upon which to construct a system of military command. In their essential opposition to escalation and their fixation on the wider social control of younger men, elders were, at best, reluctant 'commanders', especially at a strategic level. Moreover, 'command by committee' of the sort provided by congregations of elders was military nonsense. One has to agree with Baxter that 'it is difficult to see how age-sets could be [utilized as an effective military organization] except in a centralized political system' (Baxter, 1979:93). Indeed, to be effective, military command had to be centralized, but centralization was, of course, the very antithesis of many egalitarian and acephalous East African pastoralist societies. And so, military systems based on the age-class systems of these societies, for all their potential organizational, tactical and logistical sophistication, in the final analysis seem to have had little chance to transcend the limitations of ritual warfare. As Turney-High notes, the systems themselves were merely instruments which could not 'work themselves any more than a violin of finest workmanship can play itself. They require skillful handling' (Turney-High, 1991:60; Welch, 1975).

Several additional points need to be established. In the first place, the period of warriorhood in many pastoral and semi-pastoral societies was imbued with an extreme sense of assertive masculinity which was derived partly from the rugged, mobile existence of the herder. The constant protection of livestock produced hardy individuals well-skilled in the use of weapons. From the frequent slaughter of large, powerful animals was derived the art of efficient killing, the ability to deal a single decisive blow. Other elements of this assertive masculinity certainly stemmed from the tensions and frustrations of young men being dominated and controlled by their seniors. As Spencer notes, a major function of age-class systems was indeed their shouldering of 'the strain of youthful resentment' that might otherwise be vented within the family (Spencer, 1976:155). In any event, a warrior ethos, far beyond the requirements of pastoral practice or ritual battle, was a common feature. It was an ethos which gave men an affinity with the potential lethality of face-to-face shock tactics rather than the tentativeness of long-range fire fights. The heavy, socketed stabbing spears, the swords, clubs, wrist knives and shields which formed the armouries of most pastoral societies, together with their shunning of bows and light javelins, attest to the mode of combat (Spring, 1993).

As we have seen, it was the pervading sense of order and discipline imparted by age-class systems, resting on the ultimate economic and religious control of the elders, which kept assertive masculinity from becoming unbridled ferocity. But, at another level, age-class systems transmitted quite a different message: there was an essential dichotomy between the egalitarian solidarity of warrior age-sets and the highly differentiated status of elders. Power and wealth, in short, were derived by leaving the system. Furthermore, this image received additional strengthening from the presence of other functionaries, especially ritual specialists, whose offices and prestige again rested outside the age-class systems.

Finally, and very importantly, pastoral societies tended to be exceptionally dynamic ones, constantly in a state of flux. Certainly this was true of their economies, which were often notoriously unstable. Some recent studies have concluded, indeed, that specialized herding in the fragile ecology of East Africa is likely to have been historically a cyclical and ephemeral phenomenon. Under stressful conditions pastoral societies often had to make fundamental adjustments to one aspect of their culture in order to preserve others. In some instances the pastoral economy itself might be abandoned almost entirely to retain a valued cultural-linguistic identity. In other cases, the opposite choice might be made (Lamprey and Waller, 1990; Robertshaw, 1990).

In many instances, the age-class systems could become especially liable to alteration, for they were, above all, flexible systems whose rules and functions might change from generation to generation. Even the fundamental aspect of control and regulation might be relaxed under given circumstances to permit calculated and temporary escalations of hostilities (Almagor, 1977; Robertshaw, 1990; Müller, 1989).

## The Nineteenth Century: Rising Above the Military Horizon

The late eighteenth and early nineteenth centuries were a cataclysmic time in East Africa. Apparently stemming from a period of severe drought, sweeping changes were made in many societies, including profound adaptations to their military systems. For many of the pastoral communities these adaptations entailed – among other things – the emergence of centralizing figures.

A prime example of the process is that of the Maasai. While a system of increasing pastoral productivity may well have provided some stimulus to territorial expansion, what has been termed the 'active phase' of Maasai history began with the fusion of the age-class system and the office of *ol oiboni* ('chief prophet'; henceforth rendered as *'laibon'*). Apparently progressing through several intermediate stages of ritual services, the Inkidongi sub-clan of the Il Aiser group eventually gained exclusive control of key ceremonies of the age-class system. Two unique features of the Maasai system apparently facilitated the process. The first was the universal synchronization of the age-class system throughout Maasailand. The other was the institution of *manyatas*, 'warrior villages', found among many Maasai sections, which provided massed aggregations of junior *murran* ('warriors').[3]

By the beginning of the nineteenth century, the Laibon Supet had developed a close supervisory relationship over the *murran* of several sections and directed concerted expansions southwards into Tanzania. From that time, the *laibons* assumed overall control of large-scale military actions, and their preparation of charms and their cursings of enemies were deemed essential for the success of expeditions. Their effective control over the *murran* and military activity as well, was facilitated by a chain of command structure involving various grades of *Il aiguenak* (age-set spokesmen) (Bernsten, 1979; Fratkin, 1979; Fosbrooke, 1948). As the century progressed, a series of wars and expansions drove pastoral rivals out of the plains pasturelands, or sometimes absorbed them into burgeoning Maasai sections. By the second half of the century, a new *Laibon*, Mbatiany, had united no fewer than a dozen sections into the 'Purko-Kisongo' confederacy (Bernsten, 1979; Galaty, 1987 and 1993; Jacobs, 1979).

From the shares of captured livestock systematically collected for them by the *il asiguenok* after successful raids (which they had themselves, of course, planned and coordinated), the *Laibons* now built up enormous wealth, some of which could be used to attract additional followers, and even retinues of clients. Simultaneously, they gained a growing monopoly of religious control, as various sections became more and more reliant on their blessings and their supervision of vital ceremonies. All of this began to result in a serious deterioration of some roles traditionally played by the age-class system. The firestick elders, who previously had held ultimate control over the *murran*, now took a position subordinate to the *Laibon*; even their powers to curse were diminished. Increasingly, it was the *Laibon*'s growing monopolization of some areas of religious expertise that elevated him over the heads of the elders into that 'space which separates men and gods' (M. Godelier, as quoted by Bonté, 1975:395). Similarly, surplus livestock, which traditionally had been used as a currency of social reproduction and harmony, was appropriated by *Laibons* for their own private purposes. The superior status of the Inkidongi *Laibons* progressively came to be the single most important defining feature of the community (Bonte, 1975; Kipuri, 1989; Fratkin, 1979; Fosbrooke, 1948; Bernsten, 1979).

It is also of primary importance to emphasize that the *Laibons* were not bound by the same limitations on violence which had traditionally typified ritual warfare. On the contrary, it was to their direct benefit to encourage the belligerent behaviour of the *murran* and exacerbate rivalries with neighbouring societies. Certainly a degree of what might be termed 'calculated ferocity', quite beyond the effective control of elders, began to typify the Maasai military system. Some observers have even suggested that it might have stemmed from the use of drugs systematically pre-scribed for the *murran* by the *Laibon*. Others, somewhat more convincingly, have suggested that so little countervailing influence could be brought to bear that the Maasai warrior ethos became an internally motivating force fuelled by inter-group rivalries between individual units of *murran*, even providing the impetus behind some Maasai expansion (Kipuri, 1989; Lehmann and Mihalyi, 1982; Galaty, 1987 and 1993).

But on another, more fundamental level, it was the centralized leader-ship of the *Laibons* which provided the means of maximizing the demo-graphic potential of the synchronized age-class system and the *manyattas*, and of transcending the inherent limitations of the old concepts of warfare. At the height of its success, the new Maasai system had so intimidated rival communities that Maasai dominance rested largely on martial display. The simple appearance of well-drilled units of *murran* in their war panoply was enough to forestall any resistance. For a time the Maasai could police the vast areas under their control mainly through the application of 'power' (a subjective phenomenon based on others' perceptions of their military capabilities) rather than 'force' (a physical phenomenon derived from the direct application of military strength). It is the achievement of an agreed perception of power of precisely this sort that is the ultimate goal of any society practising 'true' war (Galaty, 1987; Luttwak, 1976; and cf. Lamphear, 1992, conclusion).

Increasingly, however, the Maasai began to 'turn in on themselves' in the latter part of the nineteenth century. Wars among competing Maasai sections and alliances became individualized contests between their respective *Laibons*, as other families sought to emulate the success of the Inkidongi. Even within that group itself, virulent rivalries between kins-men to secure or broaden their influence were common. While individual chief *Laibons* might dominate ritual activities associated with the age-class system and warfare, they had to accept that other religious functionaries and the elders controlled many important areas of ritual specialization (Bernsten, 1979; Fosbrooke, 1948).

By the waning years of the nineteenth century, the 'triple disasters' had wrecked the Maasai economy and the very fabric of Maasai society was severely tested. This, together with the arrival of the colonial vanguard, meant that Maasai military power could no longer be applied as it had once been. Individual *Laibons* now contracted with European officers to supply contingents of *murrans* as mercenaries for imperial expeditions, not only in order to recoup economic losses, but also, it is argued here, to act as a release for the unfettered aggression which the *Laibons* had unleashed (cf. Waller, 1976).

* * * * * *

The same sort of centralized control over military affairs gained by the Maasai *laibons* did not occur in many other East African communities. Among upland societies such as the Highland Pokot, for instance, the evolution of a sort of 'guerrilla' warfare based on militia-like organizations was apparently not compatible with strong centralization or unbridled escalation. Likewise, it was difficult for nascent centralizing figures to gain any wide control among such systems as the Sebei or Kipsigis, where autonomous territorial units provided the basis of military organization, though the Nandi *orkoiyots* came close (Peristiany, 1939 and 1951; Weatherby, 1962; LeVine and Sangree, 1962; Goldschnidt, 1976; Huntingford, 1953a). Another powerful impediment was the special degree of gerontocratic control invested in age-class systems based on generational age. Even more strongly than systems based on biological age, they typically functioned as a means of control and limitation and worked against the emergence of any real centralizing power. Generation systems, Harald Müller has observed, 'never produce a dictatorship'. Certainly many East African societies with generation systems, such as the Karimojong, Toposa and Dassanetch, retained decentralized military structures that thoroughly reflected the limitations of ritual warfare (Müller, 1989; Tornay, 1979).

Two societies, both from the Ateker group, which were organized around generation systems with powerful gerontocratic authority, were able to implement processes of military centralization, however. Elements of the first of these, the Turkana, are pictured by oral traditions as having sprung from elements of the second, the Jie, and so both societies presumably once shared the same generation system. Pushing down the Karamoja escarpment into the arid expanse west of Lake Turkana because of ecological and demographic pressures, ancestral Turkana undertook a rapid territorial expansion in the early nineteenth century, in certain respects reminiscent of that of the Maasai. Aided by a mobile and highly diversified economic system that included several types of pastoralism, and localized agriculture, gathering and fishing activities, the Turkana displaced rivals and assimilated significant numbers of them. Evidently this expansion was based far less on military activity than on successful economic adaptation, fortuitous evasions of natural disasters, and the ability of Turkana lineages to serve as 'collection boxes' for the assimilation of outsiders The process of expansion rapidly produced a highly decentralized society, spatially and structurally, with broad ethnic and cultural diversity. But one of the 'casualties' in all this was the Turkana generation system (Lamphear, 1988; Broch-Due, 1990).

During the early stages of the expansion it had been possible for the entire congregation of senior elders of the 'leading' generation-set to meet corporately and exercise strong gerontocratic direction over the evolving community. But having provided for a time a basic sense of 'Turkana-ness', the rapid expansion soon made any concerted generation-system activity impossible, and the activities of generation-sets and their constituent age-sets became more and more localized and uncoordinated. The earlier sense of corporate identity and the previous control of the senior elders were both seriously diminished.

Even as this deterioration grew, the internal integration of some neighbouring communities increased, perhaps proportionately, so that they began to present more stubborn resistance to earlier Turkana momentum. Turkana expansion ground to a halt near the Kerio River in the middle of the century. By perhaps a decade later, it had resumed with startling new vigour, largely imparted by powerful Diviners (*ngimurok*, sing. *emuron*), of the Meturona clan.

The office of Diviner is a minor one among all the other Ateker communities, and may well have been derived – directly or indirectly – from contacts with outsiders, probably southern Nilotes. In any event, the Meturona Diviners apparently had been developing a limited influence among a number of Turkana sections for some time before a new Diviner, Lokerio, began decisively to expand his activities into military affairs. And, while any very detailed reconstruction is impossible, it is clear that the transition was made possible through dramatic alterations to the generation system.

As Turkana expansion pushed further afield, biological principles had gained precedence over generational ones, so that even the fundamental alternation of 'father-son' generations gave way to the practice of initiating young men at about the age of 20, regardless of generational status. This provided an immediate solution to the problem of 'over-aging', endemic in generation systems. While the Turkana, like the other Ateker, had traditionally tackled this problem by allowing any male to raid, regardless of his generational status, substantial numbers of uninitiated men were not part of any corporate band of age-mates whose unique corporate identity provided a valuable source of *esprit de corps* and organizational sophistication.

The shift to principles of biological age now meant that each of the two generations initiated its age-sets of young men simultaneously and more or less constantly. Fresh batches of enthusiastic new initiates, whose first corporate duty was to take part in military expeditions, appeared throughout the country. Problems of coordination were also eased, as it was the individual Meturona Diviners who now became the focus of age-set activities.

It was in these circumstances[4] that Lokerio began extending his ritual leadership into military affairs by performing important ceremonies, blessings and purifications for age-sets and raiding parties. Simultaneously he gained strategic direction of military activity as a whole through prophetic dreams that identified auspicious targets and appropriate tactics for military expeditions. By the calculated extension of his influence over the war leaders, men who had traditionally been the leading tactical figures of individual territorial areas, Lokerio established a chain of command structure, facilitated by an efficient system of messengers who ran in relays from section to section. Large forces now mustered under his orders, and well-coordinated forays pushed across the Kerio to hurl back rivals and take possession of their country, women and livestock.

The impact of Lokerio's emerging military leadership on Turkana socio-political structures was strikingly similar to that made by the *Laibons* on the Maasai system. As with the *Laibons*, the Turkana Diviners did not share the elders' opposition to the escalation of hostilities, as they too began to reap a rich profit from the shares of captured livestock bestowed on them by victorious raiding expeditions. With the Turkana, moreover, there was an important additional effect. Young men taking part in the frequent, large-scale raids of Lokerio and his successors began to amass livestock of their own, allowing them to accumulate bridewealth and thus by-pass the institutionalized constraints fathers placed on their sons' early marriage, thereby escaping patriarchal control. Turkana society rapidly underwent a revolutionary process by which the cattle-raiding son became more and more revered, rather to the detriment of the cattle-owning father (Lamphear, 1988 and 1992; and cf. Meeker, 1989).

The subsequent experience of the Turkana also parallels in many respects that of the Maasai. Attracted by the success Lokerio had derived from his coordination of military activities, other contenders began to struggle for power. Just before the turn of the twentieth century a new line of Diviners from the Katekok clan usurped the office from the Meturona, although the latter, together with several other lines of minor diviners, retained control over many non-military ritual practices. Rivalries continued on into the twentieth century, until finally the leadership of Turkana resistance to the British imperial advances was taken over by a new Diviner, Loolel Kokoi, who appropriated the office for his Pucho clan.

Under Kokoi, Turkana military structures underwent even further modifications, and together with the war-leader Ebei, his field commander, Kokoi created a 'new model' army based on a virtually professional class of soldiers equipped with modern firearms, the *Ruru*. While the organization of the army continued to be based on the age-sets simultaneously recruited by the two generation-sets, any semblance of gerontocratic control completely evaporated. To counter the extraordinary pressures of the British invasion, Turkana warfare escalated steadily, both in theory and practice. By the time of its ultimate demise in 1924, the *Ruru* army was rapidly moving beyond the control even of the Diviners to become a power in its own right (Lamphear, 1992; and cf. Low, 1975).

\* \* \* \* \* \*

In many respects, the process of centralization undergone by the second Ateker community, the Jie, stands in contrast to that of the Maasai or Turkana. In the mid-nineteenth century the Jie were a small, spatially compact society that had undertaken rather little territorial expansion. Their economy, while still ideologically committed to pastoralism, was shifting increasingly to grain agriculture. The generation-system, well coordinated and utterly dominated by senior elders, provided strong notions of gerontocratic authority and group identity. There were, in addition, two hereditary offices, that of Ritual Firemaker (*ekeworon*, pl. *ngikeworok*) and War leader (*ekapalon kaajore*), but neither was vested with any real political power. The Firemakers, while performing ceremonies vital to Jie corporate integration and providing ritual preparations for military expeditions, were specifically enjoined not to concern themselves with tactical or strategic matters: indeed, they were to eschew violence entirely and be models of gentleness, arbitration and moderation. For their part, the hereditary War leaders, while theoretically 'commanders' of all the fighting men of their major division (of which the Jie had two), had minimal authority of any kind. As with the Turkana before their system took on aspects of a system based on age-sets, the Jie military organization was distinctly militia-like, with 'over-aged' men routinely participating in military operations. Age-sets played very little part in these operations. Instead, organization was built on autonomous 'private companies', loose bands of men voluntarily coalescing around 'battle leaders' who gained their (basically informal) positions through personal prowess. It was these battle leaders who controlled tactical leadership, such as it was. Strategy, or rather its limitation, was firmly dictated by the congregation of senior elders. Having very little input into either area, the hereditary War leader was thus no more than the figurehead of a system that tended to epitomize ritual war (Lamphear, 1976 and 1994).

By the latter nineteenth century, however, the Jie had come under tremendous pressure from two Ateker neighbours, the Karimojong and Dodos, as well as from several of the petty Acholi kingdoms that bordered them to the west. For a time, it seemed inevitable that the Jie would be swallowed up by these rivals. But then, at their moment of supreme crisis, Loriang, the hereditary War leader of one major division, used his office to make sweeping reforms to the Jie military system. He first replaced the system of private companies with one of much larger 'battalions' based on territorial divisions, and he transformed the battle leaders into a collective unit of their own, to which a prestigious elite status was accorded. The new battalions, vested with a rapidly increasing sense of corporate identity, functioned with stunning efficiency in several defensive campaigns. Loriang, meanwhile, forged ahead with other reforms. He created an efficient chain of command structure, induced the men of the other major division to come under his control, and forged alliances with several western peoples, including even some of the formerly belligerent Acholi, through brilliant diplomatic skills. These new allies now supplied contingents to Loriang's new model army, even forming 'specialist' units of musketeers and riflemen to work in tactical combination with Jie spearmen. By the early twentieth century, with the momentum swinging to his side, Loriang assumed the offensive, and although usually still heavily outnumbered, won a series of decisive victories which allowed the Jie to expand their grazing lands dramatically.

Quite unlike the situation with the Maasai or Turkana, Loriang's centralization presented no serious challenge to the underlying gerontocratic control of the generation system. On the contrary, Loriang was careful to work in close cooperation with the senior elders to effect his changes. Ever the diplomat, he wooed their approval with gifts and delicate rounds of negotiation. Neither he nor any individual members of his army monopolized captured livestock. While Loriang did derive large numbers of animals as his share of the booty after expeditions, it appears that many − perhaps most − of them were used as tools in his diplomacy: as inducements to allies, to smooth the ruffled feathers of battle leaders, and especially as presents to senior elders. His army remained essentially a militia organization where military activity was expected of old and young men alike, not just specific units of young 'conscripts', although the strong senses of discipline and seniority traditionally conferred by the generation system were retained. In this situation, booty was absorbed broadly into the community as a whole, functioning, as always, as a currency of corpo-rate social relations. The generation system remained, therefore, the ulti-mate source of strategic direction, even though tactical and organizational structures were now controlled by Loriang. Feeling secure in their geron-tocratic power, the elders apparently had no misgivings about acceding to what was clearly a systematically controlled escalation of hostilities in the name of community survival. Probably because of the essential lack of mobility inherent in Jie semi-pastoral practices, and because of the lack of any strong age-set identity, the younger men never threatened to break free of gerontocratic control, as with the Maasai or Turkana. With the arrival of the colonial regime, the Jie, who had probably begun to surpass the practical limits of their expansion, hastened to find an accommodation with the new order. Loriang's centralizing role quickly faded and the gerontocratic authority of the senior elders was reaffirmed.

## Conclusion

By their achievement of various degrees of centralized leadership, the three East African societies we have examined would appear to have met all the criteria cited as necessary to rise above the military horizon to 'true' war. How successfully they did so, and at what additional expense, is another matter altogether.

In all of eastern and southern Africa, the societies which most clearly and dramatically transcended the military horizon were, of course, the Zulu and the imitators of their system. In certain striking ways, the experiences of the Maasai and the Turkana bear a close resemblance to that of the Zulu. Most fundamentally, all three saw centralizing figures appropriate pre-existing age-sets, and, by converting them into more effective military units, transform the warfare of their societies. In terms of their use of a barracks system and the increasing application at the height of their success of 'power' rather than 'force', the Maasai correspondence to the Zulu system appears even closer.

But there were essential differences between the centralization provided by Zulu kings and that of the Maasai *Laibons* and Turkana Diviners. For our purposes, the most fundamental of those differences was that the *Laibons* and Diviners were, from the beginning, regarded as *outsiders*. In both societies, vivid traditions recalling their 'discovery' attest to their being outside the normal conditions of social reproduction and age-set stratification.[5] In neither case was there any thorough integration of their functions, especially their military ones, into earlier social structures: rather they stood well beyond, but also above, them. Furthermore, the institutions of the *Laibon* for the Maasai and the Diviners for the Turkana were still very much in their formative stages when British imperial intrusion made their further development impossible. In key aspects, the institutions were at that point still essentially impositions on original cultural features, and, in some ways, decidedly incompatible with them (Lamphear, 1988 and 1992; Bonte, 1975 and 1977; Fosbrooke, 1948; Kipuri, 1989).

It has been suggested that, especially with the Maasai *Laibons*, the evolution towards the hierarchical structure of a state was already under way (Galaty, 1991; Kipuri, 1989). But if that was so, the process still had a long way to go, and, it should be emphasized, it was not off to a very promising start. In the centralized politics of the Zulu and other Nguni-speakers, and indeed in those of many of the interlacustrine states of East Africa, the King was the ultimate 'father' and patriarch. By his ownership of all the society's livestock, the basic pastoral dichotomy of 'father/son' became that of 'king/army'. But while the *Laibons* and Diviners had challenged and disrupted earlier notions of patriarchal control, diminished the role of the senior elders, and taken important steps towards the privatization of economic and religious power, any suggestion of royal status was still a long way off. Far from 'owning' all the society's cattle (symbolically or otherwise), the *Laibons* and Diviners actually controlled only a very small (though, in comparison to other men, a hugely dispro-portionate) percentage, and even the systematic gifts of looted animals by victorious expeditions cannot be reckoned as real 'tribute'. In terms of religion, elders and other functionaries still controlled the myriad of family-based rituals, and, in the face of incessant, potentially fissiparous rivalries with other *Laibons* or Diviners, even the most powerful of the Maasai and Turkana centralizers had to share many ritual specializations with other practitioners (Lamphear, 1992; Bonte, 1975 and 1991; Meeker, 1989).

By their weakening of the elders' traditional control, the *Laibons* and Diviners had, above all, destroyed that deep sense of moderation which had typified age-class systems and, accordingly, unleashed a new dimension of aggressiveness among the young men. In neither case were the functionaries then able effectively to channel and coordinate that aggressiveness, again largely because their institutions were still in the process of development. With the Maasai, the aggression was channelled into the service of the imperial vanguards, as young men took up service as mercenaries for colonial armies (the image of eighteenth-century German princelings proffering the services of their own conscript armies to more powerful European states provides an uncomfortably close parallel). With the Turkana, the *Ruru* professional soldiers became power-ful enough to move even beyond the control of the Diviners, who had helped create them in the first place. If the Maasai and the Turkana did rise above the military horizon through the establishment of centralized control over their age-class systems, they did so only temporarily, for their new systems contained the seeds of their own self-destruction (Waller, 1976; Lamphear, 1992; Low, 1975).

With the Jie, on the other hand, we find utterly different processes at work. Loriang, although he expanded the parameters of his office, nevertheless worked entirely within pre-existing structures. His attainment of military centralization was marked by compromise, diplomacy and power-sharing. He managed to create effective military units without elevating age-sets to the status of conscripted regiments, while still retaining the ranked discipline of the generation system. Loriang's process of centralization was far less the dramatic imposition and the calculated monopolization of power typically associated with state formation. Some recent studies, however, have begun convincingly to demonstrate that, at its most essential level, state formation stems not from sudden outside impositions, but rather from complex and subtle interactions, compromises and adaptations within the changing social environment of the society itself: a process, in other words, much more typical of the Jie than of the Maasai or Turkana (cf. Newbury, 1991).

In the final analysis, it is evident that the Jie, too, managed to rise above the military horizon only very tentatively and temporarily. In their case, however, the reasons were quite the opposite of those of the Maasai and Turkana. Instead of creating a new order in which the privatization of power and the unbridling of the warrior ethos contradicted the basic premises upon which age-class systems were founded, Loriang's leadership ensured that the essential moderation, definitive of those systems and of ritual war, would prevail. And this was, perhaps, his greatest achievement:

> Future peacekeepers and peacemakers have much to learn from alternative military culture, not only of the Orient but of the primitive world also. There is a wisdom in the principle of intellectual restraint and even of symbolic ritual that needs to be rediscovered (Keegan, 1993:392).

# Notes

1 Much of this paper is based on oral data collected by oral historians and anthropologists working in East Africa over the past several decades. Most of the reconstruction of Ateker societies is based on my own work. I should perhaps emphasize to those unfamiliar with oral methodology that what I have presented here is my own critical synthesis of varied and complex materials from which other interpretations might be derived. For full discussions of oral methodologies, see several of the sources, including my own, listed in the bibliography at the end of the paper.

2 Although originally published in 1949, Turney-High's *Primitive War* is one of those truly exceptional volumes that has made such a fundamentally important contribution to a

field of study that anyone wishing to contribute to that field must use it as a starting point. Although open to criticism in many areas, it has stood the test of time remarkably well, and indeed is being 'rediscovered' by the contemporary generation of military historians as a seminal work.

3 To the best of my knowledge, no one has tried systematically to determine whether this universality of the age-class system and the *manyata* system preceded the rise of *laibons* or was a *result* of that process. Galaty (1993) apparently favours the former scenario but, to my mind, it is difficult to comprehend why elders would have condoned the *manyatta* system. Certainly, as Fratkin observes, the institution represents a major impediment to their control over the *murran*.

4 Müller, while acknowledging the problems attendant on the rapid expansion of the Turkana and the new coordinating roles of the Diviners, advances the argument that it was uncommonly large numbers of illegitimate sons born to the 'leading' Turkana generation-set in the mid-nineteenth century which underlay the transformation of the generation system. I do not find his argument convincing, and find hardly any support for it in the traditions I have gathered.

I am in agreement, however, with another of Müller's contentions, that while a generation system can evolve into a system based on biological age (which I feel is essentially what happened with the Turkana), it is virtually impossible for the opposite to happen. Interestingly, as Müller himself notes, the age-set principle has recently become so strong that young men from the two alternate generation-sets are being initiated into the same generation-sets.

5 In many of the centralized kingdoms of East Africa there are traditions which also picture their original kings as immigrants or 'foreigners'. But with these kingdoms, where centralizing institutions became deeply integrated into the political fabric, the message of the traditions, especially at a functionalist level, is rather different from that of the Maasai or Turkana traditions, although their structures are undeniably similar.

# 5 Generational Systems on the Threshold of the Third Millennium: An Anthropological Perspective

## SERGE A. M. TORNAY[1]

## Introduction

At the end of the twentieth century, when a new geopolitical situation has proved to be disastrous in many regions, particularly in Africa, are East African age systems in transition? Do they represent outmoded forms of social organization? In the present paper, I shall try to discuss such issues within the limited framework of some East African societies with generation systems. But let me first mention a recent, thematic, issue of *L'Homme* (no. 134, 1995) devoted to 'Age and Generations'. In her comparative paper A.M. Peatrik underlines Paul Spencer's contribution (1978) to the demography of generation systems. She illustrates the importance of demography for a global understanding of East African age and generation systems. She contrasts demographically 'restrictive' systems, the most typical example of which is that of the Meru of Kenya whom she has studied in the field, with 'fluctuating' systems which are not only far from being 'Malthusian' but, on the contrary, do everything possible to optimize the fertility of women and men alike. This is why, in the Karimojong cluster, as well as amongst the Gikuyu, women are not classified as marriageable or not marriageable by the generation system. Men's choices are limited only by the incest prohibitions, and marriage is a private affair. In order to maximize the benefits, new partners are continually thrown in. Polygamy is valued and fathers and sons are allowed to procreate at the same time: this is seen as a sign of the family's prosperity. These societies are expanding territorially and demographically. In contrast to this, amongst the Boran, Meru, Konso, Rendille and others, significant restrictions are placed on female fertility as well as on male procreation; and for parents and children to procreate at the same time is considered quite unacceptable. The population is either static or decreasing, although the deficit might be made up by immigration as amongst the Meru. Obviously there are intermediate examples in East Africa, notably the Maasai about whom Peatrik has made some interesting comments.

This typology is also interesting from a political point of view. Whereas in restricted systems there is a tendency for the short-term transmission of power between the sub-divisions of generations (see the *gada* type systems, in which a change of the set 'in power' occurs every eight years), in fluctuating systems the generational and generative period is longer drawn out: men marry late in life and there are no social limitations or constraints on paternity; men can even continue to have legal children after death, by their legitimate wives. There is no female initiation and girls are allowed to have sexual intercourse before marriage; and, even when male initiation exists, it is possible for men to ignore it in practice amongst many of these peoples. Existing models (Spencer, 1978; Müller, 1989; 1991 and Tornay, 1989a) show that there is, at the level of the system, a generational interval of a little more than fifty years, while at the level of individual families the interval is only about thirty years. It follows that power between social generations is transmitted only about every fifty years (although there is a tendency amongst the Toposa for this period to be broken up, a point further explained below). Peatrik rightly emphasizes that 'these societies try to reconcile two diverging principles: a generational political principle and domestic interests which encourage fertility' (1995: 39). It is important to bear in mind that these ideas are not necessarily capable of generalization to all East African systems. The discussion which follows is intended to apply in the first place to the peoples of the Karimojong cluster.

For my part, I have presented (1995) a sociological argument about the generational systems of the Karimojong type. I then tried to identify, with reference to a common structure, the events which reveal the specific political dynamic of the system. Obviously, one of its functions is to ensure social cohesion but, as with all segmentary systems, it has to cope periodically with tensions: (a) tensions between seniors and juniors within the same generation, which normally leads to the emergence of separate age-sets, but which may also cause a political break-up of that generation; (b) conflicts between fathers and sons which can cause the secession of the latter and the emergence of a new, autonomous political entity. Since both processes are documented in the ethno-history of the cultural cluster, the case was ideal for comparative, structural, analysis.

My aims in the present paper are (i) to give specific information on the Nyangatom system by means of a comparison with the Karimojong system; (ii) to analyze the Nyangatom institution of the *asapan*-man, which seems to be unique in the Karimojong cluster; (iii) to question the dysfunctions of two related systems (Toposa and Nyangatom) throughout history; (iv) to draw conclusions about the ideological background of the generational system.

## Two Generational Systems in a Comparative Perspective

*An outline of the system, with special reference to the Nyangatom*

If the *gada* system of the Boran is a mechanism for integrating clans which are the truly corporate units of society (Bassi, 1994), the situation is clearly different amongst the Karimojong group of peoples. Here clans are dispersed, both among the territorial sections of each tribe and among the tribes themselves. They do not function as corporate entities. It is not a lineage system either, but it rests on a structure of patriarchal families (*awuyi*: the physical settlement and the polygynic family) which are segmented into matrifocal units (*ekol*: the day hut and the mother with her progeny). The corporate units of the society are (a) generations and (b) sub-divisions into age-groups and age-sets (see below) of these generations. This corporateness is seen at four politico-territorial levels: the settlement, the territorial section, the tribe and the intertribal level, where, whether between enemies or friends, there is precise knowledge of generational differences and equivalents. How does the system work ?

(a) A multi-clanic group of contemporaries labelled *Ngiseukop*, 'Beginners of the country', is remembered in ethno-history as the generation which founded the new polity. According to the principle of patrilineal descent, all the children of this first generation, and only those, make up the second generation. The process continues, so that the entire population is distributed into successive generations which I call *species* because they are named arbitrarily after the names of animal species (Zebras, Elephants, Tortoises, etc.) or natural features such as Mountains etc.[2] Whether the naming is cyclical or linear does not have any bearing on the system itself.

(b) Each generation has to wait its turn to reach a position of pre-eminence in the society, namely the status of senior generation which I call, following the Nyangatom, Fathers of the country. In the literature, this generation is usually said to be 'in power', but it is more than power. It is also a matter of legitimacy and authority. So, for as long as a society chooses to ignore, or refuses to accept, an outside ruler, the Fathers are 'a corporate body invested with sovereignty'.[3]

(c) In age-grade systems the principle of seniority is lineal and transitive. In the generation system this rule is bent by a distribution of generations into two status-sets ('left-hand and right-hand' of the *akiriket* or ceremonial sitting order). These classes are considered to be equivalent but each has to wait its turn in order to attain senior status. If the Fathers are members of the left-hand stream, their grandfathers and grandsons are sitting with them; at the same time the Sons of the country are members of the right-hand stream and their alternate generations are assimilated to them. In other words the generation system consists of only two grades or statuses: Fathers of the country and Sons of the country.[4]

(d) A crucial moment is when there is an inversion of status between the left and the right hand. This is the moment of generational transition or succession. The demographic models show that this crucial event occurs only twice in a hundred years. The same models show that, although a generation can exist for as long as 230 years, its members can only occupy the pre-eminent status of Fathers for around fifty years. Table 5.1. shows a reconstruction of the Nyangatom system by means of a demographic simulation.

*Table 5.1 Hypothetical reconstruction of the Nyangatom generation system*

| Generation name | Date of appearance | Period in power | Date of extinction |
|---|---|---|---|
| Country Beginners | ? | around 1700 | ? |
| Wild Dogs | 1600 | 1730–80 | 1830 |
| Zebras | 1650 | 1780–1830 | 1880 |
| Tortoises | 1700 | 1830–80 | 1930 |
| Mountains | 1750 | 1880–1930 | 1980 |
| Elephants | 1800 | 1930–80 | 2030 |
| Ostriches | 1850 | (?)1980–2030 | (?) 2080 |
| Antelopes | 1900 | (?)2030–80 | (?) 2130 |
| Buffaloes | 1950 | (?)2080–2130 | (?) 2180 |

Sources: 1973 census data in Tornay 1989: 651–79; computer simulation by Müller in Tornay, 1989: 517–25).

Each generation is a lasting social entity with its own history: it appears, it grows in numbers, it reaches its demographic peak and political maturity, then it begins a long decline until it disappears. For more than a century each generation includes men of all ages, all of whom are considered brothers and ought to prove it by their solidarity. Of course, there are seniors and juniors and seniority entails coercive authority. Each generation is made up of local age-groups which, at a territorial, inter-territorial or possibly tribal level, progressively unite into age-sets. Each age-group recruits the young men of a settlement or neighbourhood (when they prove able to herd cattle and to scout in the bush), for a period of six to ten years. The senior members of the group will try to be recognized as a named age-set by the most senior members of their generation; they eventually achieve this by making payments to their senior generation-mates. At the same time, those seniors of the new age-set tend to exercise a tough authority over their juniors, imposing heavy duties on them, and beating them if they refuse to obey. This normally generates resentment and desire for autonomy among the juniors. If tension persists, they will wait till they feel strong enough to oppose their senior age-mates, when they eventually provoke an *ameto*, an open rebellion. Mock fights, but at times real stick fights, arise between the two parties, the solution of the crisis being the provisional recognition of the junior age group as an entity of its own; in the end, they will obtain full recognition when the name which they claim for themselves is accepted by the eldest living set of their generation. Thus antagonism between adjacent age-sets is both a demographic and a sociological process, while antagonism between more distant age-sets within one generation may lead to the break-up of the generation, as in the Toposa case mentioned below.[5]

In the literature, generation systems have sometimes been judged dysfunctional because generations 'artificially' bring together cohorts of all ages. In fact, this bringing together is only dysfunctional in relation to particular roles such as the military one. But Gulliver himself has stressed that the generation system of the Jie was not a military organization, a point that both John Lamphear and I have confirmed for related peoples. What are the advantages of mixed ages within the generations? What is the spirit of the system?

(a) Basic rule: *feed your fathers.* To do this in a pastoral setting you cannot use your fathers' cattle. You need cattle and small stock either of your own or from your peers. You will have your own cattle if you are an *elope*, owner of a herd, but you can only acquire this status if you have no father living, and no father's brothers or elder full brothers. Outside your family, you may obtain cattle from members of your age-group or from older members of your generation. If you honour the seniors of your generation they may help you in feeding common fathers.

(b) Secondary rule: *feed your peers.* To do this you can, of course, use your own cattle if you are an *elope*; if you are not, you may obtain cattle from elder brothers, both within your family or within your generation. Last but not least, you may receive cattle or small stock from your own father who thus encourages your goodwill as a herder and warrior.

These fraternal and filial offerings are the normal expression, at certain times on a daily basis, of public life from the local to the tribal level. Killing an ox for generation mates should be considered an offering; in contrast, killing an animal for fathers should be regarded as a sacrifice because the sons/fathers relationship has a religious dimension. After the slaughter of the animal and while the meat is being roasted, current affairs are formally laid before the audience, bad actions are denounced and criticized while good actions are held up as an example. The providers of the meat are praised and blessed. The fathers call on Akuj, 'God', to witness their words: calling for the extermination of their enemies and for the prosperity and fertility of their own sons, wives, children and animals. The filial offering (called *apeyo*, literally 'invitation') is not just an act of butchery, followed by a meat feast and a prayer after the meal: anthropologically, it is a *sacrifice*. Of course, as Luc de Heusch (1986; criticizing Evans-Pritchard, 1954 on Nuer sacrifice) and Eisei Kurimoto (1992) have aptly shown, the Judeo-Christian model of sacrifice does not fit Nilotic realities. The Nyangatom sacrifice their oxen as oxen, not as themselves,[6] and they offer them not to God but to their fathers. In doing so they pay an endless debt, that of life itself. Akuj is only summoned to witness their piety. In return, the fathers call on Akuj to witness the blessing of their children and the cursing of their enemies.[7] The Nyangatom do not rely on their dead: the generation system does not produce ancestors. Thus the living fathers, being life-givers (procreation, blessing) as well as life-takers (cursing), are in the same position as ancestors (as in South East Asia) or gods (as in Hinduism, Judaism, etc.) to whom sacrifices are offered in payment for the debt of life.

*A comparison between the Karimojong and Nyangatom systems*

Like other African social systems, the generation system rests on mechanisms of initiation. Within the Karimojong cluster, different groups have a different interpretation of, or adapt in different ways to, this demand. Since there are two fundamental statuses one would expect the system to distinguish between two steps: recognition as Sons, which can be called initiation, and accession to the status of Fathers, called succession or transition. This logic is clearly seen in the model of the Karimojong system provided by Dyson-Hudson (1963).

(a) **Karimojong.** The Karimojong conceive of their system as a repeating cycle of four generations (*nga-nyameta*, 'groups of those who eat together'), Zebras, Mountains, Gazelles and Lions. At any one moment only two generations are recognized as formally in existence: the senior generation which has stopped recruiting members and the junior generation which is still recruiting. Its growth is accompanied by the successive initiation of a series of age-sets (*nga-sapanisia*). Once the process is completed, these age-sets will constitute the new senior generation. The Karimojong make a clear distinction between the initiation (*asapan*) of age-sets and generational succession ('dividing the haunch').

*Initiation.* The first phase, which is called 'spearing the ox', takes place near the settlement. Each *initiand* spears an ox of the family herd. The fathers of the initiands anoint each of their sons with the contents of the rumen of the sacrificed ox. Then they eat the roasted meat, inviting their sons, including the initiands, to join them in the feast. For Dyson-Hudson, the symbolism and values expressed in initiation are an affirmation of the supremacy of the senior generation and a reaffirmation of paternity, which initiation extends from the domestic level to the tribal level. As for the killing of the ox by the initiand, Dyson-Hudson sees this as prefiguring his role in later public ceremonies, including that in which he will, in his turn, eventually be honoured by the members of a new generation.

*Succession.* Age-sets can only be formed within a generation which has already been formally opened. The opening of a new generation implies the retirement of its alternate senior generation and the promotion of the intermediate generation from the status of junior to that of senior. The whole ceremonial process is called *akiding amuro*, 'dividing the haunch'. This ceremony is held once for the whole tribe. It takes place at Apule, the sacred place of the tribe. Representatives of each section take part with their wives, cattle and ornaments.

The first step is called *akuwar asapanet*, 'acquiring the thing of initiation'. Those who are about to become seniors prepare a ceremonial enclosure and gather *unbroken* branches to make a new fire. One of these men, chosen by the senior elders, spears a piebald ox, yellowish-brown and white. The ox is cut up and roasted, with the exception of the haunches, from which only the perineal meat has been cut away. The perineal meat, called *elamacar*, is roasted and presented to the most senior elder present at the ceremony, who cuts it up and, contrary to normal practice, shares it with the members of the junior generation. After prayers conducted by the same elder, calling down the blessing of Akuj on the juniors who are going to assume responsibility for the country, all the participants share the roasted meat of the sacrificial animal. After the feast, the ritual of the division of the haunches takes place. The most senior elder takes hold of the blade of a spear with a long shaft, called 'the twisted spear of custom'. Behind him the largest number of members possible of the junior generation also take hold of the shaft, ranged according to their age. As the old man guides the blade, they all together divide the meat into two halves through the pelvis. The meat is then roasted and eaten in a convivial fashion by all the participants. On returning to their settlements the members of the former junior generation proclaim their new senior status by announcing that their sons are able to be initiated. Throughout the country initiations are prepared and take place *en masse*, a fact which reflects the long wait which has preceded the generational transition.

According to Dyson-Hudson, one cannot enter a Karimojong generation simply by the fact of birth, as one can amongst the Nyangatom: it is necessary to wait for the formal opening of a generation of juniors and to go through initiation, a ceremony which places each individual into a previously 'opened' and named age-set. Until his initiation, a Karimojong hardly seems to play any role in public life. From this point of view he is a minor. On the other hand, Dyson-Hudson expressly notes that, in his private life, he suffers little handicap because of his politico-religious minority: 'When a person is out of phase with the state of recruiting ... he may marry prior to initiation, but in general the Karimojong disapprove of this and require men to be socially adult before taking a wife. This puts no limit on sexual activity for the uninitiated, however, since premarital relations are considered normal for both sexes and concubinage is permitted' (1963: 388). As far as military activity is concerned, it is hardly possible for this to take place outside an age-group, formally constituted by the initiation of its members. Ideally it is the responsibility of the junior generation to take part in military activity, while it is the privilege of the senior generation to hold political authority. One can understand from this why the Karimojong are preoccupied with the problem of adjusting their system to the constraints which follow from the classification of sons according to a generational rule. By means of various adjustments, they seem (or at least they seemed at the time of Dyson-Hudson's study, from 1956 to 1958) able to achieve a reasonable degree of congruence between age and generation. The junior adults are the initiands and initiates, the active body of herders and warriors; in their private lives they are bachelors or at the beginning of their matrimonial careers; even if they are married, they remain under the authority of their father or his legal substitute such as a father's brother or an elder brother. Ideally, older adult men are the 'owners' of cattle and people. They are the men who initiate their sons and who possess political and religious authority. They are fathers of a family and Fathers of the country, invested with supernatural power.


(b) **Nyangatom.** During the 1970s there were five generations with living members: Mountains, Elephants (the titular Fathers), Ostriches (the titular Sons), Antelopes and Buffaloes. Only the Mountains and the Elephants had 'made *asapan*' and they did so age-set by age-set. No *asapan* had been given to the Ostriches, but their adults, like those of junior generations, do belong to named and recognized age-sets, wear an adult hair-style and are full legal adults. Many of them are heads of families and owners of herds who participate in public meetings; they are the most numerous sacrificers, obeying the basic injunction, 'feed your fathers', an injunction which applies to all generations with living members. This filial service is not, in Nyangatom practice, confined to men who have made *asapan*. In slaughtering animals for their fathers, the Nyangatom initiate themselves as sons and do not become real fathers themselves until their own sons begin killing animals for them.

During those years of drought, famine and warfare (Fukui and Turton, 1979), there was a high level of social tension. It was publicly debated whether the Elephants were going to hand over power voluntarily or whether the Ostriches should take the initiative by provoking the transition. The Elephants said that they were going to 'give *asapan*' to their sons. But the latter suggested that they might 'make *asapan*' of their own accord. Opinions varied according to the generational status of the actors[8] but everyone was in agreement about the structure and content of the transition rite.

## The Nyangatom *Asapan* or the Transmission of Sovereignty

In the Karimojong cluster, the word *asapan* denotes several realities.[9] According to Nyangatom tradition, the *asapan* or transmission ceremony begins when five representatives of the men who are about to become Fathers spend a night in the bush. The next morning an ox is drugged with poisonous plants before having its throat cut[10] by the *asapan*-man, a member of the retiring generation: this key-person has been previously 'bought' from his family, by means of the payment of cattle, by members of his own generation. Having cut the ox's throat he touches the forehead of the five representatives of the new generation, thus giving them *asapan*, that is making them the new Fathers of the country. After this he is supposed to lose his mind and wander off into the bush and die. The cattle given in payment for this person allow his family to obtain a wife who will bear children to him. His name seems to become tabooed afterwards and he both assumes and symbolizes, in a dramatic way, the disappearance of his generation. The *asapan* ox is offered by the sons to the retiring fathers but both generations share the meat feast. After this initial ceremony, throughout the country, the age-sets of the promoted generation collectively affirm their *asapan* by sacrificing oxen for their retiring fathers. During these great festivities the latter are the recipients of the offerings, but this will be the last time they are fed *de jure* as Fathers of the country.

This model represents a condensation of the two-stage Karimojong model. This being so, how do Nyangatom age-sets come into existence within generations? Comparative data (for example from Karimojong, Turkana and Toposa) show that the *asapan* initiation confers the right to wear the adult hair-style, a head-dress of coloured clay which can support decorative feathers. Amongst the Nyangatom, sons become members by birth, even if informally, of the generation which follows that of their fathers. Children and adults nevertheless have distinct statuses, recognizable by their hair-style. The adoption of the adult hair-style occurs independently within each generation, whatever its status position. As they approach adulthood and begin to participate in raids and to marry, young men, who have already managed to be recognized as an age-group, and who wish to be recognized as members of an age-set, demand their hair-style from their immediate seniors who give it in return for payments and gifts of tobacco, ornaments, small stock, etc. They then demand from the most senior set of the generation the right to bear the name which they have chosen for themselves and which evokes one of their exploits or the ox which they sacrificed for their seniors. In this respect, the adoption of a hair-style amongst the Nyangatom is analogous to Turkana initiation, except that the Nyangatom do not call this *asapan* and give it much less importance.[11] During the 1970s the clay head-dress was worn by a majority of Nyangatom adult men. As soon as the senior members of an age-set had obtained permission from their generational elders to wear the head-dress, junior members of the set imitated them without having again to 'bribe' their senior generation-mates.

For the Karimojong, initiation consists of the completion of the filial sacrifice. At succession a man of the new generation spears a piebald ox which is then consumed in a convivial feast. Dyson-Hudson gives us only one indication about the status of this man who is, in appearance only, similar to the *asapan*-man of the Nyangatom. He is 'nominated by the gathered seniors'. So he is chosen by them but he is a member of the new generation, while the *asapan*-man is chosen by his fellow-generation members who are retiring from their position as Fathers of the country. Furthermore, no particular fate is expected to overtake the Karimojong officiant. In any case, it is not the sacrifice which is seen by Dyson-Hudson as the mechanism of the succession but the division of the haunches, in his opinion an explicit symbol of the separation of the two generations.

The two ritual situations differ profoundly. Amongst the Nyangatom, we see a sacrifice which is quite special (a) in relation to the identity of the sacrificer (a Father of the country who is condemned to die in a state of madness); (b) in relation to the special way of putting the sacrificial animal to death; (c) in relation to the emergence of the idea of a substitution: in this unique case, the animal victim seems to stand for its sacrificer.[12] The Nyangatom say that the man will soon die: is it not from the poisonous plants[13] which have been put into the mouth of the animal before its death? The head of the ox, which has been in contact with these medicines, and which is normally eaten collectively by the sons who sacrifice for their fathers, is, in this particular case, eaten only by the sacrificer, who is a Father, but who has been 'bought' by his generation-mates for the dangerous office. Human sacrifice is therefore barely concealed, which makes succession absolutely distinct from the filial offering.

Dyson-Hudson states that, amongst the Karimojong, the sacrificial act is confined to a particular category, namely, that of the initiates. It is not easy to envisage how such a restriction would be put into practice. The non-initiates, in Dyson-Hudson's sense, could make up, according to the state of the generational system, a significant part of the adult population. Inability to act as a sacrificer, whether the sacrifice is intended to feed the fathers, cure illness or eliminate pollution, could result in a dangerous situation for the community. The Nyangatom Elephants remembered having made *asapan*, age-set by age-set, but they did not refer to the initial ceremony which should, as amongst the Karimojong, have opened their generation to initiation as sons. They considered that the *asapan* of their generation was complete; they were acting as Fathers of the country and no one denied them this status. For their part the Ostriches recognized that their defunct age-sets had disappeared without having 'made *asapan*'. They insisted, however, that it was urgent, in their eyes, that the Fathers of the country should confer *asapan* on them; and that as soon as this had been done all the Ostriches, including those not yet born, would be promoted to the rank of Fathers. It seems clear therefore that both the Fathers and the Sons conceived of *asapan* as basically not an initiation to the status of Sons, but as a transition to that of Fathers.

The generational identity of the *asapan*-man calls for comment. According to Kotol, himself an Elephant, there is no doubt that the generation which is leaving power ought to provide the officiant. His bovine substitute is provided by the new generation. In killing this animal the officiant is clearly reversing the normal direction of the filial offering (a Father killing an ox offered by his sons), committing in the process a kind of symbolic suicide. The *asapan*-man strongly resembles a divine king who is required to stop breathing. In any case he says of himself, 'It is finished for me. I am at the end.' Through him, his whole generation makes the same confession and I interpret the individual loss of reasoning as a metaphor for the collective loss of paternity. But at the same period, the Ostriches hold a different opinion about the identity of the next *asapan*-man: he ought to be one of themselves. What should one make of their view? The Ostriches, who had not 'made *asapan*', were nevertheless sacrificing, just like Karimojong initiates. Obviously it was pragmatically that the Nyangatom ignored the status of non-initiates (except for 'children' who had not yet killed any animal to feed their fathers) and conceived of the *asapan* ceremony of their Turkana neighbours and their own *asapan* as more or less the same ritual. They had simply put into practice the (analytical) assumption that whoever has sacrificed has been initiated. However, it remained clear to them that if killing oxen for Fathers means becoming true Sons, it does not turn the latter into Fathers of the country. In other words, the implicit initiation attained by killing livestock for feeding the fathers can only promote people to the first status, that of Sons; the promotion to the higher status of Fathers requires the 'hard stuff', the *asapan* ceremony with an *asapan*-man. During the 1970s both Elephants and Ostriches expressed their desire to organize the ceremony, but nothing was done. It was not until 1989 that I learned about a blockage of the *asapan* process, and until my return in 1991 that I discovered the reasons for it.

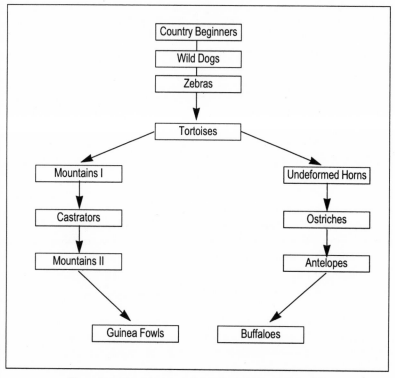

*Figure 5.1 The Toposa system (after Müller, 1991: 561)*

## Generation Systems and Their Dysfunctions

*A comparative comment on the Toposa. (Figure 5.1)*

One sequence of the Toposa generation names is practically identical to that of the Nyangatom: this underlines the close ethno-historical relationship between these two peoples and also their continuous coming together. According to Müller (1991), a quarrel occurred amongst the Toposa around 1880, which resulted in a schism amongst the sons of the Tortoises. To begin with, they were all Mountains but the quarrel led to a secession of the juniors who created a new 'league', calling themselves the 'Undeformed Horns'. Tribal unity was not broken, however, and a hundred years later, during the course of the 1980s, the descendants of the two 'leagues' were talking about reuniting. Around 1982–3 the situation was as follows. The Ostriches, more specifically their age-set called Ngikurono, were recognized as the 'set in power'.[14] At the beginning of the 1980s the Ostriches had not begun to 'give *asapan*' to their sons the Antelopes because they themselves had not yet completed the *asapan* of their own juniors. One therefore has a situation which, on the one hand, reflects the 'decompacted' Karimojong system and, on the other, the Nyangatom 'condensation' or the bringing together of making *asapan* and becoming Fathers of the country.

### The 'blockage' of the Nyangatom system

In 1989 a young Nyangatom, at that time an administrator in Jinka, wrote to tell me that the *asapan* of the Ostriches had failed because nobody agreed to play the role of *asapan*-man. I wondered if the custom had been explicitly forbidden by the (at that time communist) government, but it is clear that the Ngikumama, the section responsible for providing the officiant, had refused to do so. When I returned to the field in November 1991 the situation had not changed and I learned something which had been carefully hidden from me up to then: that a quarrel had broken out 'in the past' between the Elephants and the Ostriches, the latter demanded their *asapan*, and when their fathers refused, they hit them with sticks. Because of this unpardonable insult the refusal of the Elephants became definitive. In order to revenge themselves for this affront, the senior Ostriches cursed, not their fathers, which would be senseless and in-effective, but their own junior generation-mates: 'if you eventually accept initiation which has been refused to us, may you all die!'

What could have happened? According to the demographic model, the

Elephants should have become Fathers of the country around 1930 and 'reigned' until 1980. They confirmed that they had made *asapan*, set after set, and the chronology of the generation suggests that these initiations started at the beginning of the century, at the time of Menelik's conquest. At that time the Elephants were in fact the Sons of the country which was under the authority of the Mountains. One of the latter, Loteng, persuaded the Nyangatom that they had no choice but to submit to the Emperor and he became the first Nyangatom *balabbat*. The quarrel between Elephants and Ostriches must have occurred much later, probably during the 1930s, just before the Italian episode, at a time when the Elephants should have become Fathers of the country. The conflict would not only deprive the Ostriches of *asapan* but, equally, would fix the Elephants in the *status quo*: it would be only in a *de facto* sense that, because of the disappearance of the Mountains, they would eventually become Fathers. This position was not denied to them during the 1970s but, since they had not yet 'given *asapan*' to their sons, *de jure* they were still Sons of the country.

One understands that the system is not only an arena for political debate but functions as a political game: promoting a new generation or refusing to do so are political issues. Normally, the generation in power takes all important political decisions and is vested with religious authority. But with time the Sons gradually take decisions about pastoral and military policies. The Fathers may concede this to them, but in fact, at the end of their reign, they have no alternative but to abandon some of their authority. As regards privileges, the difference between Fathers and Sons might not be of such importance, since both generations have sons to feed them. It is possible that the Nyangatom system today is running a risk comparable to that which faced the Toposa a century ago, namely, the emergence of two concurrent leagues, each of which, as with the Turkana 'alternations', would hold its own rituals without reference to the other as a source of legitimacy. This is the implicit threat that the Ostriches have in mind when they consider making *asapan* for themselves, choosing an officiant from their own generation and, by this means, becoming Mountains, two generations above their present status. They feel that the 'blockage' of the system has kept them for too long in an *under-aged* status, that of sons of Sons who had gained only the *de facto* status of Fathers. In order to become Fathers themselves, which implies being able legitimately to initiate their own sons in the future, they must take the place of their grandfathers the Mountains who have regularly initiated their sons the Elephants. Is this how the Nyangatom system might evolve? The history of the coming decades will tell us.

The Toposa and Nyangatom systems have reflected, throughout this century, a compromise between an initiatory logic and a management of both generational time and the crises which are linked to the slowing down of the system by the generation occupying the dominant position. These systems, then, are in a *chronic state of transition* which gives them a good chance of surviving their entry, despite new disturbances, into the third millennium. Since the act of submission to the Emperor Menelik at the beginning of the century one could say that the Nyangatom Fathers have lost their sovereignty, at least vis-à-vis the outside, but internally certainly not their authority nor their power of sanction. Generational precedence continues to be respected and the filial offering continues to be the civic and religious act which confirms membership of the society.

What changes have occurred since the fall of Hailé Selassie in 1974, and what might be their impact on the generational system?

Outside influence has grown, mainly because of the presence, since 1972, of a non-governmental organization, the Swedish Philadelphia Church Mission (SPCM), which has worked in three main sectors: education, health and irrigated agriculture; and partly because of the intervention of the socialist regime, which has replaced three *balabbat* with about thirty *lokamember* or chairmen of the *kebele*.[15] At the end of the 1980s, a majority of Nyangatom *kebele* representatives were Ostriches, a generation to whom the Elephants had handed over 'the affairs of war' but who were above all preoccupied with the *asapan* ritual which would promote them to fatherhood of the country. Politically, the time of the end of the Mengistu regime (1991) was euphoric in Nyangatom: people felt liberated from a regime from which they had not suffered much but which was perceived as authoritarian; the Transitional government of 'Tigrean rebels' announced that taxes would be abolished and the people would be able to run their own affairs; within three months a purely Nyangatom militia replaced the local contingent of Mengistu's disbanded army; these twenty-five soldiers returned triumphantly with honestly acquired kalashnikovs and paraded as symbols of the liberty which had been given back to their people. These young men, some of whom had a school education, belonged mainly to the Ostriches, but some of them to the Antelopes and the Buffaloes. The Elephants, still Fathers of the country since their sons the Ostriches had not yet been promoted officially, assured me that they would keep all of these 'children' under their control. The NGO, which had been requested to feed the militia for a time, handed over the rations to the Elephants to distribute to the militia at their discretion. In this context of a new feeling of prosperity, demographic growth[16] and political autonomy, the Ostriches remembered the old curse which had prevented them from receiving *asapan* and, therefore, from being considered the true Fathers of the country.

Under the Transitional government, the *kebele* system has survived and several localities have not felt it necessary to change their representative. In general, these office-holders, who are adults with no school education,

*Photo 5.1 Nyangatom militia men
(Omo river, December 1991)*

are not politicized and their main contact is with the staff of the NGO rather than with the government. So it is unlikely that the chairmanship of the *kebele* would lead to quick changes in the society. It could be otherwise, however, with the actual emergence of a new educated elite. Formed by the SPCM and the Ethiopian Pentecostal churches, this elite is assuming new roles: as health assistants, mechanics, drivers, builders, store keepers, and a few teachers and religious leaders of the newborn local church. Despite the progressive mentality of these young people, I could find only one example of a deliberate break by a Nyangatom from his society. When he returned after a long absence a young man was beaten by his age-mates for having refused to offer them a feast. He left Nyangatom country, married an Amhara and settled in Jinka where he took on higher responsibilities. Those who, on the contrary, may need local votes, obviously do not neglect to feed their fathers and their peers as generously as possible. This is the best way to prove one's attachment to the country.

In spring 1995 several young Nyangatom were elected to the zonal, regional and national councils respectively in Jinka, Awasa and Addis Ababa. At that time, the *asapan* question did not seem to be resolved but the mechanism of the filial offering had been restarted. Important meat feasts had been offered by the Antelopes to the Ostriches and the latter intended to do the same for their fathers the Elephants. This social effervescence occurred one month after a Toposa and Nyangatom raid on a Dassanetch settlement in which they killed one person, took a boy prisoner and seized 25 cattle. An informant wrote to tell me that the Nyangatom elders at Nakua had disapproved of this raid and required the raiders to return the cattle. The letter ended with these words: 'the raided cattle have been returned'. This shows that the authority of the elders still exists and that the Nyangatom have not yet entered the era of outlaw gangs, a development which cannot, unfortunately, be ruled out and which is well described by Lamphear (in Fukui and Markakis, 1994) for the Turkana and Jie.

### Asapan-*man or … chairman?*

Let me conclude with the interesting story of E.H. As a child he, like many Nyangatom during the 1970s, experienced the death of close family members. His sister was killed by the Mursi and his father died of thirst on returning from a campaign against the Dassanetch. E.H. became the first commander of the Nyangatom militia after the fall of Mengistu. In 1993 he was elected to the South Omo Zonal Council at Jinka and soon he took higher responsibilities. Going through my genealogical data, I discovered that E.H. might have been a key figure in the generational system. He belongs in fact to the Nginyanga clan of the Ngikumama section,[17] which is supposed to provide the *asapan*-man. He himself could then be chosen as the officiant for the ceremony, but one can easily imagine that neither he nor his family and generation-mates would play this risky game.[18] Up to the present the problem remains unsolved. How do the Nyangatom live with this dilemma ? A correspondent writes:

> At the time of elections (spring 1995) my fellow Ostriches hold *apeyo*-ceremonies according to their sections: the Ngarich began, followed by the Flamingos and the Ngikumama. The question of the *asapan* of the Ostriches is not yet settled because it is the hardest method of *asapan* since it has been done by a man: everyone is afraid to be used. There is another hint of a solution: to let it be organized by Toposa, to discuss, and finally to throw *amusungipit*[19] into the sunset and to recircle the *asapan*. My suggestion for this process of *asapan* is to use a baboon instead of a man: *ejok isiwario ecom anierumor tasapanere*, 'it is good that a baboon be acquired and when this is finished the people be given *asapan*'. This is my suggestion, in order not to stop the process of *asapan*. At the present time, the generational system is just using the rank, while they haven't done the *asapan* process, so that Antelopes are considered as Elephants and the Ostriches as Mountains.

This text calls for a longer discussion than I have space for here. It shows the concern of the first Nyangatom MP in Addis Ababa to save Nyangatom custom. He said to me last year: 'not to make *asapan* is to live in ignorance'. The suggestion to replace the *asapan*-man with a baboon is based on an implicit reasoning: the baboon is an animal but at the same time it has something human in its appearance and being. The suggested substitution reinforces the sacrificial interpretation of the role of the *asapan*-man.

## The Ideological Background of the Generational System

Let me now make some comments on the remarkable absence of women in our ethnographies, an absence which can be connected with the (often male) sex of ethnographers, but which also reflects the male bias of East African societies which is shared by many other cultures. There is a well known, universal, orientation in the sexual division of labour. Nyangatom men certainly tend to monopolize political activity but they do this by means of exercising another monopoly, that of sacrificial practice. Commenting on Nancy Jay (1992), P. Erny writes:

> Everything starts from the following observation: more than any other religious institution, sacrifice has a close connection with the sexual dichotomy. Why do so many societies exclude women, during their child-bearing years, from sacrificing? Why are they only allowed to sacrifice after the menopause or as consecrated virgins? Why is the father-son relationship so often associated with sacrifice? And why is it so often associated with 'fathers' either in a real or metaphorical sense? Why, in the islands of Hawaii, is it called 'male child-birth'? (*L'Homme*, no.135, 1995: 138, my translation).

This line of questioning is equally applicable to the generational system of the Nyangatom and their neighbours. The Nyangatom perform three types of sacrifices:

(a) The filial offering which is an act of piety, an initiatory act which is repeated throughout a person's life. The statuses of Fathers and Sons are sacrificial statuses: one cannot become a Son without sacrificing to the Fathers, the Fathers themselves occupying the position of gods. The Fathers are those to whom a sacrifice is made when they receive a filial offering, but they are in turn the sacrificers for their own fathers. The chain of paternity goes back indefinitely. Akuj, 'God', is only the witness of the transmission of life. In sacrifice the body of the victim is dismembered but the convivial meal which is part of the sacrifice rebuilds the social body and reaffirms the solidarity of all its members. This is how we should interpret the rules for distributing parts of the sacrificial animal to generation- and age-set members, the constituent bodies of the society.[20]

(b) Piacular sacrifice *(ajulot*: 'skin-victim') is carried out to remove the effects of pollution from individuals and settlements, to treat sickness, to bring rain etc. In the domestic sphere, this sacrifice can be carried out by a female healer but a man is always the officiant for the community. The way of slaughtering is evisceration.[21] The first stomach (rumen) is invested with a special meaning. Its contents are the sacred substance which unites all the participants because it is obviously a mixture of all the plants and grasses eaten by the living animal.

Through these two types of sacrifice, men construct their paternity and restore life and fertility.

(c) The third type of sacrifice, that of the *asapan*-man, is infrequent but indispensable. The human victim is 'bought' by his peers in order to transmit paternity (sovereignty) from one generation to the next. This rare type of sacrifice[22] also aims at asserting the patrilineal link between successive generations.

### *Nyangatom cosmology*

The relationship between mother and child is metonymic. The child is 'flesh of her flesh'. There is natural evidence of continuity. If Malinowski did not convince us all when he said that the Melanesians were ignorant of the role of the father in procreation, it is nevertheless obvious that paternity, in traditional settings, is not subject to naturalistic proof and is, above all, a social and conceptual act, the affirmation of a discontinuity. The Fathers of the country are the living affirmation of the necessity,

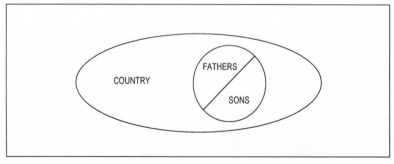

*Figure 5.2  The metaphor of patrifiliation*

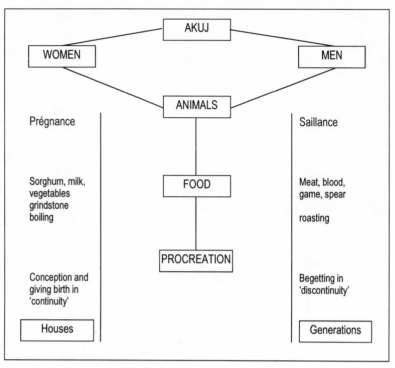

*Figure 5.3 Nyangatom cosmology*

which is underlined by the long, but limited, generational time which is given to them, of affirming paternity as discontinuity. The spatial metaphor suggests a solution. It is the 'disjunctive conjunction' of Fathers and Sons in the spatial whole, which they call the country, which creates the community as a generational system (see Figure 5.2).

But Fathers and Sons can only constitute a country through their complementary relationship to women of the same country. It is only together that they can maintain life and they do this, first of all, through the mediation of domestic animals which are destined to be sacrificed and also because they both share in a part of the principle called Akuj. This interpretation is set out in summary form in Figure 5.3.

Figure 5.3 shows the complementarity of women and men,[23] the mediation of domestic animals and the role of both sexes in producing food and descendants. We see the two fundamental social units, *houses* which consist of mothers and their progeny, and *generations* which are recruited by patrifiliation. Animals, and particularly oxen, the ideal sacrificial victims (being neither male nor female), are in the position of mediators between the human world, both masculine and feminine, and an invisible principle, Akuj, whose creative and destructive powers are shared by humans. As the Nyangatom would say, women are, or are like, Akuj because they bear children and therefore control the stream of life. On the other hand, men are, or are like, the rain, because they fertilize women. They are, or are like, Akuj in their power to take life when they sacrifice as Sons, and, this time as Fathers, in their power to bless their Sons in return for their offerings. The remarkable absence of ancestors is perhaps the most intriguing sociological characteristic of the generational system. It is a system which enables us to envisage sovereignty without the state, initiation without circumcision or masks and, finally, three modalities of sacrifice without elaborate ritual, as, for example, is found amongst polytheistic societies in Antiquity or monotheistic Judeo-Christian societies. Such are the many assets and resources which could, in my opinion, ensure a long life for this powerful mechanism for asserting links between the visible and invisible worlds, maintaining social order and potentially generating new societies.

# Notes

1 Special thanks are due to David and Pat Turton for their hospitality in Manchester while David translated an earlier version of this paper into English. Acknowledgements are due to the participants in the 'East African Age-Systems in Transition' Symposium, especially the editors of the present volume, for their remarks and constructive criticism and also to Jean Lydall for her kind reading of the final version.

2 'Species' thus has an Aristotelian meaning, both analytically and for the Nyangatom, who conceive of the generations as the various species of their society. The three main territorial sections (Storks, Ibises and Flamingos) are also named according to (migratory) bird species. Cf. Tornay, 1989: 328-407.

3 If Lewis Henry Morgan did not acknowledge the existence of the political process in tribal societies, Robert Lowie, a pioneer in political anthropology, expressed a different view. In *The Origin of the State* (1927: 2) he reminds us that the Hellenist Eduard Meyer 'pleads for the absolute universality of the state in human society' (a position opposed by all anthropologists I know), adding that 'we can hardly deny the title of governmental fabrics (*Herrschaftsgebilde*) to the illiterate peoples' (which seems a sounder anthropological opinion). On his side, Marcel Mauss writes (in 1931): 'je renonce définitivement à considérer l'État comme la seule source de cohésion dans ces sociétés' (that is, in the so-called primitive societies) and 'je crois que la notion de *souveraineté* s'est appliquée dans toute la vie sociale' (1968: 134). He thus means that there exists, in every society which claims its own identity and autonomy without reference to any rule or power from outside, a sense of its sovereignty even in the absence of a king, a state or any other form of centralized power structure. In the case discussed here, I consider that the Elephants, while recognized as Fathers of the country, collectively embody the sovereignty of Nyangatom society.

4 Even if the Sons' generation, as we shall see, can be invested with the responsibility of warfare, there is no 'warrior grade' whatsoever. Other sources of prestige and authority are: (i) the killer status. The acquisition of this status is a considerable social asset. Killers use their warrior names amongst themselves even if they are fathers and sons. Sharing warrior status helps to reduce the frustrations which arise from differences of generational status amongst contemporaries. (ii) public office. In the traditional setting,

there were only two clearly differentiated offices: *emuron*, diviner and *ekatukon*, spokesman. Since Menelik's conquest, there has existed a new office, that of *balabbat* (in Amharic 'one who has a known ancestry'), an officer responsible to the administration for his territorial section. These offices, which have no link with generational status, can confer prestige and wealth. But a diviner is in no sense a 'chief'. He is simply an adviser or healer: an interpreter who builds a bridge between visible and invisible realities. All men who speak in public are not necessarily given the title *ekatukon*, spokesman. To earn this title a man must have not only a talent for speaking but also good judgement, integrity, clear-sightedness. A spokesman is no more a chief than a diviner is. The spokesman speaks on behalf of his settlement or his section; certain spokesmen can gain tribal authority, like the great Lokuti who was called the 'mouth' of the Nyangatom (Tornay, 1989b). But intervening with the administration is the lot, not of the spokesmen, but of the *balabbat*, whom the Nyangatom call 'diviners', which means 'intermediaries' between the 'here' of Nyangatom society and the 'there' of a foreign power. The collection of taxes was one of the principal tasks of the *balabbat*. The role was outside the generational system but a *balabbat* who was accused of corruption could be cursed by the Fathers of the country.

5  Contributions to this book by Simonse and Kurimoto shed new light on age-set antagonisms. Antagonism between successive generations is addressed in the third section of this paper.

6  With one exception addressed below, the symbolic sacrifice of the *asapan*-man.

7  *Edwar angajep a ngikasukowu*: 'bitter is the tongue of the elders': this is how the Nyangatom express the dangerous power vested in the invocations and curses (*ngi-lam*) of the Fathers of the country. The Nyangatom qualitative opposition -*dwar*/-*peana* (bitter/tasteless) shares many features with similar Nilotic semantic pairs, as shown by Kurimoto (1992).

8  Of course, this was one symptom of the conflict which they revealed to me only 15 years later and on which I comment below.

9  As a noun, it means 'initiation' amongst the Karimojong or the Turkana, but 'succession' amongst the Nyangatom; for the latter, and only for them, the noun also denotes 'the person of custom' (*itwan ka etal*), the *asapan*-man, without whom transmission cannot be performed properly. The verb *a-ki-sapan* is either intransitive (*asapanete kolong Ngitome, tarau taapakec ka akop*: 'in the past, the Elephants went through or made the ceremony and thus became Fathers of the country'), or transitive (*moi esapanete Ngitome ngidekec*: 'the Elephants will soon *asapan* their sons', which means promoting them to fatherhood of the country); the latter example can also be translated as 'they will shave their sons'. A first shaving (*a-ki-bany*, not *a-ki-sapan*) is done by the mothers, a few days after giving birth, when babies are given a first name. At the *asapan* ceremony, the shaving of the sons is done by their fathers and this is universal in the Karimojong cluster. The derivative *i-sapa-t* is the common name for 'son' in all dialects of the cluster.

10  Both the intoxication and the method of slaughter are exceptional. Compare this with the Maasai special sacrifices where the victim is drugged with honeywine before being smothered. Amongst the Nyangatom, the usual way of slaughtering an ox is by spearing it. Cutting the throat is appropriate for slaughtering small stock for domestic disposal and also for killing an enemy in a hand-to-hand fight.

11  This is hardly surprising since this is the only age-ceremony which the Turkana still perform (Gulliver, 1958; Müller, 1989).

12  The idea derives from my analysis, not from Nyangatom exegesis.

13  *Euphorbia triaculeata, Caralluma russelliana, Aristida adscensionis, Aloe turkanensis*: such plants contain a poisonous milky latex or other toxic substances like alkaloïds.

14  Amongst the Toposa, power is held by successive sets of the 'generation in power'; in contrast, amongst the Nyangatom power is held collectively by the whole generation of the Fathers. So the Toposa seem to be an intermediate case between 'short-term' (e.g. *gada* system) and 'long-term' transmission of power, a case which fits well into Peatrik's paradigm (1995).

15  The *kebele* is the basic administrative entity created after the 1974 revolution by the Communist regime: a ward in a town, a locality in the countryside. Each *kebele* has an elected representative or an elected committee.

16  In the early 1970s I estimated the total Nyangatom population to be around 5,000.

**119**

According to data from the 1995 Ethiopian census, there are today at least 12,000 Nyangatom (census field workers, pers. com.).

17 The origin of this section is probably a group of (today Ugandese) Kumam emigrants which has been incorporated by the Nyangatom. In return, they have seemingly been required to provide the *asapan*-man 'for ever'.

18 Unfortunately, on my last visit in 1994, I was not able to ask Eliyas himself about his potential candidacy as an *asapan*-man.

19 According to the writer, 'the bad omen which had tied the *asapan*'.

20 This is an inversion of the Judeo-Christian schema: in the latter, the fathers sacrifice, if necessary, even their sons to God the Father in order to confirm their alliance with him, to sanctify their procreation and to guarantee an endless progeny. The son is in the position of potential victim (cf. the story of Abraham ready to sacrifice to God his son Isaac). Amongst the Eastern Nilotes, the father is a divine repository of procreative power. The son is not a potential victim but a sacrificer. He makes himself into a Son by sacrificing to the Father. Through his filial offering he pays a religious homage to the Father, who continues to exercise the power of life and death over him through his blessings and curses. The Father himself sacrifices to his father and the sacrificial debt goes back indefinitely.

21 We should note an analogy here between this operation and a caesarian. The man opens the stomach of the animal and, sometimes helped by an old woman (a wise-woman ?), presses on the stomach to force out the entrails. The entrails could be seen as symbolizing 'the child of men'.

22 The *asapan*-man is no scapegoat; if he is no king either, he is nevertheless a human being who is sacrificed to regenerate power and recreate sovereignty in his society.

23 More appropriate than the classical opposition *physis/ nomos*, the contrast between *prégnance* and *saillance* is taken from Thom, 1988.

# 6 Gada Systems on the Meta-Ethnic Level: Gabbra/Boran/Garre Interactions in the Kenyan/Ethiopian Borderland

## GÜNTHER SCHLEE

### Introduction

*Im Lande des Gada* is the title of one of the earlier works about *gada* systems (Jensen, 1936), and this title suggests that there is a '*gada*-country', a continuous geographical area marked by the presence or former presence of *gada* systems. Having learned to doubt earlier anthropological assumptions that there are as many 'cultures' as there are 'societies' and that each of these forms a 'system' of its own (assumptions which Jensen and the other representatives of *Kulturmorphologie* never shared), we may be tempted to ask whether these societies and their *gada* systems exist in isolation from each other or whether they form a meta-system, a meta-culture through which cultures interact, or, to quote another, rather better known old book, *The Political Systems of Highland Burma*, a 'single extensive structural system' (Leach, 1954:17). Our answer will be differentiated, partly 'yes', in other aspects: 'not really'. We shall find that some of those *gada* systems which are most similar run parallel in almost complete independence of each other, while some which differ greatly rely for their working on heavy inputs from each other. Paradoxical as it may look at the first glance, this is not that much of a surprise, because it combines well with a number of ideas: those about geometry (parallels never touch), and those about general sociology, that systemic interaction has to do with functional differentiation, in other words, that we interact through our differences rather than our similarities. But as these ideas have not been applied to *gada* systems so far, it may be fun to try to apply them.

What qualifies *gada* systems as *gada* systems? They are a sub-type of generation-set systems. Other such sub-types are *eigworono* and *asapan* (see Nagashima in this volume) and *monyomiji* which Kurimoto and Simonse (in

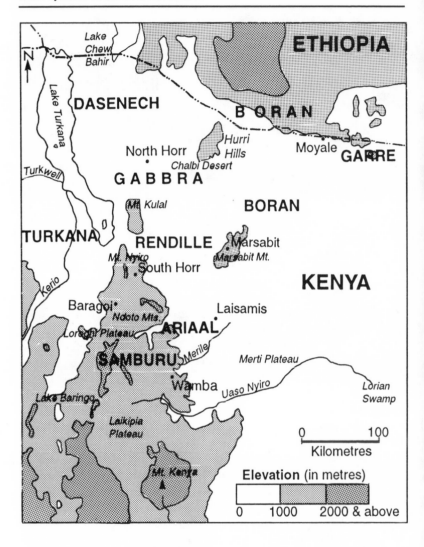

*Map 4 Northern Kenya*

this volume) examine from a similar perspective: *monyomiji* systems form a framework of interethnic exchange; in the western *monyomiji* area villages ethnically identified with at least four different groups participate in a single *monyomiji* system. Do these Nilotic peoples of the southern Sudan form a society of societies or 'a single extensive structural system' through their *monyomiji* systems? From the generation-set systems of the Nilotes the *gada* systems can be distinguished by their rigid numerical order, *starre Zahlenordnung* (Haberland, 1963:170) based on long calendrical cycles.

*Gada* systems are widespread and possibly were once universal among speakers of a certain branch of the Cushitic language family, namely, the Lowland Eastern Cushites (Ulrich Braukämper, personal communication; Schlee, 1989:82). Although providing ranks and having mechanisms of inclusion and exclusion, *gada* systems are generally described as being typical of acephalous, segmentary and basically egalitarian societies.[1] They are said to provide horizontal links which complement lineage ties by tying together age-mates belonging to different lineages which are, in terms of a feeling of relatedness, moving further and further apart with each successive generation. *Gada* systems are thus assigned an integrative force by functionalist type theories. Those Oromo groups living in a monarchical system of government, their own or alien, seem to have invariably abandoned their *gada* systems or to have greatly reduced them in their functions (Arnesen, 1996:221-9; Blackhurst, 1996:246f; Lewis, 1965).

Apart from integration as a counterforce to segmentation, one can identify other aspects of *gada* systems and other effects of their workings, not all of which combine easily with ideas about cohesion and integration. To clarify our categories, we start with a list of aspects of *gada*, relating, positively or adversely, to systemic integration at various levels. This typology of cases may look somewhat hypothetical at the beginning, but will be filled to varying degrees with empirical examples in the course of this paper.

*Gada* systems face the almost impossible task to harmonize the actual social world with a complex set of rules about how this social world should unroll, if misfortune and disaster are to be avoided. Emical descriptions of how *gada* rituals are organized often stress the heroic efforts involved in carrying them out at the appropriate time in spite of adverse circumstances like drought and interference by outside political forces. Such efforts may be viewed as community-oriented and be described under the heading of integration. As a shorthand formula to recall below, we may summarize this apect as defence of the cosmic and social order. Below the community level, i.e. considering the single parts of a society which holds joint promotion ceremonies, down to the level of individual actors, these ceremonies often appear not as a shared effort but as an arena in which people fight about ritual prerogatives. We can thus distinguish integrative and competitive aspects of the same rituals at the same level, namely, that of the single localized *gada* system, where people gather in a location (or successively a series of locations) to perform a given cycle of rituals.

The main focus of this contribution, however, is on the level above the single *gada* system. Among the forms of interaction between *gada* systems we shall find more examples both of cooperation and mutual integration, on the one hand, and of rivalry carried out in an arena provided by a shared *gada* framework, on the other. Among these forms of interaction are:

• **Synchronization**. *Direct* synchronization takes place where one society observes another and waits for it to start before it starts its own cycle of rituals. In one observed case those who take the lead themselves need some input from outside, an 'ignition key' so to speak, in the shape of a heifer given to them from a certain outside source. Only this transfer can set their *gada* rituals in motion, and if this transfer is reported to those who follow suit, they know that they, too, should get prepared.

*Indirect* synchronization takes place if the *gada* systems in their unrolling do not follow each other but have a shared reference point like a calendar. So the structurally widely different *gada* systems of the five Gabbra Malbe phratries (listed in Figure 6.1) are brought to the same rhythm because of a shared calendar.

• **Transfer.** Giving a heifer is, of course, more than a mere signal to start. It is a material input. There are many examples of objects or services which need to be provided by outsiders, including those speaking other languages and adhering to other religions.

• **Integration.** When the borders of a *gada* system which relies on outside inputs are no longer clearly defined because of the number or importance of such inputs from a given source, one might prefer to speak of one integrated *gada* system rather than two interacting ones. Integration can be on equal terms or it can take hierarchical forms.

• **Recognition**. *Gada* rituals are recognized as such by neighbours with quite different *gada* systems and even by those without such systems. They may inspire awe, fear or rejection. They may be regarded as sacred or as a pagan abomination, i.e. they are part of meta-ethnic communication and interethnic politics. Their military functions as well as their religious dimensions contribute to these effects on other ethnic groups.

## Another *Gada* Puzzle: The Discovery of a Problem

*Gada* systems, like Australian kinship, attract that minority of anthropologists who love complex calculations and formal systems. The majority of social scientists, the more social and less scientific ones, prefer looser types of discourse to 'kinship algebra' (Malinowski) as well as to *gada* mathematics. Like most people they are more attracted by subjects which give room to 'opinions', 'standpoints' and 'feelings' than by the mechanics of strictly determined systems.

The rigid generation spans demanded by (the ideal versions of) many *gada* systems, which are so hard to combine with the biographies of real people, have often caused *gada* systems to lead to under-aging: people are not yet born at the time when they should marry or they can never participate in any age-set promotion because their age-sets, and maybe even the age-sets into which their sons should fit, are already retired by the time they are born. Such discrepancies build up over the generations, and with a certain amount of data on the frequency and amount of such differences per generation, one can calculate such processes backwards and extrapolate how many centuries ago real and ideal life cycles must have coincided and *gada* have been an efficient instrument for recruiting people of the right age into military, productive, reproductive and ritual functions. On the computer screen the derailed *gada* train in such diachronic models moves backwards onto the rails. That is what Asmarom Legesse (1973) has done at a time when computers were much clumsier than they are today.[2]

The rather complex demographic calculations used for such models are one aspect of this 'ethnographic puzzle' (Legesse, 1973; Van der Loo, 1991:27). The major cycles resulting from minor ones by multiplication are another: if you have five sets per ritual generation, so that the sons of set 1 are initiated into set 6, and seven names which are used to name these sets in a cyclical succession, so that set 8 is given the same name as set 1, it is easy to calculate (5x7=35) that set 36 has the same combination of features (descent, relative position in a defined generation, first, second ... or fifth of their generation and name) as set 1. Calculating eight years between the inauguration of successive sets, you find that the system has come full circle after 280 years. Prognostic calendars based on the assumption that events repeat themselves after such cycles (major *and* minor ones, the latter also independently of the former) may cause diviners and their anthropologists to rack their brains.

The riddle I am trying to solve here (or at least to pose in a clarifying way) is of a different kind, however. Rather than getting into the internal workings of *gada* systems, I want to show, and to try to explain, some contradictory or problematic ways in which *gada* systems interact with each other. I take as a starting point my field experience in northern Kenya and southern Ethiopia. Contradictions are often mollified by the time which elapses between one experience and another which conflicts with it. If your interlocutor makes a statement which is at sharp variance with what he had said directly before, the contradiction is immediately evident. If, however, his statement is difficult to combine with something somebody else told you a decade earlier, the contradiction may dawn more slowly on you. To clarify the type of contradiction I am interested in, I therefore start with a radically abbreviated chronology of my field research. I restrict it to some mutually contradictory elements of experience and whatever context is indispensable for their description, and cut out everything in between.

All my examples are taken from southern Oromo-speaking groups. A recurrent theme is the interaction of 'original' Oromo with groups of Somali-like origin who have become associated with them in one form of the other since the Oromo expansion of the sixteenth century. To reduce the inevitable confusion caused by the many names of ethnic and clan groups I shall start with a rough diagram which 'maps' them all and shows their interrelationships. I restrict this diagram rigorously to those groups mentioned in the text, which gives a very unbalanced and incomplete

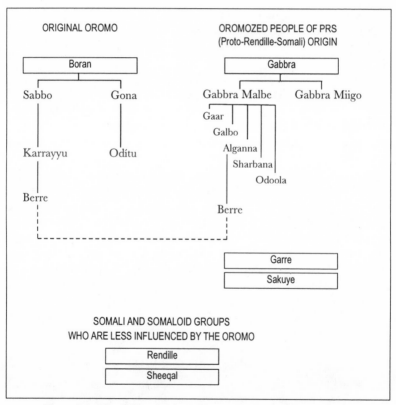

*Figure 6.1 The different origins of the groups discussed in this chapter*

representation of segmentary models but helps in finding a given name quickly (Fig. 6.1). Fuller clan lists can be found elsewhere (Schlee, 1989).

### September 1979

Boru Galgallo, an elder of the Odoola phratry of the Gabbra Malbe, who is famous for his knowledge about the past, gives me a long, quite open interview and allows me to tape it. My main interest was in clans and how the same clans have come to be represented in different ethnic/linguistic groups of the area, and I have published substantial parts of my transcriptions of this interview (and interviews with others which complement or confirm it) in that context (Schlee, 1989:123–37). I was, however, glad to get as much of a historical context of these clan histories as I could, and did not stop his explanation of the origin of the *gada* system(s) of the Gabbra.

My interest, clan histories, leads more or less directly to his *gada* origins. The Gabbra, he explains, stem from the Somali, and all Rendille are originally Gabbra, or, more specifically, Alganna (and are treated as such if they join the Gabbra as refugees from war or famine, unless clan relationships to other phratries are known). In other words: there was a time when the present-day ethnic divisions did not exist, and the fact that one frequently finds the same clans in more than one modern ethnic group is explained by the assumption that the ethnic divisions, when they occurred in a later period, separated people of shared clan affiliation. If interethnic clan identities are explained by ethnic divisions cutting through clans, then the next question, of course, is: what caused the ethnic divisions? And here *gada* systems come in: those of strangers from outside and the own ones which were established as a response to threats emanating from those of the strangers.

People stampeded and scattered like antelopes, Boru Galgallo explains, because they were attacked by the Boran. His account of this period of terror and numerous other accounts from the perspective of other clans in other ethnic groups can be combined into an historical description of how the present-day ethnic divisions have come about through warlike events which caused originally co-resident people to separate, some submitting to the Boran, others withdrawing from them either immediately or after the experience of injustice and oppression. A recurrent element also is the Exodus motif of a body of water separating and closing again, but, unlike the Israelites, the ancestors of the Cushitic-speaking pastoralists of northern Kenya and adjacent areas were not saved from their pursuers by the waters closing in again but were separated from their fellow refugees because the waters cut the trek into two parts. Cultural evidence suggests that the core of these traditions – the common origins claimed for certain clans which are found in different modern ethnic groups and the more recent character of ethnic identities in comparison with clan identities – corresponds to historical reality, whatever beautification and elaboration these accounts may have undergone.

To summarize arguments elaborated elsewhere (Schlee, 1989) we can say that the combination of oral sources with written ones (which refer, however, to other areas and only allow indirect conclusions) and with evidence from anthropological writings about the Oromo, makes it appear plausible that the period of turmoil refers to the Oromo expansion of the sixteenth century. In Kenya, the Oromo threat is mainly identified with the Boran, a major southern Oromo sub-group.[3]

Boru Galgallo goes on to describe how the ancestral Gabbra were cut off by the water from relatives to the west of Lake Turkana and how they became separated from the ancestors of the Rendille. All the moves leading to these splits had had the aim of withdrawing from the Boran, but in the end the Gabbra were nevertheless obliged to submit to the Boran and were allotted clan by clan to different Boran clans, so that now, in addition to the original clan affiliations shared with the Rendille and Garre, they are affiliated by a set of adoptive relationships, called *tiriso*, to Boran clans.

A glance at the literature about the Boran shows that the fears of the 'people of the mats', as the Boran call them, were quite justified. The *gada* system of the Boran provided the rule that each new set initiated into the *raaba* grade had to go on a ritual war expedition to procure livestock and the cut-off genitals of male strangers as trophies. As these initiations took place every eight years, the neighbours of the Boran were subjected to a regime of periodic terror. The 'people of the mats' qualified as strangers and potential victims of these expeditions because they were set apart from the Boran by a number of features, namely the PRS (Proto-Rendille-Somali) complex. This complex comprised Somaloid speech, i.e. they spoke archaic forms of Somali/Rendille rather than Oromo like the Boran, a calendar which was no less elaborate than that of the Boran but was based on quite different principles, and a complex set of rules about what to do with camels during which unit of time according to this calendar: a set of features which was sharply distinct from the 'cattle complex' of the Boran, to borrow Herskovitz' famous phrase. In emic terms 'blood' metaphors are used to point to these differences (Schlee, 1994b:134).

By submitting to the Boran and entering into adoptive clan brotherhoods with them, the ancestral Gabbra avoided being victimized by the Boran in this way. Only when the Boran at the height of their power ran out of enemies within reach, did they occasionally turn against the Gabbra to fulfill their ritual duties. The Gabbra paid tribute to the *qallu*, the ritual head of their respective adoptive Boran moiety, and underwent a change of language. Today they have ended up speaking Oromo and barely understanding the few ritual formulae remaining from their original Somali-like language. They also developed no less than three quite different *gada* systems at this period, after contact with the Boran and before finally submitting to them. At least the origin of their present *gada* systems is ascribed to this period by their oral historians, among them Boru Galgallo. But paradoxically this innovation is not described as inspired by the Boran but by the need of the Gabbra to strengthen themselves against the Boran. The creation of the *gada* order of the Gabbra is attributed to the Somali, people among whom age-sets or generation-sets have played no role for a very long time. But this does not appear to be a contradiction, because the Somali created the *gada* order for the Gabbra and not for themselves:

> So they went to a place called Au Maro by the Somali and Ababur by Odoola from where they had come before. All people of Odoola originate from Au Maro. East, east, east. In the Somali country [meaning the Somali Republic]. Near the sea. At that time the Somali installed sheikhs (*qallu*) there.
> [They were told by the big '*qallu*' of the Somali:] 'At present you are not able to deal with the book. I will set up for you something you can perform.' (Boru Galgallo. Original and fuller version in Schlee, 1989:134ff.)

What follows is an account of what the Gabbra did as a result of these instructions. They visited the different ritual sites ascribed to the different phratries and performed the *gada* promotion ceremonies.[4] These *gada* rituals are thus described as the next best thing to Islam. As the Gabbra could not read the Qur'an, they were given *gada* instead. They no longer had to run away from the Boran. They could wait for them to arrive and could trust that they would come to some arrangement with them. The Somali sheikh had told them:

> Now you do not need to be afraid of anything. I have strengthened your belly, you are not afraid of anything, stay!

Instead of describing the different routes allocated to the single Gabbra phratries in Boru Galgallo's words, we shall just map them here (Figure 6.2). The fact that, with the exception of Sharbana, the Gabbra phratries each have their own route (or alternating routes) distinguishes them not only from the Boran but also from each other.

### March/April 1985

According to the Gabbra calendar and the intentions they have told me about for years, the age-set promotion rituals, which were last performed in 1972, are to be performed next year again. Since the locations are in

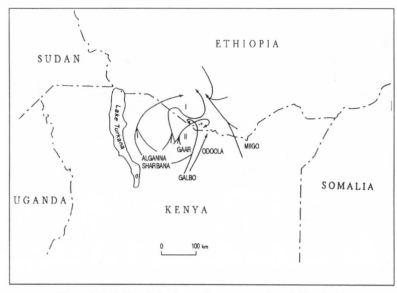

*Figure 6.2  Gabbra holy sites and movements, from Schlee, 1992.*

Ethiopia and and the authorities of socialist Ethiopia can be expected to require some persuasion before they grant a research permit to a Western anthropologist, and in order to apply for funds and leave, I want to make sure whether and when the rituals will take place.

Gaar, the most senior of the five Gabbra phratries, has to start the process. No other phratry is allowed to embark on its *jila* (ceremonial) journey before Gaar. But Gaar, I hear from different sides, cannot start before it has received a heifer as a gift from the Boran.

In other words: the cycle of *gada* rituals of the Gabbra, which had been described to me as their form of ritual defence against the Boran, has to be initiated by these very Boran.


*August/September 1985*


In the month *yaka*⁵ a Boran delegation comes to the *yaa* Gaar, the mobile ceremonial capital of the Gaar phratry of the Gabbra, which has gone on its ceremonial journey to Ethiopian territory. Its present location is Sayyole. The delegation comes from Odítu, the *qallu* clan of the Gona moiety of the Boran. The Boran bring those things which the mobile capital of the Gaar has required from them: *qumbi* (myrrh), *ruufa*, textile sheets with a black pattern which are worn by the *qallu* (ritual leaders) and the *hayyu* (generation-set leaders) of the Gabbra as turbans, and *hiitu*, the thick, stiff textile material which is woven in Ethiopia and from which the obligatory cylindrical headdress of the *dabela*, the members of the senior-most grade, the ritual elders, is made. A new set is going to be promoted to this status in the course of this ceremonial journey.[6]

*March/April 1986*

The mobile capital of the Galbo phratry, which has been gradually moving north for a couple of years to approach the ceremonial grounds, is now at Turbi from where it is going to start on the sacred part of the journey from one prescribed stage to the next (Fig. 6.3). Since I last saw it in April 1985, it has increased over four times, from ten to forty-five households. (With the hamlets that cluster around it, the final size will be 113 accompanied by thousands of camels and small stock.)

Dates are discussed in terms of lunar months. Towards the end of the moonless period the mobile capital should move to Maer, the mountain next to the even holier Farole, and with the new moon, expected on the evening of 9 April, according to my calendar, and actually observed one night later, the cycle of promotion rituals should start.

Constant discussions are held about people with essential functions for one or other ritual. On the day the final part of the journey should begin, the following people are still missing: the sacrificer of a young female sheep on Mt Farole, the owner of a ram to be sacrificed at Dakha Koi, a promontory of Mt Farole, and the owner of a billy goat to be sacrificed at another locality, Allo Korma. The owner of the strain of camels whose milk is essential for promotion to the ritual elder status is only required for the second part of the ceremonies, which is planned for the lunar month starting on 6 September.

But the first three are essential now. As they are not present, the entire cycle of rituals has to be postponed to September, and it is said that it is not feasible to fulfill all the ritual requirements in the short span of only one lunar month. The blame for this is shifted back and forth. Long-standing quarrels between a senior *qallu*, an age-set speaker and the family of the future custodian of the holy horn come to the surface. Some claim that instead of waiting for people who are prevented by the drought from crossing the long stretches of dry land or who are suspected of boycotting the events, one should replace them with others from the same lineages. But no collective decisions are taken to that extent and so nobody is exposed to the moral dilemma of having to assume the ritual function of an absent lineage brother.

Allusions are made to factions in past county council elections, and the

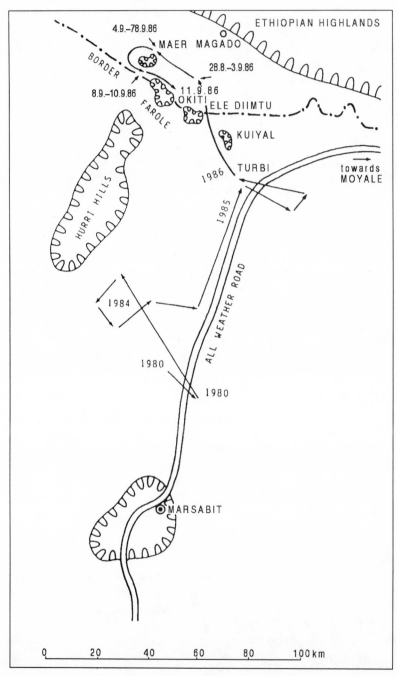

*Figure 6.3  Galbo ritual migrations*

*gada* rituals and their preparations, rather than being a celebration of community, are transformed into an arena in which rivalries are carried out. When, in September, the rituals are brought at last to completion, the participants wish me to tape-record their elaborate abuse of all those who have not managed to participate. A competitive element remains till the final moment.

For my Ethiopian field assistant, Getachew Kassa, and myself, this postponement has the consequence of a 100-km walk because we found ourselves on the wrong side of the Kenyan/Ethiopian border. After reviewing the original plans with the Gabbra, I hastened to Nairobi and took the aeroplane to Addis Ababa, where Getachew awaited me, to travel back to the border as far as the bus went. Neither of us dared to cross the border from the Kenyan side with the Gabbra, because it is oficially closed to all but the local people. From Mega we walked to Magado where we learned that the ceremonies had been postponed and that the Galbo, with all our possessions which they had promised to bring with them, were still in the location where we had left them at Turbi. In order not to be stranded without research tools and research objects, we had to walk across the plain to rejoin them there – a vivid illustration of the consequences of dissent and poor communication.

### September 1986

A year after the Gaar, the Galbo have also moved to north of the Ethiopian border. At a location called Mata Lama, 'Two Heads', because of a two-peaked little hill, they fetch water from natural rock cisterns half way up Mt Farole, their holy mountain.[7] The water is not sufficient for their camel herds which have to go the 30 km to the crater lake of Magado anyhow, but these rock cisterns are very convenient for fetching water for human consumption, because they are so nearby. The problem is quantity: 113 households have joined the mobile capital, which in profane times may only comprise about 10, and water is going to be needed not only now, but also in ten days time, when the Galbo, after visiting other obligatory sites of their ceremonial journey, will perform their promotion ceremonies here in the vicinity. They have therefore told the Boran who use the same cisterns to leave. For some of them this would mean leaving their maize fields. The Boran, who do not know about the taboos attached to the holy grounds, are anyhow regarded by the Gabbra as a polluting influence and they are told just that.

To mollify the senior *qallu* of the Galbo, the Boran invite him to take some self-distilled liquor. But the alcohol has the opposite effect on the dignitary: it adds eloquence to his threats and curses. The threats of the

Galbo include the threat that when they return to the area and move through their ritual gate (a passage which marks the transition of power from one age-set to another) they will only have to say *cirrrrr* (meant to be a scratching or sweeping noise) and the area will be swept clean of everything which does not belong there. Then all the Boran settlers on the base cone of Mt Farole will die. The Boran do not wait for them. On our return we find abandoned huts and fields, but no Boran. Later I hear that, on seeking for rock cisterns higher up, one Boran has fallen to his death. All these events are described to me with an element of pride and Gabbra self-assertion. That the Gabbra actually succeed in impressing the Boran, is quite remarkable in view of the role ascribed to them in the older literature as 'vassals' of the Boran.

The Gabbra thus assert their separate identities from the Boran by a cycle of *gada* rituals, which, however, cannot be started without the cooperation of the Boran. Instead of being rewarded for their contributions to the rituals, the Boran have to suffer the negative consequences of the process they themselves set in motion.

Conventional wisdom has it that the Oromo are the cultural source of *gada* systems in East Africa. *Gada* systems are believed to have spread through their assimilatory power. Indeed, it has happened numberless times, not only in Africa, that a weaker group has imitated the social or military organization of a stronger one. We even imitate the fashions of our enemies.[8] According to this pattern, it would have been expected that the Gabbra would have imitated the *gada* system of the Boran, especially its military aspects, in order to be better able to stand up to them. In the hypothetical case that they then failed to defend themselves against the Boran, they would have disappeared as distinct units, their remnants being incorporated into the ranks of the Boran: an identity change made easier by the circumstance that the first step of assimilation had already been made while the Boran were still their enemies. But that is not what they did. As we shall shortly see, they did not create one *gada* system but three different ones, different not only from each other, but most markedly from that of the Boran. They did not emulate their enemies. Their point seems to have been not to be alike, but to be equal but different.

## Formal Description and Comparative Analysis

This list of riddles and contradictions could easily be expanded. I refrain from doing so, because I think my point has been made. I wanted to show that there is a problem at the meta-system level, at the level of the interaction of different *gada* systems, and that this problem is interesting enough to deserve analysis.

Some questions immediately come to mind. If the *gada* systems inter-acting here are, indeed, different systems which structure time in different ways, then which of them provides the schedule? Do the Boran use their own calendar to determine the appropriate time for providing their inputs to the Gabbra system, thus imposing a Boran rhythm on Gabbra activities, or do they adjust their timing to the Gabbra calendar, following the requests of the Gabbra? The Gabbra systems are synchronized but structurally different. How do the shared intervals of promotions combine with the different structural characteristics of the units being promoted in each case? Is all interaction horizontal or can *gada* systems be arranged in a hierarchy?

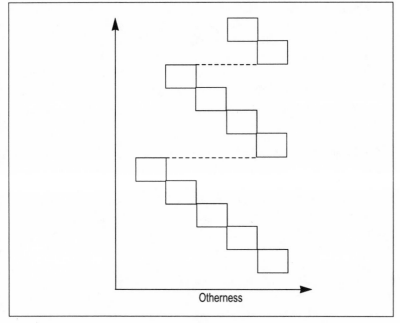

*Figure 6.4 The Boran* gada *system*

To answer these questions it is indispensable to look at some of the formal characteristics of the *gada* systems under study. Fuller descriptions can be found elsewhere. Here I simply summarize the literature to the extent necessary to understand those elements which are relevant for questions of the above type.

Baxter (1978) comprises a lucid description of the basic workings of the Boran system, which I recommend for its brevity. For our present pur-poses, I abbreviate it yet again. The timing of the Boran system is based on eight-year intervals between generation-set promotions. When a set X

**135**

leaves a given grade, successively, in eight-year steps, four other sets are initiated into that grade before the sons of X reach it. Sons can therefore not be promoted into a given grade before 40 years have passed since their fathers were promoted to that grade. If we arrange successive sets in a diagram in such a way that sets of fathers and sons are in a vertical line along the time axis, and 'otherness', i.e. the absence of such a descent relationship between sets, is marked by a step to the side, the Boran system looks as shown in Figure 6.4.

The sets which succeed each other in generational intervals, i.e. those arranged in our diagram vertically above each other, form a *goges*, a set-line, a line of sets which comprises the different generations of various patrilines. One is tempted to number them : 1–5 in generation I, 1–5 in generation II, etc. But for the Boran the starting point of these generations is shifting: one can adopt the perspective of any one set and count upwards or downwards from them. The Boran system is based on generation spans, but not on concrete generations which are made bounded entities. The Boran do not 'open' new generations and gradually fill them up as new sets are initiated, and they do not 'close' generations ritually when a given number of sets has been reached. (The Rendille, who also have a generation-set system of the *gada* type, do just that.[9])

When sons are born not to fathers who are in their forties but after a much longer generation interval, say in their sixties or eighties – a frequent case in a society where old polygynists marry young wives and even the dead have more children because the children of their widows are counted as theirs – they are too young to participate in the promotion rituals of the sets to which they belong. They can then perform these rituals with any convenient successive set, but, as non-members, they cannot acquire any *gada* office there.

A parallel system, which discards any generational considerations, has evolved among the Boran to organize the male population according to their actual age: the *hariya* or age-set system. The boys born in one eight-year interval of the *gada*-system are recruited into the same *hariya*. Successive age-sets are given two alternating names: Waakor are succeeded by Damballa, Damballa by Waakor. (It is these names, not the seven cyclical names of the *gada* sets, which we shall find again among the Gabbra.)

All Gabbra Malbe systems, like that of the Rendille, are based on multiples of seven, not eight years.[10] Any coincidences in promotion years can therefore only recur after 56 years and will, in reality, be much rarer, because the Gabbra do not hold promotions once in a seven-year cycle but once in two or three, and in adverse circumstances in even more such cycles. Intervals of 14, 21, 28, and 35 years have been recorded. I have not heard about promotion years of the Boran coinciding with those of the

Gabbra and am fairly certain that there are no rules of interaction based on such occurrences. In other words, as far as timing is concerned, the Gabbra and Boran systems are not geared to each other but are independent. If the Boran have to make inputs into the Gabbra system, they have to act on Gabbra requests at a time determined by the Gabbra, and vice versa. Their own system does not provide any clue to what the others are going to do and when.

No two Gabbra systems are alike, they all differ structurally from each other. But we can distinguish two basic types: one (Gaar, Galbo and Odoola) in which there is one set separating sons from their fathers, so that we get two set-lines, and another (Alganna, Sharbana[11]) where there are two sets separating fathers and sons with three resulting set-lines (Fig. 6.5).

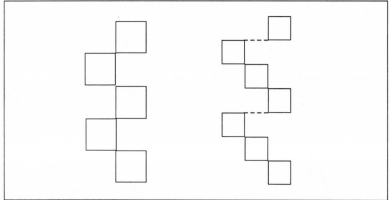

*Figure 6.5  Gaar, Galbo, Odoola (left)), Alganna, Sharbana (right)*

The consequences of this should not be underestimated. The most important promotions are the constitution of a new set of young men, *luuba*, whose office bearers, *hayyu* and *jallab*, are inaugurated on this occasion, and the promotion to the final stage before retirement, the ritually senior *dabela* status. In order not to introduce too much Oromo vocabulary into this account, we shall henceforth refer to the *luuba* as 'political elders' and the *dabela* as 'ritual elders'.[12] For *hayyu* ('king' in some archival sources), I propose 'generation-set speaker'. Among the Gaar, Galbo and Odoola a senior set is promoted to ritual elder status at the same time as their own sons are constituted as political elders. As the ritual functions in the mobile capital are divided between ritual elders and political elders, after these promotions the new mobile capital passes entirely to these ritual elders and their sons and the other set-line has no functions there. After the next promotion the capital then reverts to the other set-line.

**137**

In the Alganna/Sharbana system, on the other hand, the future ritual elders are not promoted together with their own sons, but with the men immediately junior to them of another set-line among whom the chosen leaders are then proclaimed as generation-set speakers and minor leaders (*jallab*). They share the mobile capital with another set-line. Their own sons receive office only two cycles later, when the successors of their successors are made ritual elders (Table 6.1).

*Table 6.1  Set-lines & office bearers among the Alganna & Sharbana*

| No. of cycle | Ritual elders | | Generation-set speakers | |
|:---:|---|:---:|---|:---:|
| 1 | set | 1 | set | 2 |
| 2 | | 2 | | 3 |
| 3 | | 3 | sons of | 1 |
| 4 | sons of | 1 | sons of | 2 |
| 5 | sons of | 2 | sons of | 3 |

This is simply to illustrate the level of difference, not to exhaust the topic. A further source of difference lies in the number of cyclically recurrent names which are given to the sets. These have been discussed in more detail elsewhere (Schlee, 1989:82–7). Just one example will suffice here. The Gaar have two alternating set names, the ones we know from the *hariya* system of the Boran, namely Waakhor and Dambal. As every other set belongs to the same set-line, these names also come to stand for the set-lines. Among the Galbo, whose system belongs to the same basic type (Figure 6.5), we find these two names as well, but in addition four other names. Their sequence goes: Waakhor, Gurjab, Afat, Mangub, Dambal, Waagur. The sons of Waakhor are Afat, their grand-sons Dambal, and only the great-grandsons of Waakhor are Waakhor again. A comparison of the Gaar and Galbo systems thus reveals that the same basic structure is overlaid by cycles of quite different length.

The Gabbra generation-set systems are unified only in so far as their rhythm is concerned. Their melodies are quite different. In the same year as Alganna hold their promotion ceremonies, Galbo and others also do so, but who is promoted to which status and who shares the mobile capital with whom differs widely from system to system.

## Difference and Interaction

At first glance a gear box seems to be an obvious analogy for *gada* systems which interact with each other. Gears, the cog-wheels in a gear box, like the mental representations of *gada* 'cycles', are round, and their movements are synchronized. But apart from this, comparison with a gear box yields more differences than similarities.

Gears set each other in motion when their cogs interlock. It is easy to imagine that *gada* systems interact through material inputs in this way, and there may be cases where precisely this happens. But in the Gabbra Malbe systems discussed here it is difficult to identify the 'cogs' by which one system extends into another. They are synchronized by mere observation: they observe and name (rather than count) astronomical periods – days, months and years – and determine the appropriate time for new *gada* promotions through their shared calendar, and they observe each other, or rather the junior phratries observe Gaar and start after Gaar has taken the lead.[13]

We have mentioned one material input from outside which is necessary to set a cycle of rituals in motion: the transfer of a heifer from the Boran to the Gaar. But this event is not fixed to a Boran cycle of any sort; its timing is exclusively determined by the Gaar. We may therefore – in another car analogy – compare it to an ignition key. It is like the Gaar asking the Boran to help them to start their engine.[14]

Apart from that initial impulse, the Boran, as we have seen above (August/September 1985), provide a number of ritual paraphernalia to the promotion ceremonies of the Gaar, including the textile sheets required for the *duubo*, the headdress and most visible sign of the new ritual elders. In the case of another phratry, the Galbo, this textile material is delivered by a Sheeqal Somali and has been acquired from that source for generations for the price of a young male camel – also an indispensable outside link, but a quite different one (Schlee, in prep.: chapter 4). The Sheqaal are one of those Somali clans to whom popular Islam attributes an especially efficient blessing and curse.[15] This may contribute to the ritual significance of paraphernalia from this particular source. The Sheqaal, like the other modern Somali, do not have a *gada* system of their own, however. The foreign ritual politics of *gada* and the exchanges stimulated by *gada* thus go beyond the cluster of societies who are the bearers of *gada* systems.

The Boran clearly were the dominant force in what came to be northern Kenya and southern Ethiopia for centuries, until colonial penetration. Their hegemonial role was symbolically marked by gifts which other peoples, typically the inheritors of PRS culture traits, had to take to them. What the 'vassals' received in return at the *muuda* (anointment) ceremony was the blessing of the *qallu*. The belief was widespread that without this blessing neither people nor livestock would thrive and that the value of this blessing was far in excess of the often rather modest gifts brought to the *qallu* by the Sakuye, Gabbra and other non-Boran. One may speculate that the motivation of the creation of these links by the Boran was to make themselves as ritually dependent on others as the others became on them. The rule that the Boran *qallu* may not drink water that has been transported on the back of a donkey but only water brought by camels, although no camels are bred in the highlands from which the Boran originate and where their *qallu* have to spend their lives, looks as if it were intentionally designed to make the Boran dependent on their dependants, i.e. to establish reciprocity, and at least has that effect. Here we can touch only marginally on the *muuda* institution since it primarily involves the *qallu*, not the *gada*. (For more on *muuda* see Bartels, 1983:64–6; Schlee, 1989:143, 167, 242, 1994a; Schlee and Shongolo, 1995:14f.)

But there are also *gada* rituals, i.e. rituals under the responsibility of the *Abba Gada* where the collective actors are *gada* sets or the individuals representing them, for which the Boran require the cooperation of outsiders: the *Baqala Faaji*, a banner, has to be acquired in ceremonial fashion from a certain Garre lineage. Neglect of the appropriate rituals concerning *Baqala Faaji* is said to lead to disaster (Schlee and Shongolo, 1995:15).

The Garre, like the Sheeqal, have no *gada* system of their own. Some of them speak the Boran dialect of Oromo, others different forms of the Somali language. They are one of the many clusters of people which do not fit into the 'ethnic' units on which the new regional order of Ethiopia is meant to be based. Some of them are Oromo speakers with Somali genealogies, so in a way they are Oromo *and* Somali. Modern ethnonationalism, however, is exclusive and does not favour double affiliations. This is one of the causes of the current inter-group violence in southern Ethiopia. There are, however, no clans which trace their history to the Boran or other Oromo among the Garre. Individual Boran immigrants have been incorporated into Garre clans and have not maintained separate clan identities. One can therefore say that here an originally non-Oromo group with no *gada* culture of its own performs an essential function for the Boran *gada* system (Schlee and Shongolo, 1995).

Systems form part of the environment of other systems, but the distinction between system and environment presupposes a partial independence of the system from the environment, a marked internal interdependence which stands out against relatively weak external links. When the boundaries of a *gada* system, or any other system for that matter, are no longer clearly defined because of the number or importance of outside links, one may speak of it as being integrated at a higher level with the social order of some neighbouring group rather than as being a system in itself.

The Alganna provide us with a case of a *gada* system whose independence is debatable. It is synchronized with the other Gabbra Malbe systems in the same way that these are synchronized with each other: they wait for Gaar to start in an appropriate month of a Thursday year and then perform their own rituals in appropriate months of the following Friday year, just like the Odoola, Galbo and the smallest phratry, Sharbana, who join the ceremonial journey of the Alganna. But the Alganna system does not have the same degree of independence from the Boran as the other systems have. While the Gaar only need a heifer from the Boran, the Alganna need much more: they need a Boran *qallu*. To appreciate the implications of this, we have to discuss briefly the relationship of *gada* and non-*gada* institutions.

Living *gada* systems, like these under discussion here, are interlinked with other institutions.[16] But that does not mean that all other institutions depend on the *gada* system. On the contrary, there are other institutions which exist without any need of *gada* but on which *gada* institutions depend. The *Gumi Gaayo* of the Boran,[17] the 'assembly of the multitudes', is an institution which has the power to change the rules of *gada* without being in any way dependent on or second to *gada*, because ordinary people have the same right to speak up there as *gada* officials. The strongest dependence of *gada* institutions on an outside force, however, is their dependence on the *qallu*.

The *qallu*, like all other Boran or Gabbra males, also have a *gada* set affiliation. So one can speak, at least among the Gabbra, of a *qallu* of such and such a set.[18] But a *qallu* can perform rituals for members of his own set or other sets. A mature and respected man may act as *qallu* in the mobile capital, but for promoting those elders who are not able to join the capital to ritual elder status, a very young man from a *qallu* lineage can be sent to the dispersed nomadic hamlets. Nothing of the specific ritual power of the *qallu* derives from his status in the *gada* system; all of it is inherited as a characteristic of his patrilineages. In contrast, the generation-set speakers (*hayyu*) qualify for their office by criteria which include affiliation to a non-*qallu* lineage and membership in the *gada* set whose turn it is to have officials installed in their midst. Generation-set speaker is a *gada* office. But the speakers do not derive their power to bless and curse from *gada*, but from the *qallu* who inaugurates them. *Gada* in itself is no source of such power. It all comes from God through the *qallu*. The *qallu* is an institution outside and above *gada* while *gada* depends heavily on the *qallu*. With a breakdown of the *qallu* institution *gada* would lose its divine legitimation. On the other hand, there is no reason to assume that a breakdown of the *gada* system would affect the *qallu* in any significant way.

*Hayyu nama tolc, qallu Waaqa tolc* – 'generation-set speakers are made by man, *qallu* by God'. The *qallu* derives his power to bless and curse from God and no *hayyu* elected by a *gada* council can effectively acquire any power unless it is passed on to him by the *qallu*. *Abartu qurt, eebiftu galc* is the formula used for the purpose: 'Cut down what you curse and lead home what you pray for!'

The generation-set speakers, one per set and moiety, of all other Gabbra phratries are inaugurated in this way by their own *qallu*, but not those of the Alganna. The Alganna turn to the *qallu* of the Boran moiety Sabbo, the *qallu Karrayyu*, for this purpose. This has to do with another way in which Alganna differ from all other Gabbra phratries. The latter all derive the bulk of the lineages which constitute them, and above all their nucleus of formation, the senior lineages who have gathered around themselves individuals and clan fragments from elsewhere, from bearers of the PRS complex, i.e. from Somali- or Rendille-like people. Only the Alganna derives their most senior lineage, Berre, from the Boran, and more precisely from the *qallu* lineage of the Karrayyu clan. More details of this relationship – the account of its origin and its ritual consequences like the use of cattle rather than camels[19] in Alganna rituals – have been described elsewhere (Schlee, 1989).

As nobody can become a generation-set speaker among the Alganna without the active participation of Boran dignitaries, one can legitimately ask whether the Alganna authorities are not an emanation of the ritual power of the Boran. The independence of the Alganna system from the Boran is limited to its timing: here it follows the lead of other Gabbra and is permanently out of step with the Boran system which is based on different intervals.

While the *gada* ideology of other Gabbra exemplified above by Boru Galgallo asserts independence from and equality with the Boran, the Alganna clearly place themselves at the lower end of a hierarchy: their *gada* system depends on a Boran institution, the *qallu* of the Karrayyu, who has a similar function in another *gada* system, that of the Boran themselves. This might be interpreted as equality of the two *gada* systems, because the Alganna *gada* system does not depend on the Boran *gada* system but directly on the *qallu* in the same way as the Boran system does; but clearly, at least from a Boran perspective, the functions of the Boran *qallu* for the Alganna would be regarded as a sideline activity.

From all these forms of interethnic cooperation in *gada* matters we may distinguish hostile interaction through *gada*. We have already come across the Galbo expelling the Boran from their holy grounds. The Boran were much more numerous and much better armed than the Gabbra. Why did the relevant Boran not mobilize their militia and crush the Gabbra? There must be something in the shared understanding of *gada* rituals which prevented them from doing so.[20]

*Gada* rituals are recognized as such by neighbours with quite different *gada* systems and even by those without such systems. They may inspire awe and fear, and thus protect those who perform them, as they protected

**142**

the holy grounds of the Gabbra from the Boran. On the other hand, they may provoke rejection. They may be regarded as a pagan abomination. Either way they are part of meta-ethnic communication and interethnic politics.

## Islam: the Explicit or Implicit Point of Reference

*Gada* systems recede with the advance of Islam. There is no logical necessity for this, since other pre-Islamic culture traits persist even in the core areas of Islam. Elsewhere, as among the Fulbe (Guichard, 1996), age-set systems do coexist with Islam, but, for whatever reason, it so happens that *gada* is not found anywhere in combination with advanced Islamization. But a neat complementary distribution (+Islam, −*gada*+*gada*, −Islam) does not hold true either. Islam is present in all *gada* systems as a reference point, be it as the prototypical Other or even as the Enemy, but always as that with which constant comparison is made.

Some interesting paradoxes emerge if we compare inside and outside views of *gada* systems along such dimensions as 'sacred' and 'abominable'. Earlier in this paper (September 1979) we heard that the Gabbra describe their *gada* system as based on the orders of a Muslim sheikh, as being the next best thing to the Qur'an, which the unlearned Gabbra could not master, and as being directed against the Boran who are, by implication, presented as *kufaar*, unbelievers, while the Gabbra, although themselves non-Muslims and unable to claim a Muslim identity, attribute at least a quasi-Islamic legitimacy to their own institutions. The Gabbra are not alone in viewing the Boran as the prototypical 'pagans'. Elsewhere we (Schlee and Shongolo, 1995; Schlee, 1994b) have shown how unproductive the invocation of the past glories of Boran-ness and *gada* is in many cases for providing integrating symbols for all Oromo speakers. In recent conflicts between Garre and Boran, the latter were described as op-pressors of Islam, and much more negative views of the past hegemonial role of the Boran in the area were put forward in comparison with the rather idyllic descriptions contained in traditions I had collected earlier. Because of the current political process of establishing a new regional order based on 'ethnic' distinctions in Ethiopia, the political rhetoric is rife with competing identity discourses. The political terminology of the Oromo Liberation Front (OLF) which is heavy with *gada* symbolism (*abba gada* for 'president', *raaba* for the military wing, etc.) can be shown to be counterproductive for the integration of Muslim Oromo-speakers who, through their clan histories, have the alternative option of classifying themselves as 'Somali' rather than 'Oromo' and who, in less ethno-nationalist times, have always managed to be both simultaneously. These people now recall that historically they have been the victims rather than the agents of military expansion through mechanisms of recruitment and forms of ritual warfare based on the *gada* system. *Gada* symbolism provides little attraction for those who describe themselves as the victims of *gada.*

The Boran, who in the present conflict are depicted as oppressors of Islam, paradoxically define their (undoubtedly non-Islamic) *gada* systems and the whole of their customary law with reference to Islam. Whatever the political relationship might have been between the Boran and their 'Muslim' neighbours (among whom Islam also had stronger and weaker periods) in one or the other constellation, whether the Boran were represented as anti-Islamic only by others or whether they themselves defined their social and ritual order in contradistinction to Islam, the frame of reference was always provided by Islam as the symbolic system of supra-regional currency through which the local cultures defined their relationship to each other. Christianity, the other Semitic religion with universal claims which is present in the area, also plays this role from time to time. From Baxter (1978:156) we learn that his Boran informant explained: '"Generation-sets are our Book" (*luuba Kitaabu keen'a*), that is: "They are to us [wh]at the Bible or Koran are to you."' The Boran word for customary law, i. e. for the very domain in which they differ most from their Muslim neighbours and where most conflicts arise, is of Arabo-Islamic derivation: *aada.* In an Islamic context *adat* would be that part of the law which is derived from local tradition rather than from the Islamic sources of law but the application of which is tolerated as long as it is not in contradiction with the *shari'a.* Here, however, it stands for a non-Islamic body of rules which does not care about Islam at all, except by being named in a way understandable to an Islamic environment.[21] The other Boran word which can be translated as 'law', *sera*, is derived from Ge'ez, the classical language of Christian Ethiopia (Haberland, 1963: 226; Schlee, 1994b: 195ff). Also the two Boran words for 'religion' are both of Arabic derivation. In other words, if a Boran wants to say that he is not a Muslim but has got a 'religion' of his own, he will have to use an Arabo-Islamic concept to express this idea (Schlee and Shongolo, 1995: 12, 16).[22]

On the interethnic level, *gada* systems can thus be a symbol of difference from Muslim neighbours, or they can derive legitimacy from claimed Islamic origins or analogies with Islam, or they can combine these two contradictory elements of identification simultaneously as if there were no logical problems involved.

## Conclusion

*Gada* systems have or express elements of mutual dependence and co-operation. But they also have or express the opposite: rivalry and independence. Even in their hostile interactions they form part of a wider system in a way, since rivalries are expressed in a shared medium. *Gada* systems observe each other and communicate with each other.

Beyond their actual workings in age-grading people, living *gada* systems, and even the memory of defunct ones, are important elements of identity discourses, and these discourses become increasingly important with the ethnicization of politics in a disintegrating empire.

# Notes

1  In modern political ideology this is reflected by the discussions about '*gada* democracy' and '*gada* as a possible model for a modern, but genuinely Oromo, form of democracy. Asmaron Legesse, one of the few participants in this discussion who has actually studied gada, is very cautious about this and wishes a modern constitution of Oromia to be inspired by the spirit of *gada* rather than to borrow *gada* institutions directly (Baxter, 1994:180f).

2  To enumerate the authors who have dealt with over-aging and unde-aging generation-set systems is impossible here. Apart from Legesse, substantial original research in this field has been carried out by Jensen (1936) and Haberland (1963). Secondary analyses include Stewart (1977) and Hallpike (1986:182–207) and to cite a work on a Nilotic group outside the *gada* area, Spencer (1978).

3  The earlier Warr Daya Oromo immigrants appear, just like the bearers of the Proto-Rendille-Somali (PRS) complex of cultural features which comprise the bulk of the ancestry of the Gabbra, as victims rather than as agents of this dramatic expansion.

4  I would not conclude from such accounts that, prior to contact with the Boran, the ancestors of the Gabbra had no age-set systems and no age-grading whatsoever. Distributional evidence suggests that these were part of the PRS culture already. But the social order was certainly shaken up by the Boran impact and local societies and their institutions underwent processes of rearrangement and reorganization.

5  For details of the Gabbra calendar see Schlee, 1989, chapter 4.

6  I owe my information about Gaar to Bonaya Diima, a Gaar (Rerwalan) who is literate in Swahili. (Literacy in Boran is not widespread and was even rarer then.) He wrote a record of the Gaar ceremonial journey of 1985/6 (27 typewritten pages in my German translation.) I could not observe these events myself, because they overlapped with the ceremonial journey of the Galbo phratry which I joined.

7  The ritual significance of this mountain, the taboos restricting the use of the area around it and the myths attached to it, have been described elsewhere (Schlee, 1990, 1992: 117ff).

8  The immediacy and the extent of the spread of American youth fashions in early postwar Germany may be a vivid illustration of this. Young Germans almost totally identified with (or less politely, they aped) those with whom a short while ago they had had a relationship of mutual killing.

9  The Rendille system qualifies as being of the *gada* type because it has a rigid time order and because it has set-lines like the Boran system. Sons are initiated into a grade their fathers have left after two intervening sets, or 42 years after their fathers, not earlier. As among the Boran, sons born too late can perform the promotion rituals with later sets, and unlike the Boran, they can become full members of these sets. That is how the Rendille deal with under-aging: they simply mollify the generation principle in favour of the criterion of actual age and allow more sets than the minimal number between fathers and sons in cases of long generation spans. Seen from the perspective of younger sons, the Rendille system might therefore be described as an age-set system rather than a

generation-set system. But it is the first-born who count symbolically and on whom the ideal unrolling of the system is based (Schlee, 1979: 86–96).

10 The Gabbra Malbe comprise the phratries Alganna, Gaar, Galbo, Odoola and Sharbana. They live mainly in the Marsabit District of Kenya and adjacent areas of Ethiopia. The other, related group known as 'Gabbra', the Gabbra Miigo of the Northern Wajir District who are also widespread in the former Sidamo Province of Ethiopia, do not have a *gada* system based on multiples of seven years, but one in which not only the sets of which it is made up but also the intervals between their initiations are different and recur in a cyclical fashion. These intervals are 10, 9, 9, 10, 9, 9, 10 ... years. In the Gabbra Miigo explanation, as in many emic descriptions of *gada* systems or calendars, these years are not counted, however. Instead,  reference is made to fixed sequences of named units of time (Schlee, 1989: 83).

11 Beyond the area of interaction considered here more closely, the Gabbro Miigo and Rendille also follow this pattern.

12 This takes up elements of Torry's (1978) terminology. In other ways I do not follow Torry. Among the shortcomings of his account are that he fails to notice the fundamental differences between the Gabbra *gada* systems, and that the caption of his only pictorial illustration reads 'A Gabbra political elder' but clearly depicts a 'ritual elder' with his typical headdress.

13 The analogy with a gear box should not be overstretched in any case. Gears which set each other in motion, turn in opposite senses, while *gada* cycles turn in the same sense.

14 In the editors' comments on this paper I found the beautiful expression 'green light heifer'. There seems to be no end to car and traffic metaphors. Do we have an 'automobile complex' in Europe and Japan, comparable to Herskovitz's 'cattle complex'?

15 Popular Islam shares this feature, of attributing inheritable powers to curse and bless to clan groups, with the pre-Islamic Cushitic belief systems of the area (e.g. Schlee, 1979, 1989).

16 There are other areas where *gada* has become part of folklore or historical romanticism.

17 Bassi has recently (1994) pointed to *qallu*, *Gaayo* and *gada* as three partly independent sources of power among the Boran. For a description of the last *Gumi Gaayo* see Shongolo, 1995.

18 The *qallu* of the Guji has no *gada* rank (Hinnant, 1978:234).

19 As they stem from cattle people, no matter how much their economy is based on camels today, the Alganna still rely on Rendille immigrants for their camel-oriented rituals. The Rendille clan in question has an important function among the Rendille for sacrifices tied to the *gada* cycles of the latter: one of the many links between *gada* systems which cannot be discussed here fully because of limitation of space (Schlee, 1989:200–5).

20 David Turton (1994:27f) describes an episode which I found strongly reminiscent of this Gabbra/Boran conflict in which David chases Goliath from Mt Farole. Turton describes the antagonism of two groups which have generation-set systems which do not belong to the *gada* type, but this does not seem to matter here. After having been heavily reduced and chased away by the Nyangatom, the Mursi dare to come back to their holy grounds and install a new generation-set there. They do so under the eyes of the Nyangatom who parade their kalashnikovs on the bank of the Omo. The installation of the new generation set is one of the factors which later enabled the Mursi to reverse their fate and to cut down the Nyangatom. Why did the Nyangatom just look on and allow the generation-set to be constituted? (Cf. also Tornay in this volume.)

21 In this new age of 'cultural' justifications of separate existence, the word *aada*, as we learn from Baxter, 1994:178, is now also taken to mean 'culture'.

22 Zitelmann (1994:72) discusses in a similar context the Oromo key concept *ayaano* also and points to its possible Arabo-Islamic etymology.

# 7 Women's Age Categories in a Male-Dominated Society: The Case of the Chamus in Kenya[1]

## KAORI KAWAI

### Two Age Categories of Women

*Physical development and age-grades*

To determine the relative social position of Chamus women[2] two sets of age categories are relevant. Age-grades, which are based on perceived changes in physical development, on marriage and child-bearing, and on initiation, mark the progress of women through life. Each grade is defined by a set of rights and duties, in relation to women of other grades and in relation to men. Age-sets determine the seniority of married women in relation to one another. While the age-grades are specific to women, the age-sets are derived from the age system of the men. Women do not have age-sets of their own. When they marry they join the age-set of their husbands. Women married to husbands of the same age-set share a number of responsibilities and owe respect to women married to men of age-sets senior to those of their husbands.

While men progress collectively, as members of their respective age-sets, through three successive age-grades, women advance from one age-grade to the next mainly by function of changes, biological and social, in their individual lives: initiation, marriage, the birth of their first child, menopause. In his study of the position of the Chamus women, Little (1987) states, 'Changes in socio-economic status and expected roles mainly occur at three times in a woman's life. These are (1) marriage, (2) birth of the first child, and (3) attainment of old age.' These are clearly expressed distinctions defining a woman's participation in rituals. Neighbourhood ceremonies presided over by the divine leader, the *loiboni*, in particular, are not open to unmarried women (1987: 85–7). The above distinctions

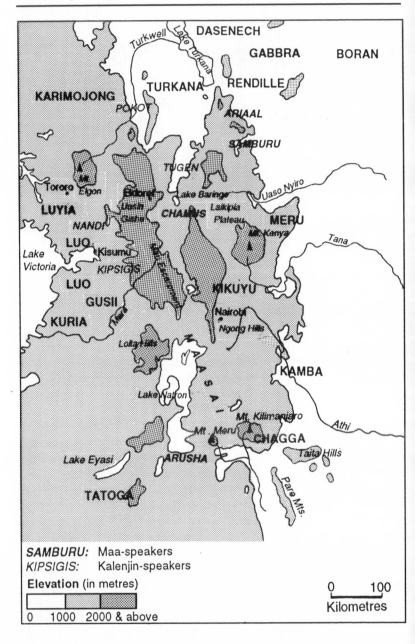

*Map 5  Maa-speaking & Kalenjin-speaking peoples & their neighbours*

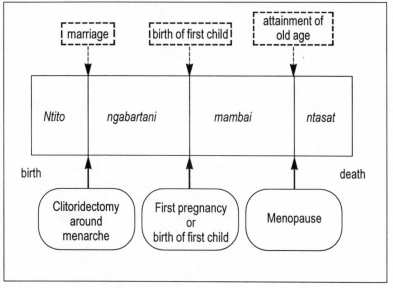

*Figure 7.1  Female physical aging categories*

generally conform to the folk categorization of a woman's age in developmental stages, primarily defined in terms of her reproductive function. *Ntito* defines 'a young girl before clitoridectomy who is sexually undeveloped', *ngabartani* is 'a young woman before pregnancy', *mambai* is 'a woman of child-bearing age', and *ntasat* is 'a woman who is no longer able to bear children'. Clitoridectomy was traditionally performed immediately before marriage. From the viewpoint of social status, the boundary between *ntito* and *ngabartani* is marriage, but the physical mark of this distinction is considered to be clitoridectomy (Figure 7.1).

In Chamus society, it is unpropitious for a girl to conceive prior to clitoridectomy, and the child is either aborted or killed at birth. *Ntito*, a girl prior to clitoridectomy, has no reproductive function socially. Clitoridectomy is a social device that transforms women's bodies from the condition of non-fertility to that of fertility.

There are socially recognized attitudes and roles appropriate for each age-grade. *Ntito* must be well-mannered and respectful to their seniors, whether male or female. They are expected to help with the household chores and with grazing small livestock. Otherwise there are few rules regulating their behaviour.

Married women are required to behave as 'adults', and being told 'you are just like a child' is considered an extreme insult. Being unable to make judgements for oneself, getting frustrated at not being able to care for a sick child, and expecting a husband to provide paternal protection, are criticized as being childish both by men and women. A married woman, however, is expected to behave in this 'adult' manner only after reaching the *mambai* stage';. women at the *ngabartani* stage are judged less severely. *Mambai* are expected to devote themselves to child-rearing and housework. While *ntito* may go out dancing every night, *mambai* generally do not leave the homestead, except when necessary, for instance to fetch water and collect firewood. They must not spend long hours at other homesteads. As the wives and their children in a polygynous family grow older, only the youngest wife remains in the husband's homestead while the older wives set up separate homesteads which they manage independently from the original homestead (Kawai, 1990). For the older wives this household segmentation coincides with the *ntasat* age-grade. A *ntasat* is free from child-rearing. Some of them make their older daughters play the role of mother in regard to homestead chores. A *ntasat* is also allowed to drink maize-beer with men, behaviour never tolerated from a *mambai*. The social roles that *ntasat* are expected to perform include that of midwife, supporting the back and legs of a girl during clitoridectomy, the performance of personal rituals such as birth-rites and ritual healing, notifying people of a case of death, and consoling mourners in their sorrow. People also expect *ntasat* to provide advice and make judgements based on knowledge obtained through their life experiences.

While the boundary between *ntito* and *ngabartani* is clearly defined by clitoridectomy and the subsequent marriage ceremony, no rites of passage mark the transition from *ngabartani* to *mambai* and from *mambai* to *ntasat*. The demarcation between these age categories is vague. Because of this vagueness the only clue to the age-grade of a woman is in many cases her actual behaviour. Individual women may manipulate this vagueness to their advantage.

In the following section I want first to show how relations between Chamus women are structured by their husbands' age-sets. Secondly I examine the recent drop in the age at which clitoridectomy is carried out. Unlike some neighbouring peoples where clitoridectomy has been abolished, the Chamus have lowered the age at which the operation takes place, resulting in the creation of a new intermediate age category of women: those who, by virtue of their initiation, can have socially recognized children but who remain, as yet, unmarried.

## *Wives'* lporar

It has been taken for granted by many ethnographic studies of East African age systems that they are male-centric and male-dominated. The position of women in the age systems, or what the systems mean to the women, has therefore, with a few notable exceptions (Bernardi, 1985; Kertzer and Madison, 1981, etc.), received very little attention. As with other societies in East Africa, the age system of the Chamus is principally a system for males. However, this does not imply that women are excluded from it. To understand this inclusion of women, it is necessary to present a summary of the framework for the male system.

*Table 7.1 Chamus Age-set (in Labori section)*

| Age-set name | Approximate initiation date | Age-grade |
|---|---|---|
| Il Kipiku | 1816 | |
| Il Tuati | 1832 | |
| Il Nyangusi | 1846 | |
| Il Peles | 1860 | |
| Il Kidemi | 1874 | |
| Il Kinyamal | 1888 | |
| Il Kileku | 1901 | |
| Ririmpot | 1914 | |
| | | Dead |
| Il Naponye | 1927 | |
| Il Paremo | 1939 | |
| Il Mirisho | 1949 | |
| Il Medoti | 1958 | *lpaiyan* |
| Il Kiapu | 1969 | |
| Il Mapoiye | 1980* | |
| No name | 1994* | *murran* |
| | | *laiyeni* |

*Source:* Little, 1983. * My data.

The age-sets come into being in initiation ceremonies that are performed every 10 to 14 years (Table 7.1). During a specific period, after being circumcised, young men participate in a series of ceremonies. Chamus society is divided into two territorial divisions, Chamus Labori and Chamus Lekeper (Anderson, 1981). Each has different age-set names and its own initiation ceremony. Unlike the Maasai and Samburu age systems, the Chamus age-set system does not have right-hand (*lporar tetene*) and left-hand (*lporar kedenye*) divisions within an age-set. However, the 'firestick relations' of the Maasai and Samburu are also found among the Chamus. The senior age-set A lights the fire for the initiation ceremony of the age-set C, the second junior one. Age-set A is also endowed with the power to bless and curse C. The firestick (*lpiron*) relationship is a father-son relationship that is both ceremonial and symbolic. The 'son' is required to pay great respect (*nkanyet*) to the 'father'. The same set of relations exists between age-sets B and D. There are ceremonies, as well as many other activities, that A and C, on the one hand, and B and D, on the other, perform together. A–C and B–D are recognized as separate groups, but there is an intimate feeling of mutual support among them. There are three age-grades among Chamus men: *laiyeni*, *lmoran*, and *lpaiyan*. All males are considered to be boys (*laiyeni*) until they have been circumcised. After circumcision they become warriors or *murran* (*moran*). After completing the *lmuget* ceremony which includes the selection of an age-set leader (*launoni*) and the giving of a name to the age-set, they become elders (*lpaiyan*). By completing the Rite of the Hair (also called 'Rite of the Stool', Chamus: *ntasim o lpapet* or *ntasim o lorikan*) they become 'elders who have become adults' (*lpaiyan lochomo an'gitie nkitoo*) or 'perfect elders' (*lpaiyan katogul*). After completing this ceremony, the circumcision ceremony for the elder's own sons can be performed. Each age-grade has well-defined behavioural standards for its members, but nowadays these rules are becoming more lenient, in particular those concerning commensality: a warrior may not drink milk alone; meat that a woman has seen may not be eaten, etc. Political, judicial and religious roles are shared by the age-sets that belong to the grade of elders.

Women have no age-set before marriage. Without further ceremony they join the age-sets of their husbands when they marry. Although a woman does not become an age-mate of her husband or a member of his age-set, she refers to the name of the husband's age-set as her *lporar* (age-set). From the day of her marriage the woman plays a supporting role in the social activities for which the husband's age-set is responsible. Women whose husbands belong to the same age-set call each other *nkaini-ai*, literally meaning 'my (*-ai*) co-wife (*nkaini*)'. This terminology does not imply, however, that Chamus men allow their wives to have sexual relations with their age-mates, which Maasai men do.

A group of women who refer to each other as *nkaini-ai*, and whose husbands belong to the same age-set, will be referred to as 'wives *lporar*' hereafter. The social roles and activities of the wives *lporar* are subordinate to the husband age-set. For example, when the husband's age-set is obliged to perform a ceremony, the wives *lporar* is in charge of collecting the funds for the ceremony, making maize beer, etc. Most of the social activities of the wives' *lporar* are related to ceremonies and rituals. The wives' *lporar* does not participate in politics or the administration of justice.

There may be a wide variation in the ages of one polygynous man's wives. Accordingly, the women whose husbands belong to the same age-set do not have the same physical age. Very young wives may join a *lporar* the majority of whose members are older women. It is not unusual for women who have spent their childhood and youth together to become members of different *lporar* after their marriages. Although they belong to the same *lporar*, the young members must display a basic attitude of respect (*nkanyet*) to their seniors. Younger women who belong to the same wives' *lporar* most of whose members are older women are rarely selected to perform important roles in ceremonies. Equality among age-mates, which is an essential characteristic of male age-sets, does not exist in wives' *lporar*. I have found no cases of young women demanding equality with their seniors in the same *lporar*, arguing that `all share the same *lporar*'. Peer equality is not a frame of reference.

While the membership of men's age-sets is formed in a collective ceremony, a woman's entry into the *lporar* is not marked by any special ceremony. Novices trickle in on an irregular basis. The wives' *lporar* is much less cohesive than are male age-sets. In their daily activities women do not have a strong sense of belonging to their *lporar* as the men do to theirs. As a result, there is no relational dissociation between two women who belong to different *lporar*. The various female groups formed in the course of daily life normally include members of different *lporar*. In conclusion, one can say that *lporar* are not a major factor in organizing women.

Women do not often utter such phrases as 'I belong to such-and-such a *lporar*', while they often say 'I am already a *ntasat*', and 'we are just *mambaï*', in daily life, especially in the domestic domain. They identify as women of a certain age rather than as members of a wives' *lporar*. Yet there are occasions when the wives' *lporar* manifests itself as a unit, namely the performance of ceremonies held only for women, the settlement of problems that affect only women, and disciplinary action as the following case illustrates.

**Case 1: A promiscuous woman punished by the wives of the ruling *lporar*.** The second wife of a man from the Mericho age-set (see Table 7.1) was unable to conceive for more than eight years following her marriage. As the deceased first wife had borne three children, the problem was not thought to lie with the husband. Many forms of traditional and modern medical treatment were tried. The woman also received treatment from a healer of the Tugen, a Kalenjin-speaking group, but none of these were effective. In 1988, the rumour spread that the woman's sterility was caused by her having had sexual intercourse with several men. The Chamus interpret conception as the result of the man's sperm mixing with the woman's menstrual flow in the uterus. They also believe that sperm from different men is mutually destructive. Therefore, frequent and repeated intercourse with more than one man results in the sperm being ineffectual, and not resulting in pregnancy.

To a woman, sterility can only mean 'misfortune' or 'evil', and the cause of the sterility must be eliminated. In 1994, six years after the woman's sterility was diagnosed as the result of her 'natural disposition', she was punished by a group of women who were wives of the Kiapo age-set. In this case, the wives *lporar* was used as the framework for an organized action. The punishment was carried out by the Kiapo wives *lporar* because the Kiapo men were 'in power', responsible for political and judicial affairs.

The next case illustrates how 'age-set logic' is strategically used in conflicts between women:

**Case 2: A wife of Mericho using the firestick relationship to demand respect from the wives of Kiapo.** While an old woman, whose husband belonged to the Mericho age-set, was going to fetch water, she made a stop at a homestead on the way. Inside one of the huts, the young wife of a member of Kiapo, and another woman of the same age, were eating sheep's feet. The older woman asked the younger women to cook some for her as well, and said that she would stop to eat on her way back. When she returned, she found that not only had the meat not been cooked, but the fire had been left to go out. The older woman protested, asking why they had not done as she asked. The young wife replied that she did not have to follow her orders. The older woman became furious, accusing the women of having no *nkanyet* (respect) for their elders. In the end, the older woman said, 'Is this the attitude you show to your mother? All right! I will never again participate in any of your rituals' and left.

Six months later the Kiapo wives prepared a *ntasim o nkerr* (Rite of Sheep). At the time the Mericho wives *lporar* in the region had only three members. If the old woman refused to participate, the rituals for the Kiapo wives *lporar* could not be held. The end of the story was that all members of the Kiapo wives *lporar* in the region apologized to the older woman, offering her maize beer and slaughtering livestock to obtain her forgiveness.

It should be noted that Mericho are the firestick patrons of the Kiapo. When the old lady called herself 'mother', she referred to their ritual parent-child relationship. The firestick relationship between male *lporar* is mirrored by an analogous relationship between the *lporar* of the wives of the two age-sets. Senior women perform ceremonies for members of junior *lporar*, and members of junior *lporar* must show the highest *nkanyet* (respect) to women who are senior according to the age system.

The case illustrates women's manipulation of the power differential between age-sets. By using the wives *lporar* as the framework for attack, the old lady turned a trivial, personal battle into a political problem. This is rather an unusual case, but it does show that wives *lporar* can be mobilized for a political action

Between these two parties with their age difference also lies the self-evident and universal proposition that 'one must respect one's seniors' , in this case *ntasat*. There is a 'justifiable' curse called *ldeketa* that can be activated to support claims of seniors to be respected. Fear of *ldeketa* may have been a factor in the compliance of the Kiapo wives.

Occasionally, the wives *lporar* is used as a unit for discipline and punishment by their husbands.

**Case 3: The collective responsibility of wives *lporar*.** In a series of three wedding ceremonies, the wives of Kiapo joined the dance and were said to have tempted the *murran*. The men of Kiapo held many meetings to discuss the behaviour and attitudes of their wives, individually and as a group. They decided to build a *wwata*, an enclosure made of the branches of thorn trees. There, they planned to punish all their wives, as a group. The news spread rapidly among the wives' of Kiapo. Some of them had not attended the weddings in question, but all the wives were likely to be beaten. They discussed countermeasures. Although the Kiapo men sensed their wives' agitation, they stuck to their original plan and fixed the date for administering the punishment. The wives then decided to send two delegates to the Mericho elders, their *lporar*'s firestick patrons, to ask them to intervene on their behalf. The Mericho elders succeeded in persuading the Kiapo men to forgive their wives. Consequently, the wives made a large quantity of maize beer, danced with their husbands to make peace, and promised they would never dance with *murran* again.

In this case the wives' *lporar* mobilized its members to defend itself against its male counterpart, by seeking an intervention by the firestick patrons. All the members of the wives *lporar* were at the *mambai* stage. The behaviour of a married *mambai* is under the strict control of her husband. A husband not only scolds his wife but beats her severely, even for minor offences such as when she returns late from drawing water or stays too long chatting in other homesteads. Husbands use their own physical force as well as the public force of their *lporar* to restrict and control their wives' behaviour.

**Case 4: *Mambai* as the target of male discipline.** A male elder of the Naponye age-set had five wives. The first wife had died, the second and third wives had already left their husband's homestead, but the fourth and the fifth wives were living with their husband. One day, the fifth wife returned late from a wedding ceremony. The husband went to look for her and found her in the middle of a circle of dancers, many of whom were *murran*. The husband took his fifth wife home and reprimanded her violently. The reason he gave was that she had been negligent in her housework. On the same day, the fourth wife was also late in returning home, but no assault was made on her. This was because she was considered to be a *ntasat*, as more than six years had passed since she had had her last child.

In this case, the reproach of the husband was based on what the wife was expected to do as a *mambai*: namely, devote herself to housework and child-rearing. In their efforts to control their wives' behaviour Chamus husbands focus on *mambai* wives who are capable of bearing children. They change their attitudes after the wife becomes *ntasat*. I observed several times that the behaviour of *ntasat* was judged according to different standards from that of *mambai*.

**Case 5: The prohibitions of the firestick relationship should also be respected by the wives' *lporar*.** The second wife of a man of the Medoti was drinking maize beer at the hut of a member of the Mopoiye age-set. The husband happened to see this, and shouted accusingly, 'What is this, are you drinking with your son?' and then beat her severely. Since Medoti and Mopoiye have a firestick relationship, the wife was considered to have been drinking with the husband's son, in other words, with her own son.

In this case, the husband called upon the age-set code that closeness between members of *lporar* with a firestick relationship is regarded as incest. The husband in this case could also have reproached his wife, a *mambai*, for being negligent in her housework and child-rearing duties. It seems that arguments taken from the rules of the age-set system and of the women's age-grades are not used at the same time.

The last two cases highlight the sensitivity of husbands with regard to the behaviour of their *mambai* wives. Their main preoccupation is the fear that their young wives may commit adultery with young men.

## Girls' Initiation

### *The* moratale nkerai', *the clitoridectomy of the girl*

In the afternoon of the day before the clitoridectomy operation a large number of *murran, laiok* (uncircumcised boys) and *ntito* gather to dance and sing around a tree near the homestead of the girl undergoing the operation. A married woman and three uncircumcised girls are selected from the girl's clan members to collect the twigs of the *lamarkweny* (*Cadaba farinosa*) that will be put round the bed of the mother of the initiand. They also gather two branches of *ldepe* (*Acacia nubica*) and set them on either side of the entrance to the hut.

In the evening the initiand sits, with her legs stretched out, on a cow-skin beside the entrance to her mother's hut. There the circumciser shaves off her hair and puts it in the hollow of the seat of a stool which has been filled with milk. The stool is kept under the bed. After that her head is smeared with a mixture of ferric oxide and butter.

The dancing and singing continue till midnight, often all night through. After dark, another type of song is sung. Each singer composes a song ad-lib and sings it in turn. The themes are 'you will be adult tomorrow', 'it is not so bad, so don't run away', 'stare at the eyes of the circumciser and don't blink', etc.

Before dawn the initiand and the girls enter the hut and all sit down on the bed continuing to sing the songs. The elders enter the corral which is still full of cattle, while the *murran* and young boys leave the homestead. The girls then leave the hut and wait around the entrance. A little later the initiand, her mother, the circumciser and two or three old women who will hold the girl's legs (or her right leg) appear after they have been blessed (*maiyan*). The girl's mother then puts a cow-skin on the ground, drawing four lines on it with butter. The girl then stands on the cattle skin, takes off her sheepskin cape, and is stripped naked. The circumciser takes a calabash bowl of milk and pours some milk on to the girl's palms and sprinkles it on the people who have gathered around. This is repeated four times. Then the circumciser pours milk on the girl's head and on the bead necklaces she is still wearing.

The girl is now made to sit on the cow-skin. One woman sits behind her holding her head while another holds her legs or her right leg. The circumciser smears ash on her pubic parts and carries out the operation. People then spit on her. The circumciser then smears butter and ash on her pubic parts, on the inside of her legs, her forehead,. throat and the middle of her chest. The circumciser put the razor-blade into the girl's mouth and spits on her body. This is also repeated four times.

The skin is then rolled up. The girl enters the hut with the skin between her legs. She takes off a bead necklace and gives it to the girl who is expected to be the next to be circumcised.

Married women start to sing the *saiyaakeya* song. The girls and old women join in. Two women come out singing and holding a branch of ldepe and lean against the entrance to the hut.

The blood is covered with soil and swept under the bed. The circumciser washes the razor and her hands with milk from the bowl. The spilt milk is also swept under the bed. The four participants wash their hands in water. The remainder of the milk is given to the girl.

The girl is blessed (*maiyan*) by the men of her father's *lporar*. A pair of elders spit milk on her, each one four times. The milk bowl is given to the girl. She spits the milk on the middle of her chest, four times. The girl is made to drink a lot of milk and blood. I know of a girl who drank four bowls full. They say that if you drink a lot, the wound will be cured quickly. The milk is brought by old women.

After circumcision the girl wears a black necklace and a sheepskin cape or black cloth. She also puts on a headband (*limeresen*) with a decoration (*sulimorei*) made of cowry shells (*sekera*) and black and white beads and a thread of the *lpaluai* plant.

Before the circumcision she is also blessed by her mother's brothers., who are given beer by her father. They come to ensure that the ties with the mother's lineage will continue after the girl is married. The girl's father dresses in a cape of sheepskin and puts strips of sheepskin on his head. His age-mates put a lump of butter on his head as a blessing. This butter shows that he has completed his daughter's circumcision. After this his age-mates and some of his firestick elders enter the hut to receive chewing tobacco and to bless him once more. This ceremony concludes the '*moratale e nkerai*'.

### *The prevention of uncircumcised motherhood*

In the clitoridectomy ceremony practised by the Chamus the entire clitoris and a portion of the labia minora are removed. This causes immense physical pain. Clitoridectomy has been the subject of various debates over the past several years (e.g. Hosken, 1982). Whether it is a violation of women's rights or not, and despite the fact that it is prohibited by both the government and the church, the practice still continues today as a necessary and essential custom for the Chamus.

In this the Chamus contrast with their neighbours. Most of the girls of the Tugen, their southern neighbours from whom many Chamus are believed to be descended, are no longer circumcised. Such girls are no longer considered eligible partners for the mainly Christian Chamus who consider them as lost to Tugen society; 'it is just as well that they are carried off by their churches'.

It should be noted that both parents and daughters, including those who like to be considered modern, are eager that clitoridectomy should be carried out. The modern ranchers living in the suburbs of Nakuru town, away from Chamusland, continue to observe the practice as well as a local chief who has completed higher education. There have been numerous cases of dedicated members of the African Inland Church and the Catholic Church, who oppose the practice, leaving the church by the time their daughters approach the age for the clitoridectomy ceremony. Traditionally, the clitoridectomy ceremony is a rite of passage performed just before the marriage ceremony. Two days after the ceremony the woman enters the homestead of the bridegroom. Circumcision for males and clitoridectomy for females can be considered as a 'physical marking', giving social recognition that the person is now an 'adult'. For women it also means the transition to marriage. However, in recent years, young women are undergoing clitoridectomy despite the fact that no decision regarding their marriage has been made.

In 1986, when I first visited the Chamus, this situation was still rare, but since then clitoridectomy has rapidly been becoming detached from marriage. Nearly half the girls having a clitoridectomy today do so without a marriage in prospect. The explanation given by the parents who take the responsibility for their daughter's initiation is that it is a means of preventing the girl becoming pregnant while she is still uncircumcised. They also explain that the clitoridectomy is performed when the girl has 'physically matured'. They do not specifically mention the onset of menstruation as the time for the girl to undergo clitoridectomy. Menarche is not ritually marked by the Chamus, nor do they make the onset of menstruation publicly known. When a girl has her first period, she will definitely not tell her father, and in some cases may not even tell her mother. Therefore, the physical maturity mentioned above must refer to the appearance of secondary sexual characteristics around the time of the first menstruation.

As noted earlier, the Chamus believe that pregnancy results from the mixing of menstrual blood with sperm. They clearly recognize the relationship between menstruation and the capacity for pregnancy and child-bearing. According to their indigenous reproduction theory, women are thought capable of becoming pregnant after the first menstruation. Although there are no regulations regarding the sexual activity of uncircumcised girls, it is unpropitious and dreadful to conceive before clitoridectomy. It brings shame on the family. Traditionally, the child would be aborted or killed at birth, and the girl would henceforth be excluded from all rituals and ceremonies. In the past, it was not uncommon for a girl to marry before menarche. In those conditions, very few women became pregnant before marriage. The Chamus explain this by pointing out that girls nowadays reach menarche at a younger age, thought to be the result of improved nutrition, and marry when they are older, a practice which is attributed to the spread of education.

During the last few years the Chamus have become increasingly preoccupied with the possibility of pregnancies before marriage and clitoridectomy are performed. This preoccupation should be seen in the light of the increased influence of the churches and the government administration, who denounce and prohibit abortion and infanticide and thus make it difficult for the Chamus to resort to these traditional solutions. The Chamus refused social recognition to children of uncircumcised women. Such children were expelled from society. So a new solution had to be found to preclude this type of unwanted pregnancy.

The solution invented by the Chamus is to dissociate clitoridectomy from marriage and perform the operation well in advance of the moment a girl can get pregnant. Nowadays, elders, both men and women, seem to have accepted the separation of marriage and clitoridectomy. In order to maintain the principle that a woman who has not yet undergone clitoridectomy should not have a child, this solution seems a satisfactory safeguard. But other solutions would have been possible. By establishing rules prohibiting sexual activity, there would be no need to separate clitoridectomy from marriage. Unmarried women in the Gabbra society of the Kenya-Ethiopia border, for example, are strictly prohibited from having sexual intercourse, even after the clitoridectomy operation (Harako, 1982). A girl's virginity is very important, and if a man violates it he must marry the girl, or he will be exiled from the society. Among the Rendille of northern Kenya unmarried women may not become pregnant. If they do, they will have their illegitimate children aborted or killed at birth (Sato, 1980). Spencer (1973) states that Rendille women are circumcised on the morning following the day on which the bridegroom enters the bridal settlement. He also relates that if an uncircumcised girl should conceive, she must abort. After the abortion the head of the family may drive her away from his home. He adds that such women generally settle down as concubines with the neighbouring Samburu or drift to the towns. The man who caused the pregnancy would be barred from any of the Rendille age-set ceremonies. The Chamus, however, nowadays accept the pregnancy of unmarried girls provided that the girl has been marked as an adult, capable of reproduction, by the performance of clitoridectomy.

### *The meaning of clitoridectomy to the girls*

What does clitoridectomy mean to girls? When a Maasai girl is undergoing a clitoridectomy, she is permitted to scream and cry as much as she wants (Llewelyn-Davies, 1981). But among the Chamus, if they scream and cry, or even if they squirm a bit during the operation, the girls dishonour themselves and their families, and will be criticized as boys are during circumcision. Accordingly, clitoridectomy is not performed until the girl reaches an age at which she can bear the pain dauntlessly. Even so, almost all girls want to have a clitoridectomy. 'Aren't you afraid of clitoridectomy?' is a question that makes no sense to them. The ordeal is a source of invaluable pride to the girl. Elderly women still take pride in their brave attitude many years before.

Matsuzono (1994), who carried out research among the Gusii of western Kenya, has pointed to the clear contrast in attitude to initiation between boys and girls. He argues that Gusii boys have positive and affirmative views about circumcision as a transition to 'adulthood', while, on the other hand, when girls talk about initiation, they emphasize the serious pain of the clitoridectomy operation and the sickness caused by the loss of blood afterwards. The method of Gusii clitoridectomy is for the tip of the clitoris to be cut off with a razor. They insist that clitoridectomy is harmful to health. Girls also claim that clitoridectomy is not an indispensable custom because it is not practised among the neighbouring Luo and there is no notable difference between Luo and Gusii women.

Such contrasts between the two genders are not recognized in Chamus society. Both circumcision and clitoridectomy are considered to be indispensable steps in the transition to adulthood. All Chamus boys eagerly want to undergo circumcision in order to become *murran*. The same thing can be said of girls. Completing clitoridectomy is, more than anything else, understood as the passage to 'adulthood'. Although girls are worried about the operation, they look forward to the day of their clitoridectomy ceremony as their traditional introduction to becoming 'proper Chamus women'. Chamus girls frequently express their willingness to undergo clitoridectomy. In particular, those who have reached puberty without completing this rite of passage admit that they feel 'disgraceful' (*keata hanyet*) about their condition.

While it is usually the parents who take the initiative for their daughter's initiation, sometimes it is the daughter herself, as in the case of the following schoolgirl who made all the arrangements and had the operation done during her Christmas holidays.

**Case 6: Clitoridectomy during the school holidays.** During the Christmas vacation of 1994, initiation ceremonies for boys to constitute the new age-set began, including circumcision. A girl, a standard seven primary school student of approximately 15 years of age, insisted that she needed to go through clitoridectomy before going back to school. Otherwise she would feel disgraceful. Eventually, she succeeded in having the operation just before the end of the vacation. Her parents had also agreed that she should have a clitoridectomy ceremony; their only disappointment was that, due to the short notice, they could not make full arrangements including providing food for the participants.

Why are girls so eager to have a clitoridectomy? Do they have more freedom or independence after it? As far as girls sexual behaviour is concerned, the answer is negative because Chamus girls are sexually active even before clitoridectomy. Lowering the age of clitoridectomy does not seem to have led to a rapid increase in the number of unmarried mothers. Girls do not want to be unmarried mothers. When a girl gets pregnant, her father will insist that her sexual partner marries her. She is married to him as soon as possible or to any other suitor. Unmarried mothers are not uncommon, but they are still a small minority. The notion of adulthood, the social recognition of a woman's capacity to reproduce, is presumably a key factor in explaining a girl's eagerness to have a clitoridectomy.

A parallel phenomenon to the lowering of the age of clitoridectomy may be the lowering of the age of marriage for the *moran*. Among the Matapato Maasai, *murran* are not expected to marry before the *eunoto* ceremony which includes selection of the leader of their age-set (Spencer, 1988: 172). This was also the case for the Chamus *murran*. However, when the *lmuget leunoto* ceremony of the Mopoiye age-set, which corresponds to the *eunoto* ceremony of the Maasai, was held in 1989, some boys had already married. During the ceremony, their wives were sent back to their natal homesteads. Each *murran* who had married before the ceremony had to slaughter two goats for the members of his firestick-patron age-set. Elders explain this transition in terms of the colonial pacification. In the past, they say, there were frequent raids by neighbouring peoples. A married *murran* would not be a brave fighter because he would be thinking of his wife and children. Therefore, the *murran* were prohibited from getting married.

In Chamus society an unmarried pregnant woman has two options: she can marry either the physical father of her child or another man. In the first case, she will take her child to the husband's homestead and legal paternity will then equate with physical paternity. It does happen, however, that the presumed physical father refuses to marry her. He may insist that she has other partners and deny that he made her pregnant. If the partner is not Chamus, which is often the case, he can escape from Chamus land to the town or to his homeland. In these cases, the girl eventually becomes an unmarried mother because abortion and infanticide are no longer practiced these days. Unmarried Chamus mothers are usually in this category. However, nowadays almost all of them are still young, and the general expectation is that they will eventually get married. Some unmarried mothers have been married to Tugen elders as second or third wives. Others married Chamus men. In most cases where the husband is considered not to be the father of the child the unmarried mother leaves the child at her natal homestead. It then becomes the legal sibling of its mother.

### *The* sapadei, *a new women's age-grade*

The new category of women who have undergone clitoridectomy but are not yet married, are called *ngabartani*. The term was originally used to indicate a newly married wife before the birth of her first child. Nowadays, this meaning has been replaced with the term *ntuaa*. *Ntomononi* is used for a nursing mother and *nmorani* for a woman who has finished nursing, until her next pregnancy. *Ntuaa, ntomononi* and *nmorani* are sequences of the *mambai* stage. A *ntuaa* is considered to have already become a *mambai*. A

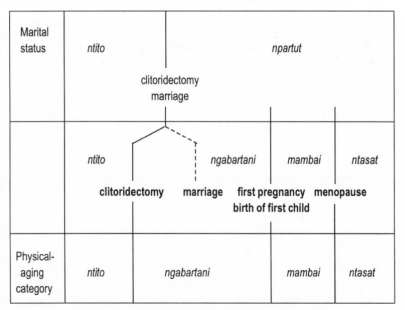

*Figure 7.2 Dissociation of clitoridectomy from marriage*

**163**

circumcised and unmarried woman is neither *ntito* (uncircumcised girl) nor a *npartut* (married woman). If the Chamus had wanted to give priority to the distinction between married and unmarried women, they would have classified her as *ntito*. However, the Chamus have put the greater emphasis on the physical 'mark' of clitoridectomy. So the *ngabartani* boundary has slid downward, towards the unmarried side of the category system (Figure 7.2). From the meaning of the term of *ngabartani*, the idea of bridal status seems to have been removed. A *ngabartani* is no longer necessarily a married woman.[3]

Recently, another new women's age category was created. When I revisited Chamus land in 1996, I came across a girl who had undergone clitoridectomy about six months earlier and who was called *sapadei*. The term *sapadei* originally referred to a woman who was unable to marry mainly because of a mental or physical disability. However, it does not have a derogatory meaning. According to this new categorization, a circumcised and unmarried woman is at first called *ngabartani*. Later, about three to six months after clitoridectomy, she is called *sapadei*. When a *sapadei* woman gets pregnant, she becomes *mambai*. A circumcised and unmarried woman, whether she is *sapadei* or *mambai*, will be called *ngabartani* again when she gets married.

An elder explained this last use of the term as follows. When a woman gets married she becomes a new member of the age-set of her husband. That is why she is called *ngabartani*. In this sense, the term stands for a novice of an age-set. Apparently *ngabartani* has a double meaning. On the one hand, a woman is *ngabartani* as a novice in the group of 'adults' who have the capacity for reproduction thanks to the completion of clitoridectomy. On the other hand, a woman is *ngabartani* as a novice in the age-set of the husband whom she has married.

How are these new categories of *ngabartani*, *sapadei* and unmarried *mambai* dealt with in relation to rituals? Participation in rituals used to be

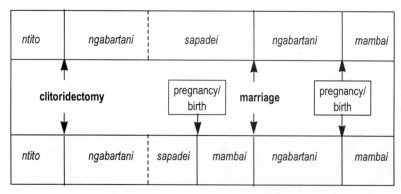

*Figure 7.3* Sapadei, *a new category and* ngabartani *stage*

limited to married women (*npartut*), with the exception of individual rites of passage and healing rituals. However, nowadays, unmarried women who are pregnant or have already borne children formally participate in the Rite of the Sheep (*ntasim o nkerr*) that is held to pray for women's fertility. They are treated in the same way as other women. Here, the criterion for participation is not only marriage but marriage and/or child-bearing age. Participation is allowed for both married and unmarried *mambai* (Figure 7.3).

In fact, the reason why *mambai* take part is that the ritual is related to women's fertility. So the *mambai* aging category, usually relevant only in the domestic context, also counts in participation in the domain of public rituals. However, most rituals for women are performed in wives *lporar* units, and the Rite of Sheep is no exception. When a circumcised but unmarried woman perceives herself to be *mambai*, she herself chooses which *lporar* to join, normally selecting the one which consists primarily of women of her own biological age. Her participation in wives *lporar* rituals and gatherings differs from that of ordinary *lporar* members, because for her it is not an obligation. Eventually, when she gets married she will join a *lporar* as determined by her husband's age-set.

Women's age categories serve as a compromise between socio-cultural constructivism and biological pragmatism. The concept of age is currently regarded as a socio-cultural construct. Like the categories of kinship, ethnicity, gender and illness, age is considered to be a cultural and not a natural ahistorical and biological fact. Perspectives that try to minimize the physical attributes of age are popular. To be sure, the 'age' concept of the Chamus is constructed in social discourse and cultural practice. The wives *lporar* do not take the physical age of their members into account. Similarly, the importance attached to clitoridectomy, as a cultural operation, in determining a woman's capacity to produce socially acceptable offspring, highlights the cultural constructivism of age categories. However, the changes in respect to clitoridectomy indicate that, although age categories are determined by systems and rules, they also take the natural facts of fertility and birth into account. The lowering of the age at which clitoridectomy is practised is the adaptation of a social construct to the biological realities of life.

As I have shown elsewhere (Kawai, 1994a), the way the Chamus deal with the issue of children's legitimacy is another conspicuous demonstration of this type of compromise between cultural constructs and 'facts of life'. Chamus society consists of patrilineal descent groups. In principle, a new-born child automatically becomes a member of the group of its mother's husband, even if it is born long after his death, and whoever may be the biological father. In actual fact, the Chamus are very much preoccupied with the issue of who is the biological father, because of their indigenous theory of reproduction, according to which the formation of the foetus begins with the mixing of menstrual blood and sperm in the uterus following the menstrual period, when blood still remains in the woman's body. The menstrual period is considered to last for four days for almost all women. Blood is believed to stay in the body for a few days, counting from the fourth day after the onset of menstruation. Sexual intercourse on the fifth day after the onset of menstruation gives the highest probability that a woman will become pregnant. They also believe that the duration of gestation varies from nine to eleven months according to the patrilineal clan of the male partner. If a man's wife has become pregnant, and he did not have intercourse with her during those days, he has good reason to conclude that the pregnancy was caused by adultery. Traditionally, such a child was likely to be killed by abortion or infanticide. Husbands were not inclined to pretend that they did have intercourse. Although abortion and infanticide are avoided in more recent times, a husband still refuses to accept a child conceived in adultery as his legitimate offspring. Usually, such a child will be adopted by its maternal grandparents. As with the age categories the cultural constructs of legitimacy and paternity have to take biological facts, as understood by indigenous theory, into account.

Another example demonstrating the relevance of biological facts for ethno-medical science is the way the Chamus interpret human bodily conditions, especially bad health (Kawai, 1994b). In addition to the modern medical facilities (available in the National Hospital and the Dispensary of the Africa Inland Church) and the modern medicines in the shops of Marigat town, the healing powers of the traditional diviners (*loiboni*) are still respected. People rely on the *loiboni* to diagnose and remove the supernatural causes of their poor health. Both modern and traditional medical treatment are believed to help against a range of specific diseases. Self-treatment is also very popular among the Chamus. Before going to the diviner or doctor, people try to treat themselves. The Chamus have a rich folk-knowledge of the human body and its condition. They interpret their discomfort both from an anatomical and a physiological viewpoint, based on the recognition that the bodies of all human beings have common structures and similar functions. While the concept of illness is a cultural construct, the Chamus are well aware of biological realities.

From these observations one general point emerges. In addition to their cultural construction of the body and of illness, the Chamus keep an eye open for the biological realities of aging, reproduction and physical discomfort. Biological notions have been integrated into folk knowledge. This may seem obvious, but it is often overlooked.

**166**

# Notes

1    The research on which this paper is based was supported by the Grants-in-Aid for Overseas Scientific Research of the Japanese Ministry of Education, Science, Sports and Culture (Nos. 61041077, 63041026 and 05041028) and the Noma Asian and African Scholarship Fund of Kodansha Publishers Ltd.
2    The agropastoral Chamus, numbering approximately 11,500 persons (Kenya Population Census, 1994), live around Lake Baringo in northern Kenya. Like the Maasai and Samburu, their language belongs to the Maa, one of the Eastern-Nilotic languages (Gregerson, 1977). They are considered to have originated from various peoples, such as the Maasai, Samburu, Ntorobo (Okiek), Turkana, and Kalenjin peoples (Anderson, 1981).
3    A circumcised and unmarried girl is represented as '*enkanyakuai*' in Maasai (Mol, 1978: 74), but I have not come across such a word in Chamus society.

# 8 Age Systems and Modes of Predatory Expansion
## PAUL SPENCER

In 1988 at the 'assembly of multitudes', convened by the Boran every eighth year at Gayo in southern Ethiopia, it was resolved to enforce a return to traditional values associated with their age system, the *gada*. This was aimed to reverse the creeping spread of Somali influence that was felt to be destroying their society. Over the years, an increasing number of Boran and of their allies within the Oromo federation had converted to Islam, adopting Somali practices and intermarrying with Somali, and now Somali claims to territory were reaching towards the ritual heartlands of Borana. Faced with this threat, it was held to be the discipline imposed by *gada* alone that could arrest this trend. Commenting on this decision, a Boran representative maintained that, over the generations, it had been *gada* that had mobilized effective resistance to the territorial incursions of the Somali, and had served as a unifying force for Oromo over a wide area. Without *gada*, he claimed, the Somalization of local populations would by now reach as far south as Tanzania.[1] It was a claim that repeated the more general view of Trimingham (1968: 40), that the spread of Islam into northeastern Africa had been resisted by societies with age systems, but it gave this insight an unexpectedly contemporary ring.

There is also an intriguing link at a more theoretical level. In his analysis of the segmentary lineage as an organization for predatory expansion Marshall Sahlins (1961) took the Nuer and the Tiv as his model, but he might equally well have taken the Somali. The ethnic identity of Somali through their lineage system and under the banner of Islam has been prominent in the process of territorial annexation as they have shifted their boundaries with non-Islamic neighbours, rather as the notion of Nuerhood in Sahlins' model was prominent in their steady expansion against the disorganized Dinka. Among the Somali as among the Nuer, the strength of their lineage system was also its weakness, with endemic feuding and shifting allegiances as segments at various more basic levels turned against one another at different times. The expansion of the Somali into the hinterland of eastern Africa and also the fragility of their parochial loyalties appear to follow Sahlins' model quite well. The historical premiss of this approach to the Nuer has been questioned and elaborated by various writers, and Kathleen Gough (1971) has undermined it, noting the key role of charismatic leadership rather than lineage loyalties, in the areas where the Nuer had most recently expanded, leading to a more individualistic network of affiliation. This shifts the interpretation of Nuer warfare towards a pattern recently and vividly described by John Lamphear (1992) for the Turkana at the turn of the century. In the arid conditions of Turkana, such leadership was necessary to inspire and synchronize a surge of support towards a limited end before the mustering was forced to disperse. Significantly, changes in the nature of Turkana leadership corresponded to a modification of their age organization, adapting it pragmatically towards a new form of warfare (Lamphear, 1992: 19–20, 30–1).

While the role of the Nuer lineage system may be questioned, the fact of their expansion against the Dinka remains uncontested. In this context, a feature of their age organization that has been generally overlooked is at least worth noting. In discounting the wider significance of this system, Evans-Pritchard emphasized that the Nuer did not fight as age-sets, and he noted that 'it is easy to conceive of the political system existing without an age-set organization' (1940a: 260). Yet there remain some suggestive links between the age system and their territorial expansion. Within the Nuer federation, the individual tribe was the principal fighting unit against the Dinka, on the one hand, and it was also the level at which age-sets were organized, on the other, integrating the tribe, structuring respect for age seniority, and creating close fellowship among age peers. It was young men following their initiation into an age-set who played a prominent role in the raiding to establish their reputation, and such fighting as a result was often spoken of as the action of a particular age-set (Evans-Pritchard, 1940a: 253–7, 260; Lamphear, 1992: 23–4). In other words, while Nuer did not organize themselves along age-set lines in their raiding, the notion of age-set loyalties and pride appears to have imbued the predatory nature of their warfare. If lineage loyalties are in question during these raids, age-set reputations at least appear to be quite central and close to Nuer ideals of warriorhood. Among the Dinka, who were the victims of Nuer expansion, on the other hand, age-sets appear to have been more parochial and subject to factional secessions in which rivalries between big men seem to have been more significant than age affiliations as such (Lienhardt, 1958: 103, 131–2). To the extent that this contrast provided a consistent pattern before the Nuer age system declined with pacification,

there appears to be evidence that the weakness of Nuer lineage organization as an explanation for their success in expanding against the Dinka
was compensated for by the relative strength and cohesiveness of their age
system. To the extent that young men in the vanguard of Nuer expansion
were spurred by the need to establish the reputation of their new age-set,
the Nuer age organization deserves a prominent place in any analysis of
their political system as an organization for predatory success.

Applying Sahlins' argument to age systems can be taken a step further
with reference to the history of the Boran in southern Ethiopia. During
the sixteenth and seventeenth centuries especially, they mounted systematic raids on a series of neighbours, expanding their area of dominance.
According to their oral traditions, this warfare was linked to a particular
ritual in the eight-year cycle of their *gada* age system, and each successive
age-set was expected to attack a new territory. This led to the emigration
of Boran and the absorption of new peoples into the expanding Oromo
federation under the umbrella of *gada*. This process of colonization seems
to have been linked to the structure of authority and inheritance within
the Boran family, which was based on strict primogeniture and associated
with considerable rivalry between brothers. After their conquests as
warriors, eldest sons tended to return to the Borana homeland, eventually
to take up their inheritance, while younger sons tended to establish themselves within the conquered areas, mending their fortunes and resolving
tensions within the family by means of this migration.

The dramatic successes claimed in these accounts could not be
sustained indefinitely, especially when faced with the powerful response
from the Abyssinian state, and *gada* appears to have lost its significance in
the northwestern areas of expansion (Legesse, 1973: 74–5; Hultin, 1979:
283–6). The Boran continued to be a dominant expanding force southwards, however; and on their eastern flank *gada* appears to have been the
principal cohesive force through which to contend with sustained Somali
aggression. In other words, what had been an organization for predatory
expansion against relatively weak neighbours was transformed into a more
defensive role when faced with a more determined foe. Given the history
of conflict between the two peoples, one is led to consider *gada* as an
alternative organizational principle that has developed up to a point as a
counter-measure to Somali aggression and is even structurally opposed to
the segmentary lineage principle among the Somali. *Gada* stresses the
unity of all Boran and the role of age and generational loyalties in
maintaining the Peace of Boran, *Nagaa*, as opposed to the Somali *jihad*.
Elaborating on the term *jihad*, another Boran elder did not perceive this as
an Islamic holy war conducted against unbelieving Boran, but as a
manifestation of endemic Somali greed and factionalism at all levels. He
perceived *Nagaa* as a religious concept associated with Boran identity and

their future survival as a united people, while he regarded *jihad* as an expression of chaos, with special reference to destructive Somali behaviour.[2] For the Somali, *jihad* is equally a religious concept with corresponding implications for their identity, rising above their parochial lineage loyalties and the shifting relevance of segmentation with circumstance. The Boran elder cited earlier drew attention to the defensive role of *gada* in the face of Somali aggression, and the second elder emphasized the mindless destructiveness of this external threat. Thus one has diametrically opposed views of the significance of *jihad* from Boran and Somali points of view. But among the Boran, the significance of *gada* also appears to vary according to circumstance, adapted to aggression in one context and to defence in another.

Turning to a third pastoral group in East Africa, the Maasai, one again has an example of a society with an age system to which the principle of predatory expansion seems to have applied at one time. According to oral history, the Maasai migrated from the north, occupying a massive stretch of East Africa through warrior conquest governed by their age system. However, this refers to the distant past, whereas more detailed oral histories of more recent campaigns by specific age-sets display mixed fortunes rather than sustained expansion, overshadowed by disastrous internecine civil wars during the nineteenth century. In one respect, the Maasai shared a ritualized feature with Boran and Nuer warfare. Corresponding to the ritualized Boran raid performed within a *gada* cycle, and Nuer raiding following the inauguration of each new age-set, the culminating feature of the Maasai ceremony of promotion (*eunoto*) for their *murran* (warriors) to senior warriorhood within each tribal section was a triumphal raid against one of their enemies. However, there is no evidence of expansion of the Maasai specifically linked to these raids. The aim was to acquire cattle rather than territory and the raids were intended to establish the reputation of each successive age-set at the height of its power, and to reinforce the military supremacy of the Maasai throughout the region. Thus, the Maasai without doubt were predatory through their age system, but the period of expansion belongs to an almost mythical past.

Within this region, the Nuer, Boran and Maasai are well-established examples of age-organized pastoralists who have expanded in the course of their histories. However, under what conditions do age systems develop rather than other forms of organization? Why should the expansive Somali or Tiv, for instance, have developed an elaborate form of patrilineal segmentation rather than an age system? Why should identity and primary affiliation be with kinsmen in one situation and towards peers in another? To the extent that organization was based on age (and especially generation), this could limit the number of able-bodied men available for fighting as compared with other systems, or could it have the advantage of limiting the divisiveness of opposed loyalties that occurred among the Somali?

The success of age organization as a device for the pursuit of warfare may be judged by the extent to which different forms of age system spread to neighbouring peoples. The expansion of *gada* under Boran leadership in the northeast has already been noted. In the far south, the Nyakyusa expanded into the surrounding area, incorporating their neighbours into their age-village system (Wilson, 1951:3–5). In the centre, the expansion of the Maasai tended to involve domination rather than annexation, raiding their adversaries or serving as mercenaries among their allies, and the typical response was for these neighbours to adopt aspects of the Maasai age system as a defensive measure. In effect, the Maasai age system infiltrated their area of influence, which was an ambiguous mix of alliance and conflict. In the northwest, the Jie/Karimojong cluster expanded from a single ancestral group, and certain neighbours, such as the Labwor and Pokot adopted their age-generation system. Thus Somalization has historical parallels in Boran-ization, Nyakyusa-ization and Maasai-ization, each referring to the diffusion of a successful cultural formula. We cannot know, of course, the manner in which age systems originally came into being. But the extent of their spread throughout the region as a means of aggression and defence does emphasize that their military aspects were crucial. These systems were the basis for organized warfare among the more successful pastoralists over a wide region and they were adopted by their less successful neighbours.

Leadership, as we have already noted, was another ingredient for success in warfare. The leaders were prophets and outstanding spokesmen among the Maasai, for instance, or those elevated to high office in *gada*. However, unlike the Nuer or Turkana instances, the outstanding quality underpinning success in these societies was the discipline imposed by the age system itself. Even among the Maasai prophets are thought to have provided an ingredient for military initiative, but accounts of the spectacular success appear to focus both on the cohesive courage of the warriors (*murran*) and on the cool-headedness of their age-set leader. He was surrounded by his advisers and, if necessary, constrained by them. He was the 'head' and they were his 'feathers', using the metaphor of a warrior headdress that enhanced the power of the individual. In Weber's terms, confidence in leadership stemmed from the charisma of the office rather than the charisma of the person (as in Nuer and Turkana), and this was true also of the Maasai prophets (Spencer, 1988: 104–6). In the Boran situation, it appears to have been the charisma of *gada* as a manifestation of collective will, associated with the age-set of elders in office.

## Adaptation and Change

In the process of maintaining age systems, each innovation should be seen as a conscious adaptation to current events. It is not that the systems as such were functionally self-regulating in the sense of being guided by some unperceived hidden hand, but that elders in particular took collective measures to adapt to pressing problems, rather as judges, in applying the spirit of the law to novel situations, create precedents that implicitly change the law. An outstanding example of this was provided by the *gada* assembly which met every eighth year to assess any aspect of Oromo custom that appeared anachronous. In a less systematic way, a similar procedure was followed by elders elsewhere, adapting to circumstance in a more *ad hoc* fashion. To the extent that the elders in concert comprehended the essential features of the system, there was an element of (conscious) self-regulation, as they adjusted their system to the perceived needs of their time. The Maasai age system, with relatively simple rules and an age-set span of some fifteen years, appears to have had this characteristic. Local shifts and adjustments led to a certain diversity between sections of the Maasai federation; and neighbouring peoples who have adapted Maasai characteristics show greater diversity still. It is not just the fact of diversity that has to be stressed here, but the fact of diversification that is inevitable in the handing on of oral tradition, notably in changing times. If one compares the Samburu and Maasai age systems alongside their oral traditions, for instance, it is tempting to assume that the more rudimentary version in Samburu represents a proto-Maasai form before the Maasai migrated southwards and elaborated their system in the process of extending their domination. The mechanism for adaptation step-by-step lay with successive age-sets of elders (firestick patrons, *ilpiron*) and *murran* acting in concert as the scope of opportunity unfolded.

A useful illustration of the spread of the Maasai system was among the Chamus of Lake Baringo whose oral traditions provide a rich example of this process of diffusion and adaptation. When pastoralism displaced irrigation as the principal thrust of their economy from the latter part of the nineteenth century, they first adopted some aspects of Samburu age organization and then some Maasai features associated with the formation of warrior villages (*manyata*). Virtually every age-set modified the system in some way in response to circumstance. Whereas Maasai and Samburu oral traditions tend to view the past as a projection of the present imposed on a scenario of warfare and shifting territories, the Chamus are unusually conscious of their institutional history and of the factors that led to successive adaptations. It is an aspect of their society that gives their tradition a dynamic quality and provides an especially useful insight into the process of perceived change in relation to age systems.

To describe such adaptations as a process of self-regulation at a conscious level is not to assume that there are no underlying aspects hidden from the elders' purview and no unintended consequences of their piecemeal adjustments. However, when the periodic cycle of an age system is relatively short, there can be a greater awareness of its nuances and ramifications. Thus with age-set cycles ranging from eight years (*gada*) to typically fifteen (Maasai), senior elders can accumulate considerable experience of the subtle mechanics of their systems over a number of cycles. However, when these cycles span a generation of fifty years or more, as among the Jie and Karimojong for instance, the system would appear altogether more opaque, with intricacies that lie beyond the immediate comprehension of even the most experienced men. In such circumstances, it does not follow that any immediate adjustment reached by the elders to meet some exigency will also serve to maintain the system in the longer term. Thus, I have argued elsewhere (1978) that John Lamphear's material on Jie history (1976) appears actually to point towards a breakdown of their system as a result of a short-term accommodation reached by the elders. The same argument questioned whether Dyson-Hudson's (1966) analysis of the breakdown of the Karimojong system really did point towards some irreversible change, as he suggested, or simply revealed a critical point of the generation-set cycle of succession as it ran its unaffected course. Generational crises appeared to be a characteristic of the stability of the Karimojong system, whereas the Jie data suggested irreversible change in a system that had been returned to meet a critical problem, sending it into decline.

Thus short-term adaptations of the organization of age and generation-sets under the pressure of expediency can have longer-term implications that are not fully recognized. The wider the span of the cycle, notably where generations and not just age-sets are involved, the more concealed are the inner workings of the system.

## Age and the Balance of Power

While the argument so far has focused on the external aspects of age systems in terms of their military value, it is in their internal dynamics that they contrast so essentially with alternative modes of social organization such as segmentary lineage systems. Affiliation and loyalty emphasize the peer bond rather than the bond of kinship and descent. In the (ideal) lineage model, members of the same family are united and to this extent the father's authority and lineage seniority are respected, whereas grouping by age highlights the scope for conflict between generations and also between brothers of a different age. In any attempt to accommodate age systems into a sociology of age and ageing, I take it as self-evident that these systems are concerned with the balance of power between young and old. By controlling the rates of promotion of boys to warriorhood and then of warriors to elderhood, elders command a privileged position. This is linked to the control of women also through the marriage market in what tend to be highly polygynous societies (although not always). So long as they can regulate the system, the elders hold a monopoly of property extending from cattle to the exchange of women and to the destinies of children, and ultimately of younger men.

There is nevertheless a certain balance of power between young and old which involves two very different kinds of excelling: as youths, on the one hand, with abundant physical vitality and as elders, on the other, with the knowledge and political wisdom that accrue with experience. Within the family throughout the region, relative age and generation are of vital importance in the allocation of resources, especially with regard to the transfer of marriage payments, and this creates an inherent tension that contradicts the ideal lineage model. Cutting across families, an age system creates separate domains that highlight the opposed characteristics of young and old. The extent to which age systems tend to focus attention on the most recently formed age-set is broadly correlated with the problems of youth: flamboyant and virile, but dispossessed and less than fully committed to a system run by elders. In a situation of conflict, younger men are vital for defence and have much to gain or lose where this involves an element of cattle raiding or territorial domination. They excel in what may be called the predatory domain. However, in the absence of conflict, the elders have an investment in the domain of peaceful husbandry which can promote the growth of their herds. Data collected among the Maasai suggest that an average stock-owner in an average year could add as many animals to his herd through peaceful husbandry as an unusually successful *murran* (young man) in his whole career as a warrior (Spencer, 1988: 20). A general sense of peace and security, extending even across tribal boundaries, was essential for herd growth; and the elders excelled in diplomacy through their personal networks and through shared institutions across the region. In general, they had more to gain from peace and more to lose from warfare. But in times of frustration, impoverished younger men could perceive that they had more to gain through predation, raiding to build up their herds in the short term and leaving the problems of the longer term for the future.

In Marxist literature, any notion of a pastoral mode of production has been rightly questioned on the grounds that a variety of political and economic structures are found among pastoralists and there are no relations of production that are uniquely associated with pastoralism as such (Asad, 1979: 425–6). Here, however, it seems equally pertinent to point out that this literature also acknowledges a variety of domains within any one society, that is, several modes of production, each associated with a discrete set of relations of production and displaying its own sub-culture (ideological superstructure). The critical feature is then to identify the relations of dominance between these domains at any historical moment; and the contradictions of the system extend to ambiguities which obscure such patterns of dominance (Foster-Carter, 1978: 216). Among pastoralists in East Africa, peaceful husbandry and predation appear to offer two such modes of production, with different premises concerning the reproduction of property and the legitimacy of accruing herds. Each is involved in a quite different array of relations of production: acting as a family enter-prise under the authority of the family head, on the one hand, as against exploiting alien producers across the tribal boundary and depriving them of their herds, on the other. The balance of power between these modes is between older and younger men: that is, the extent to which the elders dominate their juniors or fail to do so, and this may vary with the phase of the age-set cycle and less predictably with the wider regional context between times of instability and stability, war and relative peace (Spencer, 1989). Again, this balance may vary from one pastoral group to another. The Boran elders whom I cited at the beginning of this chapter were in effect arguing that *gada* in its peaceful mode, with an emphasis on organized defence, has to cope with the Somali who (from a Boran view-point) have no control over their warriors and are caught up in a vicious circle of predation.

This switches attention from the external military aspects of an age system as an organization for defence or aggression to its internal aspect of maintaining the balance of power between older and younger men. It is not simply that age-sets cut across local communities and kinship networks to provide a wider cohesiveness, but that the hierarchy of these age-sets within an age system serves as a means whereby older men can aim to control younger men, and especially the most recently formed age-set who have more to gain than to lose from predation (especially in the past) or at least from greater freedom nowadays and are less committed to the longer-term benefits of peaceful husbandry. The elders' problem is that they may lose control in the process of trying to pursue their own interests by delaying the induction of a new age-set into the system. The system itself may then be threatened as younger men seek to assert their independence. There is a widespread myth that this was how the Turkana came to be what they are, breaking away from the generation-set discipline of their Jie forebears. Various studies emphasize different aspects of this problem of the succession of age-sets and generations. My own study of the Samburu emphasized the gerontocratic aspect (Spencer, 1965). Wilson (1951) drew attention to the more juventocratic aspect of the Nyakyusa system with power handed over to younger men in their youth: Gulliver's model for the Arusha (1963) switched attention to ageing among the elders in their political prime competing with more senior age-sets whose ability to command respect dwindled as their numbers diminished together with their political agility. As boys aspiring to be warriors, these elders had previously replaced their seniors of the preceding age-set, and now, at a later stage in their careers, they were again hurrying these same men further up the age ladder into retirement.

It is evident from the literature that these are stereotypes of aspects of age organization that apply more generally. The problem is not simply that systems differ in degree, but also that they change over time and even from one phase of an age cycle to another. Competition among younger men of different age-sets may be symptomatic of one point, among elders of another, and a certain loss of control by the elders of yet another. Given that both Samburu and Arusha are within the same cultural complex as the Maasai, for instance, how far do the various models simply represent different phases within the Maasai age-set cycle when the studies were undertaken (see Spencer, 1976: 154–5; 1989: 315–16)? Or again, there may be a kind of oscillation built into the system, as in Samburu where strong and weak age-sets appeared to alternate: a strong age-set would build on high expectations and remain open for recruitment longer, attracting larger numbers and being more troublesome. To this extent, there would be few men waiting for initiation into the following age-set, spirits and expectations would be lower, it would be more docile, and there would be more pressure to close it earlier, building up a backlog of uninitiated youths and paving the way for a regeneration of spirits and expectations in the next age-set (Spencer, 1965: 169–71).

Viewing age systems historically, it is almost inevitable that there would have been changes in the profiles of power with age, but anthropologists, whose span of fieldwork tends to cover only one phase of an age cycle, face the problem of extrapolating to the age cycle as a whole, let alone to broader oscillations or historical trends. The opportunity to visit the same society at another point of the age cycle is rare enough, and rarer still are the conditions in which it is possible to disentangle age-set phases and oscillations from broader historical trends. Again, perceptive elders can provide some essential clues within the contemporary setting, but wider insights are open to the distortion of false perspectives of the past and to parochial views of the present. Corresponding to the unintended consequences of elders' decisions noted in the previous section are the unperceived nuances of historical development. And, as suggested earlier, corresponding to the ethnographic analyses of these systems based on contemporary evidence, there is scope for alternative interpretations based on different premises.

Here we face the problem of reconstructing historical processes and cycles from the sort of synchronic data collected by anthropologists over a limited period of time, certainly much shorter than the duration of one cycle in any of these age systems, let alone change in the longer term. Unlike the study of the life course of a family, where we can sample households at different stages of development, in any study of the life course of an age-set we have a very limited sample and are faced with the problem of the weighting to place on our informants' views of change. Where, for instance, older men state that they had more respect for the elders and were less adulterous than younger men today, then we have to decide how far this is a historical statement and how far it is a characteristic of the system – that older men have always held this view. How far is today's youngest age-set an accurate replica of the more senior age-sets when they were young, and how far does it represent a novel form in the general process of irreversible change? To cite the earlier example, if there appears to be evidence of a weakening of the power of elders to control younger men, then does this reflect a fundamental change or does it merely echo a characteristic of the system over time: an oscillation or perhaps a phase within the age-set cycle?

Oral traditions among East African age-set societies tend to stress the functional persistence of earlier practices before their more recent modifications, and pay less attention to indigenous processes of change. However, given the extent to which 'traditions' were obliged to respond democratically to circumstance and given the fallibility of collective memories, earlier shifts in practice are altogether more likely than changelessness persisting over time. In this context, the balance of power between old and young, and even the profile of ageing itself, could well have varied from generation to generation and from age-set to age-set. Early visitors to the Maasai, for instance, gave conflicting impressions of the degree to which elders actually controlled the *murran*: sometimes they were seen to do so, and at other times the *murran* apparently were uncontrollable (Spencer, 1988: 20). Again, in the Nyakyusa region there are accounts that give the impression of stability when peaceful husbandry seems to have prevailed under the watchful eyes of the elders, as against accounts that emphasize local hostilities, suspicion, and the breakdown of diplomatic networks of communication as power shifted away from the indigenous establishment towards predation (Charsley, 1969: 47). Various ethnographies can be read either way. Among the Nyakyusa, for instance, Monica Wilson's early model of juventocracy (if one may coin this term) remains an anthropological classic, but her later writings point towards a background of ultimate power in the hands of the senior generation. On the one hand, this was as fathers who retained control over women, cattle and any other resources that were scarce; and on the other, it was as ritual elders who tended the shrine of the dead chief, enabling them to retain authority over the age system, except for a brief flurry of independence by the younger men on 'coming out' (Wilson, 1951: 22–32; 1959: 4–5, 91–3, 96).

There is an intriguing parallel between Nyakyusa and Maasai in the extent to which popular attention focused on proud young men whose flamboyant glamour and separateness in democratically controlled villages appear to have given them a distinct advantage over older men. Yet, in each case, it was the elders who claimed a higher ritual power and authority to control all processes associated with age-set development and the promotion of young men. Beyond this and giving legitimacy to their authority, there was the extensive knowledge credited to older men alone and associated with their broader experience and opportunity over time to build up strategic networks among their peers. In this very age-conscious region, older men who had lost the glamour and sheer physical energy of youth were still able to cultivate an inviolable moral domain from which they could overawe. Through their claim to knowledge concerning the esoteric aspects of ritual, they controlled the arrangements for marriages and for new age-sets and hence the destinies of younger people. From this stance, the arena controlled by younger men was central to their own affairs, but might be viewed by the elders as a theatre that they themselves ultimately stage-managed. This initiative might slip to the younger men at critical times, providing a temporary release from the regime of the elders, on the one hand, but also a warning indication of the moral as well as physical strength of the opposition, and an intimation that as they grew older so younger men were maturing and must eventually take over the reins of power. The key for elders retaining their authority was to be sensitive to the build-up of forces leading towards the promotion of the younger men before their spirit of protest burgeoned to a point of rebellion.

Generally in traditional age-based systems, it was at a time leading up to a major promotion (for example, Karimojong) or following it (Nyakyusa) or either (Maasai), that younger men might slip out of control. The Maasai pattern seems quite typical of the region. At the point of changeover in the cycle, a relatively young age-set of elders was handed authority over a new age-set of novices, and their credibility as future ritual patrons was tested. With less experience than older men, the reputation of these patrons, and ultimately the authority of the establishment of elders at large, hinged on their ability to wrest the initiative, in asserting control over the new age-set. Each age-set established its own reputation. To the extent that an age-set of novice warriors was seen to take the initiative against traditional enemies, this reflected well on them and their novice patrons. To the extent that they were seen to cause trouble and be out of control, their strength was also seen as a weakness of their patrons. The reputations of more senior age-sets as well as the newly formed ones were at stake. Predatory expansion may also be regarded as a metaphor that describes the career of a high-flying age-set as it builds up a reputation at the expense of less successful predecessors and successors. The orderly procession of ageing described by the age system may conceal a background of uneven achievement.

The involvement of pristine age systems in warfare – the predatory mode of production – is largely a matter for the historical record. In this respect, the survival of such systems to the present may be regarded as an anachronism. Yet this survival is also a historical fact and to this extent I would argue that one has to examine the internal aspects, that is, the role of age systems in the balance of power with age, between older and younger men to account for their persistence in times of peace. Among the Samburu, for instance, my earlier study (1965) suggested that it was the elders' prcference for polygyny that created a shortage of marriageable women and hence the need to suspend young men in a state of prolonged bachelorhood that gave their age system a continuing relevance. The elders retained a regime that perpetuatcd their power to dominate. They created an atmosphere in which they could overawe through a display of ritual superiority and esoteric knowledge, hinging on a belief in their power to curse. In their political prime, they had to sustain the credibility of their ultimate power over younger men in their physical prime. Each new age-set of younger men had to be convinced of the immaturity of their ways and of their understanding, marginalizing them, pinning them down in a prolonged state of adolescence even throughout their twenties with no final purpose other than to play for time while the older men retained their monopoly over marriagable girls for a decade or more. The persistence of polygyny sustained the institution of *murranhood* and hence the age system which controlled the *murran*. In my later work among the Maasai, the *manyata* system of warrior villages appeared to resolve tensions within the family by separating patriarchal fathers and their growing sons, and a similar explanation seemed to underpin the system of age villages in Nyakyusa over a more prolonged period. The regulations of the *gada* generational system served to support the position of the father, on the one hand, and to underpin the rule of primogeniture within the family, on the other. Clearly, while warfare associated with age systems has largely been overtaken by events, cultural preferences underpinning the family survive: and to this extent age systems have survived this transition, albeit in modified form.

## The Growth of the Market Economy and the Demise of Age Systems

In relation to an elder's defence of *gada* as a means towards stemming Somali expansion, I noted that this seemed to echo Trimingham's view of age systems more generally in stemming the advance of Islam. However, this is to lose sight of a counter-argument which is a major aspect of Trimingham's work: that Islam spread into Africa along established trade routes. In other words, it is not the existence of age systems that has prevented the penetration of Islam beyond the coastal hinterland so much as the limits of long-distance trade into areas where age systems have flourished. That is, until comparatively recently when the spread of Somali influence would seem to have followed the further development of trade routes, with Somali traders playing a pioneering role. More generally, I would argue, it is the spread of trade (with or without Islam) that is eroding systems based on age.

Taking a broader view, the process of civilization, by which I mean the spread of urban culture and of capitalism in one form or another, appears to have reduced age systems in various parts of the world, leaving East Africa as the single most important area in which they still survive. But even there, this same process appears on balance to be undermining age as a principle of social stratification.

The Chamus were previously cited as an example of the elaboration of age organization with circumstance, and it is useful to follow their more recent experience as an extension of this. Indeed, Peter Little's (1992) account of the decreasing significance of the Chamus age system may be regarded as a microcosm of what seems poised to occur elsewhere in pastoralist East Africa as popular expectations become ensnared by the insidious growth of self-interest. As the Chamus perceived their traditional society, it had always been the elders who controlled property and the destinies of younger men, as fathers individually and as guardians collectively. In the previous transitions, however, it had been the younger men rather than the elders who had tended to be the pioneers of adaptation, and notably it had been successive age-sets of *murran* during the development of the pastoral dimension of their economy.

Consistent with this pattern, as the advantages of involvement in the market economy began to outweigh those of dispersed pastoralism, it was the younger men especially who seized the initiative and collected the immediate benefits. With successive age-sets, an increasing number became involved in new forms of investment. It was not so much a conversion by a whole age-set of *murran* as a widening gulf over successive age-sets among those who remained close to the pastoralist ideal, those who became wage labourers as a temporary expedient, and those who exploited the backwardness of their area for personal gain. At first, government-sponsored projects and the monetary economy were treated with suspicion and the majority held themselves aloof: cattle as a form of investment over which they had direct control seemed altogether more reliable. Where fathers encouraged their sons to seek some form of wage labour, migrating if necessary and returning with their savings to invest in the family economy, this was seen as an alternative path through *murranhood*. However, a vital link with their age peers was broken, and over the years the expectations of the age system dwindled as increasing numbers sought work elsewhere and as new schooling offered even better job prospects and insights into alternative life-styles and career patterns for those who cared to take the initiative in an arena of enterprise that extended beyond Chamus. On this occasion, it was not normally *murran* who precipitated these innovations, but younger elders who had managed to bypass *murranhood* in the normally accepted sense. The constraints of *murranhood* and the age system were significant by default. Increasingly among younger men, notions of peer group solidarity became strained by new opportunities.

Within a few decades, as the best claims to pasture and irrigation land were taken up by the more enterprising, the options open to others diminished, forcing them into some form of subservience. Increasingly, poorer families lost the ability to tend their own herds and cultivate their own land, and they drifted towards tending the herds and cultivating the land of others as underpaid clients. Hunger then forced them to sell their remaining stock to more successful men, and they became trapped in their poverty, caring for the growing fortunes of others. Even older men found themselves increasingly dependent on the more successful younger men, exchanging their daughters, their stock and their land for cash, because they did not have the means of becoming involved in the cash economy more directly. Whereas the form of stratification in Chamus previously had followed the divisions of the age system, with older men tending to be the more wealthy and younger men sharing similar aspirations for accumulating wealth in the longer term, the new form of stratification now began to divide the society between the minority whose success seemed invincible and the remainder who were increasingly dependent. Age was no longer a relevant factor in control over wealth or opportunity and the age system itself started to become an ossified relic as the fortunes of younger men diversified and the bonds of shared interest no longer drew peers together.

More generally, with the advent of the market economy, recent pastoralist studies no longer focus on the ramifications and nuances of age systems, but rather stress the process of innovation and social and economic differentiation, challenging the traditional balance of power that once lay with older men.[3] It is not younger men as such who have necessarily been in the forefront of change, but those who have been on the fringes of tradition and in direct contact with new economic forces throughout their adult careers. Tradition has persisted for a time, but increasingly it has been tradition that has been relegated to the fringe and the capitalist economy that is in the process of dominating the centre.

In these pastoral societies, there appear always to have been differences in wealth between families, and clearly some men had better prospects than others; but there was also a premise of equality in status between peers and a general notion of equality of opportunity. The best investment open to wealthy men was to cultivate a broad network of stock associates through open-ended gifts as an insurance against hard times. For poorer men, their best chance was to cultivate a reputation for trustworthiness and a commitment to herding which could reverse their fortunes. The concept of equality was displayed in the sharing of good and bad times. As against this pastoralist ideal, it is a characteristic of the market economy that careers diverge and that the networks of commerce create and perpetuate inequalities. Such networks are more selective and consolidate established elites; and as a byproduct they produce the underswell of poverty. In such a situation, relations between rich and poor are based on the denial of shared responsibility. It is in the breakdown of the traditional balance of pastoral wealth, opportunity and expectation, that age systems have become outmoded.

Thus the spread of age systems in the region has been displaced most recently by the spread of the market economy as a more penetrating form of predatory expansion. Sahlins does not appear to have had a Marxist model of capitalism specifically in mind when he emphasized the acquisitive and divisive process of unlimited expansion in his segmentary lineage model, but the two are not incompatible. To this extent, the model – applied to the Somali and not the Nuer – can be equated with the frontal shock-wave of the predatory expansion of the capitalist market. Indeed, I. M. Lewis (1975: 437) has described Somali pastoralists in particular as 'some of the thickest-skinned capitalists on earth'.

## Conclusion

Contributions to this volume range from age systems that have been radically modified under modern conditions to those that continue to operate in situations of regional conflict. The effectiveness of various forms of age organization had a marked relevance for the military balance of power throughout the region in earlier times. However, these military aspects alone could not account for the non-military complexities of these systems, nor for their ramifications across other institutional structures, nor for their persistence after the formal abolition of warfare during the colonial period.

In traditional age systems, control over the process of arriving at elderhood lay with the elders, bolstering their power as heads of families and within the public domain at large. It was in their interest to generate a mixture of consent and discord among younger men, prolonging the period of 'youth' while taking care to build up the stake of these younger men in a system that they would in time inherit. This and the uncertainties of warfare lent a dynamic quality to the process of ageing. The ethos of each age-set and the changing pressures on the age system itself to change varied with the thrust of youth. It was younger men who constantly tested the system and it is they who appear to have been in the forefront of the need to adjust to changing circumstance; and this has been especially true of the most recent adaptations to change.

The intrusion of colonial powers, which reversed the fortunes of successful age-based societies, may be seen as a more potent form of predatory expansion. Ostensibly, the colonial period was typified by a protective barrier not only between rival groups, but also between remoter peoples with intact age systems and the market economy which was restricted as a monopoly for those in the developing areas. In this sense, the first ripples of world capitalism were felt before the shock-wave. Having argued previously that age systems survived the pacification of the area because they were more than just military institutions, it is now clear that this very pacification, and even the earlier pincer penetration of Islamic trading from the north and from the east, were steps towards involvement in world capitalism. Generally, the area was being infiltrated with developing trade, and it is plausible to argue that subsequent developments have been steps along a path that was already predetermined. Over time, and especially since independence, the cash economy and commercial values have penetrated to these remoter areas, and age systems have increasingly been a clear casualty as the market principle has imposed its own less democratic or age-bound patterns of stratification. As a form of predatory expansion, it is without equal.

# Notes

1   Kodola Digali (Legile, 1 August 1994). I am grateful to Getachew Kassa for arranging these meetings and acting as interpreter.
2   Aba Liban Mattarri (Legile, 2 August 1994).
3   For example, Hogg, 1986 (Uaso Boran and Turkana); Sperling, 1987 (Samburu); Kituyi, 1990 (Maasai); Fratkin, 1991 (Ariaal); and also Baxter and Hogg (1990); Markakis (1993); Galaty *et al.* (1981).

# 9 Peacemakers, Prophets, Chiefs & Warriors: Age-Set Antagonisms as a Factor of Political Change among the Kipsigis of Kenya

## TORU KOMMA

The Kipsigis[1] of western Kenya, like their neighbours the Nandi, belong to the Kalenjin cluster of Southern Nilotes. They have a Nandi-type age-set system (*ipinda*). Since the latter half of the nineteenth century their society has undergone profound social change as a result of the incursions led by the Maasai prophets, or *laibon*, from Nandiland, whom the Kipsigis, like the Nandi, call *orkoiik*, and British colonial rule, in particular, the imposition of administrative chiefs. In this chapter I shall try to account for the reaction of the Kipsigis age-set system to these changes.

My main points are as follows. First, the Kipsigis system was quite different from the Nandi one in its social function, for the two ethnic groups had started to follow different courses of political development in the mid-nineteenth century. Secondly, when the warrior grade had recaptured its social function through the recruitment to the King's African Rifles (KAR), the *ipinda* came to terms with the colonial administration, so that administrative chiefs who were ex-KAR veterans elemena ted the prophets. Thus the age-set system facilitated a comparatively smooth transition of Kipsigis society up to the 1910s. Thirdly, although the system's social function became more or less paralyzed during the 1920s and 1930s, owing to the decline of the recruitment demands of the KAR, it acquired, during the 1950s and 1960s, a completely new social function in the context of an ethnic movement called the Kalenjin phenomemon.

### The Differentiation of the Nandi and Kipsigis Age-systems

The Kipsigis age system as it existed before the end of the nineteenth century can be reconstructed as follows based on oral tradition. The central social institution was the male age-sets (*ipinwek*) which were organized on the basis of the entire Kipsigis territory. The seven age-sets followed a cyclical pattern with consolidated names, existing simultaneously. Each age-set consisted of a number of sub-sets which were formed every few years through circumcision and the subsequent initiation ceremonies. Members of the same age-set had a very strong sense of group identity. The age-sets passed through three age-grades: boys, warriors and elders. Special importance was attached to the warrior grade, while the boys' grade existed only as a transitional stage. After the first sub-set of a new age-set had been circumcised and had completed its period of seclusion, the incumbent warrior grade retired to elderhood. Young elders, however, still continued to participate in raids and warfare, although they had only a supportive role. As successive sub-sets were formed, the age-set of warriors accumulated members and power. The span of age-sets might be assessed as between fifteen and twenty years; no exact data are available to scrutinize it from other than oral tradition. The warriors were organized into four military units or regiments (*boriosiek*), membership of which was inherited patrilineally. Members of all four regiments lived scattered throughout Kipsigisland.

A paradox of the Kipsigis age system is that it is more difficult to reconstruct it during the 'historical era' than during the pre-colonial period. Let us examine the differing lists of Kipsigis age-set and sub-set sequences from various sources presented in Table 9.1. While two early studies (Dobbs, 1921: 56–7; Barton, 1923: 60) list a number of age-set names with their initiation years, they apparently fail to distinguish between age-sets and sub-sets. Peristiany (1939: 42–3) and I myself list sub-sets as extensively as possible. There are, however, considerable differences between the two lists and neither of us has been able to identify the opening years of initiation of the sub-sets. In fact, it is not easy to figure out the real time sequence of age-sets and sub-sets over the whole period.

Despite contradictions in the data and their fragmentation, Table 9.1 may be useful for our discussion. Although it has been generally assumed, both by the Kipsigis and the Nandi themselves and by outside scholars, that the two age systems are homologous, the contrast between the Kipsigis and the Nandi systems is remarkable. The Nandi system, if we believe Huntingford (1953b: 49), has been extremely stable and consistent over a long period of time. New age-sets are formed precisely every fifteen years and an age-set consists of four sub-sets which have consolidated cyclical names. Among the Kipsigis, on the other hand, the interval between age-sets is irregular and the number of sub-sets in an age-set is not fixed. Each sub-set has a specific name taken from an event that took place during its formation. Insufficiency of data is not solely responsible for the partial understanding of the Kipsigis age-set system. Other reasons

Table 9.1 *Comparative table of Kipsigis (and Nandi) age-sets and sub-sets*

| Dobbs, 1921:56–7 | Barton, 1923:60 | Peristiany, 1939:42–3 | Komma | Nandi (Huntingford 1953b:49) |
|---|---|---|---|---|
| Maina 1856 | | | | *Saawe:* 1851<br>Chong'iniek<br>Kipalkong'ek<br>Tetekatik<br>Kiptoiinik |
| Chuma 1861 | | | | |
| Sowee 1866 | Sowee 1866 | *Sawee* | *Saawe* | *Kipkoimet* 1866<br>Chong'iniek<br>Kipalkong'ek<br>Tetekatik<br>Kiptoiinik |
| Kiptaimen 1871 | Korongoro 1871 | *Kipkoimet.* | *Korongoro (=Kipkoimet)*<br>Kiptoinen<br>Kimuguchen<br>Kiptor-mesendet<br>Kibelkot<br>Kimariri | |
| Kipturmesendet 1876 | Kiptil-mesendet 1876 | Kiptormesendet<br>Kibelkot<br>Kimerere | | |
| Kaboloin 1881 | Kimororik 1881 | *Kaplelach:*<br>Kipalayeng<br>Kimutawet<br>Masiba | *Kaplelach:*<br>Kibal-oeng' (commet) 1882<br>Kimut-aiywet<br>Kimasiba | *Kaplelach:* 1881<br>Chong'iniek<br>Kipalkong'ek<br>Tetekatik<br>Kiptoiinik |
| Kimasiba 1886 | Kimut-Aiyuet 1886 | | | |
| Kabaocha 1891 | Ka-papucha 1891 | *Kimnyige:*<br>Kibebucha<br>Kipsiljoget | *Kimnyige:*<br>Kebebucha (leaf-hopper) 1891<br>Kipsil-choget | *Kimnyike.* 1896<br>Chong'iniek<br>Kipalkong'ek<br>Tetekatik |
| Kipsiljoget 1896 | Kipsin-joget 1896 | | | |
| Tabarit 1901 | Kapar-iit 1901 | Tabarit<br>Kiptilosiek | Tabarit | |

| Set | Yr | Set | Yr | Keptechoret subsets | Yr | Names & events | Kiptoiinik subsets | Yr |
|---|---|---|---|---|---|---|---|---|
| Kosigo | 1906 | Kosigo | 1906 | Keptechoret / *Nyongi:* Kiptilgarit, Kosigo, Kipterangerek, Martartebeit | 1902 | Kipirtyorik, Kiptechoret / *Nyongi:* Kiptil-garit (Uganda railway)1901, Kipter-angerek, Kosigo, Kimatar-tebe[-it] | Kiptoiinik / *Nyongi:* Chong'iniek, Kipalkong'ek, Tetekatik, Kiptoiinik | 1911 |
| Kipsirgot | 1911 | Kipsia-kot | 1911 | Kipsirgot | | Kipsir-got (Halley's comet) 1910, Kiptil-barwa (poll tax) | | |
| Buloo | 1916 | Buloo | 1916 | Kipsorbosiek, Boulou | | Bulu (blue finger stamp for proving obedience) | | |
| | | Mesiawa | 1921 | *Maina:* Mesiewa, Kassie, Silling | 1921 | *Maina:* Mesiewa (=Kasie) / Siling' (shilling coinage) 1922-3, Kiptiltiliet, Chemorta, Silo-bai (Orchardson 1961)1929 | *Maina:* Chong'iniek, Kipalkong'ek, Tetekatik, Kiptoiinik | 1926 |
| | | | | Silobai, Kipkulmengit, Kiptindinie / *Chuma:* Kimingiet | 1931 | *Chuma:* Tuberet / Kiptabot (famine of cassava)1941 / *Sawe:* (no sub-sets) | *Juma:* Chong'iniek, Kipalkong'ek, Tetekatik, Kiptoiinik | 1940 |

*Notes:* Main set names are in italics. Nandi set names are modified in accordance with the present Kipsigis orthography are the structural-functional bias of the analyses and their predominant focus on the morphological aspect, as is the case with Prins (1953), and the assumption of homology with the Nandi system. It appears that they all neglect the actual ethnographic and historical contexts.

Table 9.1 by itself suggests that by the middle of the nineteenth century Kipsigis society had already started to diverge from the common model. This was the precise period when the two ethnic groups, under circumstances specific to each, started to take different courses of political development.

It is generally assumed that all the peoples of the Kalenjin group shared a uniform age-system.

> It appears that at some stage in the past, at least two hundred years ago, all the Kalenjin shared, or adopted from a common source, be it internal or external, a uniform system of eight successive age-set names – Maina, Chuma, Sawe, Korongoro, Kipkoiimet, Kaplelach, Kimnyike and Nyongi (Sutton, 1973:10–11).

If the above assumption is correct, at one stage the Kipsigis must have dropped the Kipkoiimet age-set while the Nandi dropped Korongoro. It is also possible that the two merged into a single age-set, thus forming systems with seven age-sets. Three or four centuries ago, the Proto-Kalenjin presumably migrated in *pororiet* (pl. *pororosiek*), the largest territorial, military, and administrative unit. The Nandi were a federation of a number of *pororosiek* which settled on the Chemungal plateau (Magut, 1969: 96–7), while the Kipsigis were another federation of four *pororosiek* which migrated southwards and occupied its present residence, i.e. the present Kericho and Bomet Districts, at approximately the same time as the Nandi did.

According to oral tradition, the four Kipsigis' *pororosiek* originated in the following way:

> Another development which had taken place by the time of the Kalenjin occupation of Mt Elgon was the emergence of fighting units amongst the separate groups. Among the Kipsigis, these fighting units (*poriosiek*) [*pororosiek* in Nandi] were named Kipkaige, Ngetunyo, Kasanet and Kebeni. It is said that the time when some young men ran away with cattle and girls the elders sent a deputation of other young men to find them and to hear their reasons for deserting. These messengers were named kasanet, a word derived from *kas* ('to listen'). Under threat of a curse some of the deserters returned and were named Kebeni, which means 'to stay longer'. Those who did not return became known as Kipkaige, 'those who separated', while those who had never run away were given the name of Ngetunyo (*kenget* 'to remain', or *kutuny*, 'to kneel'). These names became the names of the fighting units. The old men foretold that the Kipkaige and Kebeni would at first be great enemies, but that one day they would join forces (Lang'at, 1969: 78).

Note that this oral tradition tells us the origin of the four military units of the Kipsigis, and that even divisive opposition between age-grades, i.e. elders plus warriors vs youths, was a fundamental element of the Kipsigis' political dynamism, just as it has always been.

In the course of events, a differentiation in social organization emerged between the two groups. Among the Nandi, the *pororosiek* remained autonomous. Among the Kipsigis, on the other hand, members of the four *pororosiek* started to reside intermingled during the latter half of the nineteenth century (Lang'at, 1969: 84–5). In contemporary Kipsigis language *pororiet* has the general meaning of 'tribe', 'ethnic group' or 'nation', while the original territorial, military, and administrative unit, which, probably in the middle of the century, was turned into a mere military unit, is now called *poriet* (pl. *poriosiek*). Thus, in modern usage, *pororiet* and *poriet* have clearly distinct meanings.

The political system of the Nandi was one of acephalous segmentation with the *pororosiek* as the largest sections, although at times of crisis representatives of the *pororosiek* used to gather as a kind of 'federal council'. The Maasai *laibon*, who came to Nandiland in the middle of the nineteenth century, facilitated the political integration of the Nandi to the extent that before long they established themselves as the central authority (Magut, 1969: 97). Among the Kipsigis, however, political rivalry and conflict between the *poriosiek* had been completely resolved as a result of their intermingled settlement. The sense of unity of the Kipsigis seems to have been growing throughout the political innovation. It is my argument that this could be an essential factor in explaining why the Kipsigis did not accept the Maasai prophets, while the Nandi did.

The political dynamics of the age-set system in a segmentary society appears to be determined by two variables: the relations between territorial units, and the relations between age-sets. Relations between senior and junior age-sets were characterized by tension and conflict. The Kipsigis expression *lugetap ipinwek*, literally meaning 'inter-age-set warfare', refers to this latter aspect. There is abundant evidence in the oral tradition telling of 'revolts' or 'defection' by junior age-sets. Peristiany refers to the inter-age-set warfare fought between the Kipkoiimet warriors (more properly speaking the Korongoro, for they had abandoned Kipkoiimet) and the would-be Kaplelach who were pushing for initiation, early in the 1880s. From his accounts it seems Peristiany mistakenly took *legutap ipinwek* to be a proper noun:

> I have met some old Kabelelach who related to me the hardship their age-set had to undergo before persuading the Kipkoymet to retire. When they were sufficiently strong, they made a sortie and attacked the Kipkoymet; but the elders acted as mediators and the Kipkoymet retired. This is known to this day as the war of the Ipinwek (Peristiany, 1939: 31–2).

We have already seen, in the oral tradition cited above by Lang'at, that a somewhat similar kind of conflict resulted in the creation of the four *poriosiek* among the Kipsigis. Note that it says, 'Some young men ran away with cattle and girls'. Another version I know refers distinctly to well matured boys instead of the ambiguous 'young men'.

One oral tradition tells us of a case where runaways formed a new ethnic group outside the Kalenjin. They were said to be cowards who could not endure the ordeal of circumcision. The old men pursued them and there was fighting, but the deserters refused to return. They grew up uncircumcised and their descendants became the Luo and the Lango (Lang'at, 1969: 76–7). Although this story may not reflect historical fact, it does reflect the general idea that inter-age-set conflict may be maximized before the opening of a new age-set, and that it may have disastrous consequences. While among the Nandi the prophets became the ultimate authority deciding the timing of the opening and closing of age-sets, among the Kipsigis inter-age-set rivalry and conflict continued to play an essential role in the acephalous political structure. As Fortes has argued, initiation ceremonies provide an effective way of transforming the rebellious power of youngsters into constructive power (Fortes, 1956: 91–3). In order to achieve this end, it was necessary to maximize generation conflict, or inter-age-set conflict in the Kipsigis context, between youngsters and warriors. The oral traditions mentioned above fully support this argument.

Seen from a different perspective, however, Kipsigis society, at the end of the last century, had already paved the way for a central political leadership covering the entire society. Though Kipsigis society has been seen as highly egalitarian throughout pre-colonial times, in fact even then a charismatic personality did emerge. His name was arap Kisiara, a successful *kirwogindet* or peacemaker (see below). According to Manners, he must have been a person of considerable status and personal charisma to have left the image – with even a few people – that he was truly a chief of all the Kipsigis (Manners, 1967: 251). He was the one who played the leading role in the federal council meeting which endorsed the reorganization of the *pororosiek*. In a sense, the Kipsigis as a whole became a single *pororiet* when the council decided that the initiation of any sub-sets was to be held throughout Kipsigisland at the same time, while the Nandi *pororosiek* continued to hold theirs independently of each other.

Another factor which reinforced the tendency towards differentiation of the two systems was the lowering of the age of initiation among the Kipsigis. It used to be the rule, among both the Nandi and the Kipsigis, that a new age-set could not be opened until all members (and their wives) of the former age-set with the same name had died out. After the devastating defeat in the battle of Mogori, around 1890, against the agricultural Bantu-speaking Gusii, which wiped out almost an entire generation of warriors and brought Kisiara's leadership into open question, the youngsters were initiated in a hurry to create a new body of warriors. The long-lived rule of waiting for the death of the name-sake set of retired elders was pigeonholed for a period.

## Marginal Men as Peacemakers

A grasp of the political structure around the turn of the century is indispensable for understanding the way the Kipsigis age-set system reacted to modernization. The neighbourhood (*kokwet*) was and still is the basic social unit of Kipsigis society. Although there are exogamous patrilineal clans, clan members are dispersed widely all over Kipsigisland and lineage cohesion is not very strong. Neighbourhood is therefore more important than clan. It should be remembered, however, that each of the neighbourhoods, clans, age-sets and military units had a different functional domain. Moreover, membership of each of these groups was cross-cutting. A person's group identity was therefore multiple and tessellated. A neighbourhood, in turn, was a mosaic of members with tessellated identity. It was an administrative and judicial unit under the collective responsibility of all male adult members. Among these the neighbourhood leader (*kiptaiyatap kokwet*), who was also called neighbourhood elder (*boiyotap kokwet*) , played a leading role. And the peacemakers ('advisory judges'), or *kirwogik*, were even more important, although they had no specific area under their jurisdiction. One or a few peacemakers were invited from outside the relevant neighbourhood, or neighbourhoods in the case of a dispute involving more than one, and were put in charge of the court. They were seen as personalities transcending parochial neighbourhood interests and embodying universal Kipsigis values. Their position and role hold the key to understanding Kipsigis society.

Other political offices of significance were as follows. The married warriors of a neighbourhood had a 'war leader' (*kiptaiyatap murenik*) and fought defensive warfare under his command. The prerequisites for being a war leader were valour and eloquence. A loosely organized cluster of neighbourhoods also had a 'military unit leader' (*kiptaiyatap boriet*), and each of three territorial sections, Belgut, Buret, and Sot, had a 'great regiment leader' (*kiptaiyatneo nebo boriet*), who organized offensive warfare. Peacemakers were chosen from retired military unit and great military unit leaders. Eloquence was also a prerequisite for them. 'Initiation elders' (*boisiekap tumdo*) presided over the initiation ceremonies of the age-sets from several neighbourhoods. They had a considerable influence over the timing of opening and closing the age-sets, and consequently over the retirement of warriors into elderhood. These leaders were chosen because of their personal abilities. Their offices were not inherited. Their authority was limited to particular contexts and they enjoyed no privileges in daily life.

The eloquence of the peacemakers was described by a special verb:

**193**

*berir.* Among their principal tasks was the making of peace between the Kipsigis and other ethnic groups, especially with the Maasai. Kisiara, who united the Kipsigis, was very famous for his eloquence. His tongue was said to keep moving like a snake. Yet he was a marginal man. When young, he lived among the Kisonko Maasai. He was a *kipsagarindet* ('stranger'), someone who had left Kipsigis society, or who was adopted into it from outside. Kisiara was able to become a political leader because of his command of Maasai. His rhetorical powers are still clearly remembered today. They resembled the style used in riddles (*tangochik*) and by tricksters in Kipsigis folklore. The term *kiptangoiyan* ('riddle man') is used for another category of marginal person: a man who behaves childishly even after initiation. A 'riddle man' can be thought to be a 'stranger', so to speak, precipitated from within the Kipsigis society (Komma, 1991).

Besides peacemaking, peacemakers were in charge of the neighbour-hood courts and of supposedly impartial distribution of raided cattle. They were not only peacemakers but also mediators. In other words, they were responsible for adjusting people's reciprocal activities in general. Herein lay the uniqueness of their role.

Although adopted foreigners were treated as equals, they were kept under social supervision for two generations. Many of the war leaders and peacemakers came from this category of marginal people. Their power of speech was kept in check by another kind of power of speech: the collective curse of the elders. The source of the cursing power of the elders lies in their closeness to the spirits of the ancestors. Some clans have special powers of cursing, such as the Kipsamaek and Kibaek. They are said to represent the 'real Kipsigis', in contrast to clans of non-Kalenjin origin, which had a large membership, especially in the southern part of Kipsigisland. While Kipsigis society absorbed a lot of foreigners and was quite adaptive to new situations, it also had its mechanisms for keeping foreigners under control and for suppressing rebellions against the religious authority of the elders who were at the centre of Kipsigis society.

Oda takes chiefly office as being necessarily placed outside the com-munity in order to promote the reciprocity of exchange and prevent the emergence of individualistic and divisive interests, and construct a focus of public concern (Oda, 1994: 110). If we accept his definition, we may well call peacemakers chiefs. They regulated specific interests in and between neighbourhoods, and were always invited in from outside. They had no particular area attached to their office. Although they were in charge of the redistribution of cattle raided by warriors, as retired elders they were never part of military units. They were internalized foreigners, marginal men, standing between Kipsigis society and its enemies. Their authority derived from their outsideness and marginality.

## Centralism Under the Prophets

It seems that Kisiara exercised extraordinary and unprecedented power. He had led the epoch-making reform of the military units system. The four originally independently operating military units, which were organized in two competing or rival moieties, were unified and brought under a single high command (Lang'at, 1969: 84–5). This had a remarkable effect on the military strength of the Kipsigis and enhanced Kisiara's authority. Manners attributes his consolidation of power to the need to meet the threats from Arab caravans (Manners, 1967: 250–1). In any event, it became a rule that people could not go raiding without his permission and only members of the Kapkerichek, his clansmen, could become war leaders (1969: 249–50). At one time Kisiara himself resorted to *latet*, the irrevocable ritual of becoming betrothed to a girl of his own clan, a certain chebo Chepkok. This was a bold challenge to the rule of clan exogamy and to the clan elders. It meant that he challenged the accepted horizontal segmentation of Kipsigis society that structured the system of reciprocal exchange, and tried to establish a new system of redistribution with himself at the top. If this incestuous marriage had been approved, the Kipsigis political structure would have collapsed and Kisiara would have been like a 'king' (*laitoriat*). The Kapkerichek elders sought a compromise. A clan-separation ritual was carried out creating the Kapkaon clan to which Kisiara belonged. The elders then approved the marriage. It is said that an awful, deadly oath (*muma*) was part of the ritual. Thus Kisiara's arbitrary exercise of power was brought under control.

Kisiara's authority was further undermined by the disastrous defeat in the battle of Mogori (ca. 1890) against the Gusii, which is believed to have annihilated almost all the Kipsigis warriors. On the eve of the battle, a Nandi prophet, Kipchonber arap Koilegen, sought refuge in Kipsigisland, allegedly after having lost a power-contest with his younger brother,[2] the sixth chief prophet of the Nandi, Koitalel arap Samoei. At that time Koilegen's influence among the Kipsigis was almost non-existent. He sent a messenger (*maotiyot*) to the warriors conveying the prophetic message that they would be defeated and that they should cancel the military expedition. The warriors abused and ridiculed him, saying 'Does the prophet bring us cattle? You coward!', and they drove him away. The fact that his prophecy came true dramatically enhanced his authority. From then on he was held in fear. At that point it seemed that the Kipsigis might adopt prophets along the same lines as the Nandi seemingly had done a few decades before.

According to Kipsigis oral traditions, Nandi prophets were originally refugees from the Sigilai Maasai (the Uas Nkishu Maasai in reality). The first prophet, an ancestor of Koilegen, was believed to be the son of a snake which had been adopted by a childless Maasai woman. When the man grew up, he could obtain water from underground, as he wished, even during drought, and his cattle grew fat. Sensing that other Maasai, in fear of his power, were making plans to assassinate him, he first fled to the Keiyo, a group of Kalenjin speakers, and then to the neighbouring Nandi, who were suffering from hunger at the time. He called in a large herd of buffaloes by means of his magic, and let the people hunt them. In the meantime, he also sent a herd of buffaloes to Luoland in the southwest. While the Luo were busy hunting, he sent the Nandi to raid the cattle of the Luo. On another occasion he made the Nandi raid the cattle of a group of foreigners he had called in. In this way he made the Nandi prosperous. Be it true or not, this oral tradition is a fair representation of the Kipsigis view of prophets. Koilegen was essentially a stranger, even in his homeland, who brought in wealth from outside, relying on supernatural power whose source, symbolized by the snake, was again derived from outside the community. At the same time, he was always under threat of being murdered.

They say that Koilegen could control rain. He foretold where and when people could raid cattle with certainty, indicating the exact colour configuration of the cattle to be stolen. He also dispensed war medicine to make warriors immune to the enemy's attack. He set up messengers (*maotiik*) at different localities throughout Kipsigisland to make his will known. In return for his guidance, Koilegen received a share of the booty. He took any woman, unmarried or married, for himself without paying bridewealth. These wives neither cultivated nor carried out domestic duties other than cooking. At times they mobilized people to work in their fields. A certain portion of the first harvest was given to them. Koilegen had a few old male servants (*otwagiik*) from poor families who fetched water and cut firewood, tasks normally carried out by wives, and took care of his domestic animals.

There is a sharp contrast between the prophets and the peacemakers. The latter mediated in relations of reciprocity and in a fair distribution of booty, but did not generate wealth themselves. The prophets, on the other hand, did generate new wealth, but they also exploited the people. They remained outside and transcended the system of traditional reciprocal relations such as those between kinsfolk and affines which integrated clans. The principle of reciprocal exchange is also a prerequisite for the resolution of inter-clan feuds through the payment of blood wealth. Negation of the principle undermines the system of compensation and leads to chronic feuding. As Oda has argued,

> Killing between brothers of the same agnatic kin is against the rule of reciprocal exchange of violence between kin groups, and makes the groups

invalid as exchange units. Thus the killing is the same as incest [my translation] (Oda, 1994: 119).

Koilegen and Koitalel bitterly contested the position of chief prophet among the Nandi. The fact that people could not directly approach prophets but had to communicate with them through messengers, suggests that they rejected reciprocal relations even at the level of language communication. From these and similar indications we can understand that the Kipsigis eventually started to call their prophets 'rulers of the land' (*biikap emet*) (Toweett, 1979: 45).

Among the Kipsigis the consolidation of power by the prophets came to an abrupt end with the advent of British colonial rule. Punitive expeditions against the Kipsigis started in 1905 in retaliation for a raid by the Sot (so-called Sotik),[3] one of the three territorial sections of the Kipsigis, on the Maasai. In April 1905, Donald Stewart, then Commissioner of the East African Protectorate, reported that the Sot had raided the Maasai of Elburgon, killing fourteen Maasai and capturing a large number of cattle, sheep, and goats (Mungeam, 1966: 141). The Maasai reported this to the colonial government. A punitive patrol was sent, in which Maasai irregulars took part. As a result, all the Maasai women and children taken by the Sot, together with almost all the captured stock, were recovered. In addition, 2,000 head of cattle and 3,000 sheep and goats were captured from the Soti as 'loot stock'. It was reported that 92 Soti were killed (ibid.: 143).

In 1913 the Sot raided the Maasai at Melili and looted their cattle. The government did not miss this chance to teach the Sot another lesson. Before dispatching a patrol, it sent an ultimatum to the Belgut and Buret sections, declaring that the government intended to punish the Sot and inquiring whether the Belgut and Buret belonged to the same tribe as the Sot. If so, they would also be punished; if not, they would be spared. It should be remembered that at the time the government did not always recognize the Kipsigis as a separate and unified tribe, although this was simply to suit their own convenience in order to 'divide and rule'. The decision always lay in the government's hands, never the Kipsigis'. Even today, scholars often share the same attitude.

> ... the Kipsigis did not achieve the same degree of unification as the Nandi; and, in the early days of British administration, the three main divisions ... were sometimes regarded as separate tribes (Sutton, 1973: 8).

Koilegen's network of messengers had not reached the Sot at the time.[4] However, the government chief of the southern Buret was a former 'military unit leader' and a messenger of the prophet. His name was Kibii arap Cheriro. He answered, in accordance with the interests of the prophet, that the Sot were not Kipsigis. However, the Belgut and Buret protested against this. A big meeting was held in which the Belgut and Buret confirmed that the Sot were their own people and that they would stand by them. They offered shelter to the cattle of the Sot, and were also punished by the patrol which confiscated as many cattle as possible, chased the Kipsigis into the bush, and fined them 16,000 rupees. Soon afterwards, the whole of Kipsigisland, deserted by its inhabitants, was burnt by the government in order to turn it into land suitable for European settlement. This is how Kipsigisland was devastated and the Kipsigis became a single 'tribe' within the framework of a British colony.

## The Era of the Chiefs

During the early stages of the colonial administration, the government demarcated the territory of the various tribes and, within its framework, allocated administrative units such as districts and locations. Thus in each location of Kipsigisland an administrative chief was appointed, based on the recommendations of the people. What sort of men were recommended? According to Manners, they were usually 'lesser known and even obscure' men (Manners, 1967: 321). In fact, they were often strangers, messengers of prophets, and 'riddle men'.[5] There was arap Taptugen who learned English by working as a servant for a white man. Arap Tengecha was one of them. Tengecha belonged to the Omotik, a group of hunter-gatherers who live in a symbiotic and subordinate relation with the Ikwobek Maasai. In due time Tengecha came to be known as an excellent government chief, and in present-day Kericho, the centre of Kipsigisland, a busy street has been named after him. A certain 'riddle man' called Kiplanykot ('roof climber') was also said to have been recommended. He was feared because of his peculiar and evil habit of climbing up (*lany*) the roofs of people's huts (*kot*), and breaking the apex pole which symbolizes the reproductive power of the hut owner.

This marginality of the administrative chiefs is a reminder of the marginality of the peacemakers. Like them, the chiefs were often opposed by the elders and turned into the object of their curses. Many early chiefs did not live long because, as people say, they were cursed by elders (Komma, 1992).

After the bulk of the warriors died in the battle of Mogori, a lot of cattle were simply grazing around without being used for bridewealth. By lowering the age of initiation and shortening the interval between successive sub-sets the Kipsigis tried to make better use of this wealth. Thus, within a short period, Kipsir-choget and Tabarit, sub-sets of the Kimnyige age-set, were formed, and the Kipsigis again obtained warriors.

The prophets, however, now began to oppose the formation of new and more age-sets by threatening that it would bring death to the cattle, because they wanted to strengthen their authority and influence by means of regulating the age-sets. In any event, the new age-set of Nyongi was formed around 1901. The sub-set names of the new age-set offer vivid illustrations of the conflicts among the Kipsigis, the prophets, and the colonial government. The first sub-set was called Kiptil-garit, which means 'those who bought railroad tickets'. These were the youngsters who were impatient and took the Uganda railroad train in order to be initiated in Nandiland. Kiptil-garit and the next sub-set, Kipter-ankeret, were therefore not considered to be properly formed sub-sets. They had only a minor and transitional status between the age-sets of Kimnyige and Nyongi.

In 1906, a group of young men secretly underwent initiation in Koiwa, a remote bush area in Sot. This sub-set was named Kosigo (implying 'bush or somewhere'). They acted against the will of even the chief prophet, Koilegen, who was said to have overwhelmed minor groups by then who came into Kipsigisland from around the time of the defeat of Mogori onwards. When other young men followed suit, the prophets were obliged to recognize the new sub-set. This was a blow to their authority. It is interesting to note that the initiation of the Kosigo almost coincided with the establishment of colonial rule in Kipsigisland by the Soti punitive expedition of 1905. Subsequent names of sub-sets and their literal meanings are as follows:

| | |
|---|---|
| Kimatar-tebe | – those who did not even finish a four gallon tin, |
| Kipsir-got | – those who mark huts, |
| Kiptil-barwa | – those who issue receipts, |
| Bulu | – blue stamps. |

The first name refers to the fact that their initiation period was so drastically cut short that an initiate did not even finish a four gallon tin of grain by the time he came out. The second and third were respectively formed during the introduction of hut and poll taxes. The last refers to the custom of putting blue ink on the thumb as a sign of loyalty during their employment as squatters at the plantations of white settlers.

Koilegen was also said to have opposed the formation of the Kipsir-got sub-set. In this case his messengers tried hard to mediate in the relationship between the prophet and the people.

The chief 'orkoiyot' (seer), Kipchomber arap Koilegen again, had declared that no circumcision should be done in any part of Kipsigis because, as he 'foresaw', this would bring disaster upon the land. This 'orkoiyot' was an extremely powerful figure, being a brother of the famous Koitalel arap Samo ei of Nandi. Besides, his 'maotik' (consultants) included such chiefs as arap Mastamet himself, arap Cheriro, and arap Tombo. But he was prevailed upon eventually – by persuasion – and he allowed the circumcision of boys in only one seclusion hut ('menjet') to be built in arap Mastamet's homestead . To this hut, a total of 175(?) [sic] boys flocked from all over Kipsigis (Korir, 1974: 165).

T. Toweett, the Kipsigis politician and linguist, and the first Kipsigis graduate of the then Makerere High School in Kampala, sheds further light on the mediating role of messengers: 'The Laibon [prophets] were like the District Commissioners and their messengers were like chiefs who act between the District Commissioners and the people' (1979: 44). Manners expresses a similar view. 'It is significant ... for they are the link between the administrators and the people' (1967: 264).

I would argue that some messengers (*maotiik*) were appointed as government chiefs because the Kipsigis saw something in common between the old office and the new one of government chief. Administrative chiefs were mediators like the peacemakers, but, more importantly, they also received tribute (taxes) and levied forced labour, like the prophets. If this analogy can be extended further, one can say that the colonial administrators were seen as prophet-like rather than peacemaker-like rulers in the sense that they exercised arbitrary power as collectors of taxes and acted as redistribution agents. This redistributive function was apparent especially in relation to the distribution of food in periods of famine.

The nineteenth-century Kipsigis suffered a series of famines, just as their ancestors did, and these are still well remembered today. For instance, in the period preceding colonization they were successively stricken by the 'famine of leather' (*lubetap magatet*), during which people ended up eating leather artefacts, the 'famine of no donkey's bray' (*kimaut sigiriet*) during which people ate even the most ominous animals, donkeys, and the 'hunger of the Gusii' '(*lubetap kosobek*) in which the Kipsigis gave their children to the Gusii in exchange for food. During the colonial era, the 'hunger of the road' (*lubetap barabara*) came, when the government supplied relief gain to those who worked on road construction. During the 'hunger of cassava' (*lubetap taptoiyat*), Gregory Smith, the British administrator at the time, searched the loft (*tabot*) of every hut, to see whether the occupant qualified for the distribution of grain. Thereafter he was known as the 'loft man' (Kiptabot).

Elders could influence messengers and administrative chiefs by their collective curses (*chubisiet*). Cheriro, who was both a particularly loyal messenger of the chief prophet and an administrative chief, is said to have been cursed to death. The cursing method was only effective, however, among the Kipsigis in particular and the Kalenjin in general. It had no effect on prophets of Maasai origin, whom the Kipsigis people regarded as immune to this form of control, since they were foreigners, or at most strangers. The only alternatives open to the elders were to kill them, as the

Nandi did, or to swear a reciprocal oath on one another's life, a combination of curse and sorcery which was termed *muma*. *Muma* is also considered effective between Kipsigis and foreigners and is sworn as part of peacemaking ceremonies. This also demonstrates the 'stranger-hood' of prophets in Kipsigis society.

Although warriors continued to consult the prophets about the auspiciousness of cattle raids and thefts, the prophets, as the *Pax Britannica* was established, were no longer able lawfully to mobilize warriors for raids. As a result, they largely lost their redistributive function. In the eyes of the bulk of the Kipsigis public, they remained only as exploiters, which was in marked contrast to British administrators at the time.

The confrontation between prophets and people entered the final stage during the 1930s. Between 1933 and 1935 there were persistent incidents in which huts belonging to opponents of the prophets, such as Christian converts, were burnt down. With the government firmly in place, the people were not able to open a counterattack. The attacks were reported to the government and the prophets were blamed as sorcerers of foreign origin, who had their own government and levied their own taxes. In 1935 all members of the prophets' clan, regardless of sex, were arrested and detained on the uninhabited island of Gwasi in Lake Victoria. This was an unprecedented measure, taking into account that the prophets' clan of the Nandi, which was less deeply implicated in armed resistance but was nonetheless suspected of involvement in cattle thefts, was allowed to remain in its own location in the Nandi Reserve, where, at a later stage, they were also placed under government scrutiny (Anderson, 1995: 185). Before their detention, an oath-taking ceremony was held at Kericho by elders and prophets. The prophets admitted that they had been practising sorcery (*ponisiet*) and swore that they would never come back. Any breach of this oath was to result in death. Both parties drank sacred salty water (*sugutek*) from a human skull, as the severest type of *muma*.

It is significant that the leaders who arose to eliminate the prophets were government chiefs who had been KAR (King's African Rifles) veterans. Many young men were recruited to the KAR during the First World War, most of them members of the Kosigo sub-set. According to Toweett, Torongei arap Taptugen, the former government chief mentioned above, claimed that the Kosigo were forced to join the army and to fight on behalf of the British (Toweett, 1979: 71). That is why the Kipsigis call the First World War the 'war of Kosigo' (*lugetap Kosigo*). After the war the British administrator Gregory Smith, alias Kiptabot, reduced the number of Kipsigis administrative chiefs from seventeen to five (1979: 70–1), and all five of the newly appointed chiefs were ex-KAR veterans and, as is generally believed, Kosigo age-mates. Thus, the same Kosigo who, in the first decade of the century, struggled to form their own sub-set against the stern opposition of the chief prophet, were, in the 1930s, the main force behind the expulsion of the prophets from Kipsigisland. It should be added that Kipsigis men recruited to the KAR were generally from a poor background and from families which had suffered most from exploitation and oppression at the hands of the prophets.

The elimination of the prophets by the Kosigo can be seen as a triumph of the traditional political structure, the dynamism of which has been maintained in the balancing of inter-age-set opposition, over the domination of the prophets. This victory finds expression when people say that it was the Kosigo who reconstructed the society, and when they treat the Kosigo as if it was an age-set, not a sub-set. It is true that the *Pax Britannica* deprived the warriors of their military role, but the KAR provided the Kosigo with a new role as soldiers in the colonial context.

Just as the traditional peace makers and prophets could act as mediators because of their 'stranger-hood', so Kosigo men, in their capacity as administrative chiefs, became mediators between the colonial government and society. In this context, it is significant that the term the Kipsigis use for government chief is *kirwogindet*, that is, peacemaker (Komma, 1995). During the 1930s people saw no contradiction in using the same folk term for the two offices. This was also in conformity with the traditional age-set system. Since it was a rule to choose the peacemakers (*kirwogiik*) from the newly retired warriors, it was quite natural for ex-KAR veterans to be appointed as administrative chiefs.

## From Subversive Organization to Ethnic Emblem

The harmony between the traditional and colonial systems did not last long. From the point of view of the government the behaviour of the ex-KAR veterans became too arrogant, and they were eventually replaced by former policemen. In the 1920s a new challenge presented itself: the ambitions of a new generation of young people. As the end of the First World War had meant a fall in the KAR recruitment demand, it became difficult for members of subsequent sub-sets of Kosigo to be enrolled in the KAR. Nor was it easy to find jobs in the towns and plantations. As a result, some of the new warriors of the Maina age-set, which was formed in 1921, had recourse to the traditional practice: cattle raiding.

The 1929 annual report of South Lumbwa District gives a vivid description of the situation:

> The year has been marked by an increase of stock thieving on the part of the Lumbwa [Kipsigis], in spite of a line of Police which has been maintained along the border between the Buret-Sotik farms and the Kisii [Gusii] Reserve since the end of 1926. Thieving, which had practically ceased in 1927 and

1928, broke out with renewed vigour early in 1929, and continued to the month of October, when a climax was reached which necessitated the employment of the King's African Rifles and an increased Police force (His Majesty's Stationery Office, 1931: 20).

The Maina warriors not only raided neighbouring people but also fellow Kipsigis. This was not exceptional for Kipsigis warriors. For instance, the Kimasiba sub-set of the Kaplelach, formed in the 1880s, had done the same when the *kimkusi* epidemic, an uncertain disease which could have been rinderpest, had killed Nandi and Kipsigis cattle *en masse*.[6] The Kimasiba threatened the country by stealing the remaining cattle from their fellow Kipsigis. People had to live by trapping moles and mice (*murek*), and by stealing other people's livestock; many people in Buret committed suicide because they could not stand the situation (Toweett, 1979: 65). The Kimasiba posed a serious challenge to the authority of the elders, but the raiding should be seen as a manifestation of the dynamics of the Kipsigis political structure.

While sub-set names of the Nyongi reflect the conflicts among elders, prophets and government, those of the Maina emphasize their own maladjustment and misbehaviour. During this seclusion period, initiation members of the Mesiewa (or Kasie) sub-set used to say 'I have belched (*kasyie*)', which is why they were named Kasie or Mesiewa. Kiptiltiliet literally means a woodpecker. This is because the elders had abused them with the words: 'May the woodpecker hate you'; the implication being that they would fail to understand the messages of the woodpecker which is believed to be an ominous bird (Orchardson, 1961: 31), and would perish as a consequence. The name Silobai was given to ridicule those who committed sodomy during the seclusion period. People were quick to compose limericks teasing them about this very misdemeanour. These are still well remembered.

The elders punished the warriors of the Maina by abruptly closing recruitment to it in 1930, only nine years after its formation (Peristiany, 1939: 43–4). This was not very effective, for the Chuma age-set, next to the Maina, followed in the latter's footsteps. The Kosigo/KAR chiefs also made their contribution in bringing the raiders under control. When the cattle-rustlers of the Chuma age-set burnt down the huts of their seniors and circulated the rumour that the fires had been caused by falling stars, the chiefs reacted decisively. With the cooperation of the neighbourhood leaders (*kiptainiik*), who were asked to report any movement of rustlers, the chiefs successfully brought the situation under control. This was the final blow to Kipsigis warrior age-sets manifesting themselves militarily.

Throughout the 1940s, while the social functions of the age-set system were paralyzed, initiation and circumcision continued to be carried out as essential steps to attain adulthood. The rule that a man cannot marry his age-mate's daughter was maintained. Then, in the 1950s the age system came to fulfill a completely new function in the context of the newly emerging Kalenjin phenomenon.[7] As a large number of people from major agricultural ethnic groups such as Luo, Gikuyu and Luhya had been brought into Kipsigisland to work on the white settlers' plantations, and with Kenyan independence near at hand, the suspicion grew among the different Kalenjin groups that the Gikuyu-Luo regime of independent Kenya would take over the land (Manners, 1967: 323-331). Under these circumstances a political movement arose to unite the Kalenjin as a single ethnic entity. The language and the age-set system were signalled in the first place as the core of this common identity.

As a result of this new sense of unity, differences among various Kalenjin groups with regard to the number of age-sets (eight/seven), the length of age-set intervals, the number of sub-sets, and their names were played down and gradually forgotten. The fact that, during the 1940s, the Kipsigis stopped naming sub-sets, should be seen in the context of the rising importance of the Kalenjin identity and not as a simple decline.

The last sub-set to be formed was Kiptabot in 1941, significantly named after the colonial official, Gregory Smith, in his role as a redistributor of wealth. The name symbolizes the incorporation of the Kipsigis into the Kenyan cash economy. In this respect, it is noteworthy that, from the 1940s, women's temporary pseudo-age-sets[8] were no longer given new names, but were henceforth monotonously called Cheptonglo, literally meaning 'ladies of the 10-cent coin', which is another token of their incorporation into the cash economy.[9] As a marker of ethnic identity the age-set system continues to play a significant role in the present-day life of the Kipsigis.

# Notes

1 The present population is inferred to be a little below 1 million. They are now settled agro-pastoralists, but prior to colonization they led a much more pastoral life. I intermittently conducted fieldwork among the Kipsigis between 1979 and 1994. Data on the Kipsigis without reference were collected by me.
2 The existence of three or more conflicting genealogies and its political implications have been persuasively analyzed by Anderson (1995:186–9).
3 The residents of Sot are Sotik. The *ik* of the vernacular term is a suffix, meaning plural. In referring to the area itself, one must say Sot instead of Sotik, although not a few writers have referred to it as Sotik.
4 In fact, Kipchomber arap Koilegen was at first recognized by the colonial administration as the senior chief of the district (South Lumbwa District) and paid an annual salary of 600 rupees (Anderson, 1995:175). But, after 1910, the colonial administrators reported increasingly that many Nandi and Kipsigis elders presented the *orkoiik* as a subversive and unwelcome influence. From having initially sought to utilize the *orkoiik* as agents of colonial government, by the early 1920s the British had come to perceive them as

dangerous miscreants, posing a potentially serious threat to law and order (Anderson, 1995:167).

5  Of course, there were a few exceptions. The above-mentioned arap Cheriro was the most significant one. He was an ex-military unit leader, and is said to have applied for the post voluntarily.

6  Here it is never implied that the raids took place between territorial sections, as this was never known in their history. The Kimasiba despoiled Kipsgisland as a whole.

7  According to Kipkorir, a Kalenjin (Marakwet) historian, the origins of the Kalenjin phenomenon can be traced to the early 1940s. But it only took deep root in the mid-1950s, and matured as a political force to be reckoned with in the early 1960s (Kipkorir, 1973: 72).

8  Among the Kipsigis, it was the tradition for a lady to get married just after she had come out of seclusion. She was then regarded as an honourable member of her husband's age-set. Even now, this tradition still persists. Women's age-sets were therefore only temporary, as well as pseudo in character. Their names were quickly forgotten. Barton (1923: 67–8) named six instances as follows: Chemachul (opened in 1909), Chepandek (1913), Chepperesi (1917), Chepkokoiek (1918), Chepkiskawa (1918), Cheptilangit (1919). I myself can add some more including Cheptabaget, Tuimereng', Chepsanit (Chepsaniik). These names, just like those of men's sub-sets, derived from certain incidents which took place during their initiation periods, above all at the opening. Compared with men's age-sets, it is more difficult to reconstruct the sequence of women's age-sets.

9  According to one source (Republic of Kenya, 1979: 54), the introduction of the 10 cent coin was recorded in the history of the Luo in Kisumu District, since the famine which took place in 1943 was called the 'famine of 10 cent coin' (*ke otonglo*). Its introduction into Kipsigisland, which the sub-set name, Cheptonglo, commemorates, could be around the same year.

# 10 The Rendille and The Adaptive Strategies of East African Pastoralists

## SHUN SATO

The Rendille, who number about 20,000, are East Cushitic people, inhabiting arid lowland areas of northern Kenya.[1] They are a nomadic pastoral people who subsist almost exclusively on the products of their camels and small stock (sheep and goats); a few cattle and donkeys are kept as subsidiary livestock. They do not practise cultivation and are only marginally involved in the market economy (Sato, 1987). Rendilleland is situated in the Marsabit District of northern Kenya. To the north and east live East Cushitic peoples such as the Dassanetch, Gabbra, Boran, Sakuye, Garri, and Somali, and to the west and south, Eastern Nilotic peoples such as the Turkana and Samburu.

I have argued elsewhere from a socio-ecological viewpoint that two adaptive strategies, i.e. collectivity-centred and individuality-centred, and an intermediate strategy exist among East African pastoral societies (Sato, 1984a, 1988). The perspective of adaptive strategies encompasses differences in social institutions such as the polygyny rate, decisions about the amount of bridewealth, type of inheritance, population control, clan and territorial systems. I shall outline my argument below, because the typology of adaptive strategies is fundamental to understanding East African pastoral societies and is relevant for our discussion of the Rendille age system.

Typical examples of collectivity-centred strategies are found among the Rendille, Boran and Gabbra. These are East Cushitic speakers and are engaged in a mono-resource-based economy, which is predominantly pastoral with little dependence on cultivation, hunting or fishing. The size of household is small, and cooperation among households within the framework of more corporate patrilineal descent groups stabilizes pastoral production. Marriage and reproduction and inheritance are strictly regulated by age system and primogeniture, respectively. The amount of bridewealth is fixed and the polygyny rate is relatively low. The reproductive capacity of women is institutionally restrained, and so this strategy is supposed to have the effect of controlling population growth.

The second type of strategy is the individuality-centred strategy, which is adopted typically by the Eastern Nilotic Karimojong, Jie and Turkana. Their economy is multi-resource-based, and not only pastoralism but also cultivation, hunting and fishing are practised. Pastoral production is maintained by the maximization of individual household size as well as of herd size within a setting of less corporate patrilineal descent groups. The amount of bridewealth is not fixed, but determined by negotiation. The polygyny rate is relatively high. The utilization of the reproductive capacity of women is much higher than that among the peoples following the first strategy. The age system seems to play little role in restraining population growth. The third strategy is midway between the above-mentioned two in every aspect. Typical examples are found among Southern and Eastern Nilotic pastoral peoples, such as the Datoga, Maasai, Chamus and Samburu.

In this paper, I shall examine the functions of the age system in the Rendille society which follows a collectivity-centred adaptive strategy. This means that the age system will not be dealt with as an independent institution with a specific cultural ideology, but in the socio-ecological context of other factors such as the descent groups, the developmental cycle of the household, the cooperative nature of herding, and the camel transactions. This approach follows the same lines as Baxter's (1978) comments on the study of the generation-set of the *gada* system by Legesse (1973), Gulliver's (1979) comments on the comparative study of the rules of the age system by Stewart (1977), Almagor's (1978a) viewpoint from which he examined the ethos of equality among the Dassanetch, and Spencer's (1976) approach to the gerontocratic ladder.

Generally speaking, age systems have various functions such as military, political, social, economic and ritual (Baxter and Almagor, 1978) and are governed by a number of rules (Stewart, 1977). In a review article on age systems, Nagashima (1974) notes that they are organized both by the ranking order between different ages and by the equality principle among the same age, that the resemblance in form does not necessarily mean similarity in functions, and that they are easily changeable. Allegedly, an age system is easily modified through cultural contacts such as inter-marriage and inter-ethnic relations (Tomikawa, 1979; Gulliver, 1958; 920–1; de Wolf, 1980).

From the socio-ecological point of view, the variation and changeability of age systems seem to be relevant to the methods of social control over the most scarce and valuable resources in society. Among the pastoral societies in East Africa, marriageable girls and livestock are regarded as such resources. Girls are controlled by many institutions. Livestock are vested with high value because they can be used as bridewealth, which means that they are regarded as equivalent to marriageable girls. Households, which are the critical component of the descent group, are assured by marriage, and pastoral subsistence by livestock. In addition, the age system prescribes the socialization of its members which is accompanied by livestock transactions. Thus, various functions of age systems are closely interconnected with the adaptation process of the society in question.

## Structural Framework of the Age System

### *Outline of the system*

Since Spencer (1973) published his original study of the Rendille age system, Schlee (1979, 1989), Stewart (1977), Beaman (1981), Sato (1980), Roth (1986, 1993), and Fratkin (1987) have accumulated substantial material on the topic from the various viewpoints of socio-economics, demography and cultural history. Interestingly, there are considerable differences in the description and interpretation of the system. Before examining the discrepancies, let me present a general feature of the Rendille age system.

The Rendille age system is composed of age-grades (*ueinan*), age-sets (*kholo*) and generation-sets. All males pass through three age-grades: boyhood (*inam*), youth (*her*) and elderhood (*aram*). Boys are not organized into any age-set. When they are circumcised, they form a new age-set and enter the youth grade. When the next age-set is formed after fourteen years, they are promoted to the elderhood. Elderhood is sub-divided into four sub-grades: junior, middle, senior and retired, each of which is occupied by an age-set. As a new age-set is formed, elders move as an age-set sequentially through a series of sub-grades (see Table 10.1).

There are four major ceremonies to mark the transition of men's positions in the age system: the ceremonies of circumcision, name-giving (*gaalgurme*), marriage-opening (*nabo*), and *fahan*, the ceremony by which elders acquire a special status and power. These ceremonies are performed by the whole Rendille society according to their own calendar.[2] The ritual offices of each ceremony are attached to specific descent groups. Circumcision[3] is performed collectively in each settlement in the first year within the fourteen-year cycle of an age-set. Recently, circumcision ceremonies took place in 1965, 1979 and 1993. In the year following the circumcision, the new name is given to the age-set at the name-giving ceremony which takes place in a gigantic ritual settlement. At

*Table 10.1 Framework of the Rendille age system (as of 1995)*

| Age grade | Age sub-grade | Age-set (initiation year) Ref. of age-set | Generation-set | Age-set of Samburu (initiation year) |
|---|---|---|---|---|
| | | As-1; Irbandif (c.1825) | gaal-dahano-F (war times) | Kipayang (c. 1823) |
| | | As-2t; Ikubuku (c. 1839) | gaal-daayo-F (peace times) | Kipeko (c. 1837) |
| | | As-3; Libale (c.1853( | | Kiteku (c. 1851) |
| | | As-4; Dibgudo (c. 1867) | | Taragirik (c. 1865) |
| | | As-5t; Dismaala (c. 1881) | gaal-dahano-f (war times) | Marikon (c. 1879) |
| | | As-6; Irbangudo (1895) | | Terito (1893) |
| | | As-7; Difgudo (c. 1909*) | | Merisho (1912) |
| No member alive | | As-8t; Irbales (1923) | gaal-daayo-F (peace times) | Kiliaku (1921)[#] |
| | Retired elder | As-9; Libale (1937) | | Mekuri (1936)[#] |
| Elderhood [aram, pl. arame] | Senior elder | As-10; Irbandif (1951) | | Kilmaniki (1948)[#] |
| | Middle elder | As-11t; Difgudo (1965_ | gaal-dahano (war times) | Kichiri (1962) |
| | Junior elder | As-12; Irbangudo (1979) | | Kororo (1977) |
| Youthhood [her, pl. here] | | As-13; Dibgudo (1993) | | Imore (1990) |
| Boyhood [inam. pl. yele] | | No formed age-set | | |

* There are different views: 1909 (Sobania, 1980:135), 1910 (Schlee, 1989:76), 1909 to 1910 (Grum, 1976: 81), 1912 (Fratkin, 1991:30), and 1916 (Spencer, 1973: 33). -F: generation-set with fahan, t:constituent age-set of teeria. The Rendille pronounce 'Kiliaku', 'Mekuri' and 'Kilmaniki' as 'Ikileku', 'Imauri' and 'Ikimaniki' respectively.
Sources: Spencer (1973: 33), Sobania (1980: 135) and my own data.

this point, in principle, recruitment into the age-set is closed except for a few cases which are mentioned later in this paper. In the eleventh year after the circumcision ceremony, the young men from all the clans gather together in the bush and perform the marriage-opening ceremony. Within three years after this ceremony, they eventually get married. When the circumcision ceremony for the following age-set is performed, they move up to the junior sub-grade.

The *fahan* ceremony is performed for all the elders of the senior, middle and junior sub-grades every forty-two years, which is equivalent to the time span of three age-set cycles. After this ceremony, these elders are vested with *fahan* power and regarded as *fahan* elders,[4] whose sticks are called the sticks of *fahan* (*usi-fahan*). The last *fahan* ceremony took place in 1966 between the circumcision and the name-giving ceremonies of age-set, As-11t (Table 10.1). At that time, the elders of the three age-sets (As-8t, As-9, and As-10) simultaneously became *fahan* elders. The next *fahan* ceremony for the elders of As-11t, As-12, and As-13 is to take place in 2008.

The *fahan* elders are expected to pray for the well-being and prosperity of the Rendille and to restrain their power to curse people. Although the power of *fahan* elders is considered to be ambiguous, i.e., both of blessing and curse, more emphasis is put on blessing than on curse. It is believed, however, that if a *fahan* elder is mistreated or insulted, he could severely harm the wrongdoer by means of the power of his *fahan* stick. *Fahan* elders are therefore treated very carefully. Irrespective of their power in manipulating private affairs, however, *fahan* elders do not constitute any political entity that controls the society as a whole. There are no takeover or handover ceremonies in which political or ritual responsibility is formally transferred from one age group to another as in the *gada* system among the Boran (Legesse, 1973; 81–92) or the *mojomiji* system among the Pari (Kurimoto, 1995). Moreover, since Rendille age-set ceremonies are regulated by the prognostic calendar which is based on a fourteen-year-cycle, no-one can manipulate the timing of the age-set ceremonies. There is thus no opportunity to cause political conflict over the timing of the takeover ceremony for age-set offices.

Those three consecutive age-sets which hold the *fahan* ceremony together are a case in point for our argument here. Whether we regard the three age-sets as a generation-set or not is the source of major discrepancies in the interpretations of the Rendille age system.

### Different interpretations of the system

Historically, although they originally derived from the East Cushitic group, the Rendille have increasingly been in socio-economic alliance with the

Samburu (Spencer, 1973: 153–4; Sobania, 1980; Schlee, 1989: 6, 39-40, 91). This fact is very important in our examination of their age system. Spencer (1973: 33–6, 73–4), the pioneer anthropologist who studied the Rendille age system as well as that of the Samburu, attached greater importance to the age-grades and age-sets than to the generation-sets in order to emphasize the similarity to the Samburu. Following his study from the viewpoint of the age-set model, Stewart (1977: 108) claimed that the Rendille age system is very similar to that of the Samburu, but that the Rendille also have some rules that are entirely their own. Another significant point that Spencer (1973: 33) discovered is the age-set line. In a linear sequence of age-sets, every third one makes up an age-set line. Of the two adjacent age-sets in the same age-set line, the senior age-set is referred to as 'the age-set of the father (*oyo*)' by the junior. There are three age-set lines, and one of them is specifically called *teeria*, and is composed of As-2t, As-5t, As-8t and As-11t (Table 10.1). Although Spencer gives no description of *fahan*, among the three age-sets of the elders who perform the *fahan* ceremony together, the seniormost age-set is always in the *teeria* line. However, Spencer does not regard these three age-sets as constituting a generation-set.

Later studies (Schlee: 1989; 73–9, 91, 247–8, Beaman: 1981; 374–5, 382, 426-427, 447–8) have argued that the Rendille age system has a composite structure of age-grades, age-sets and generation-sets, and that it should be interpreted from the viewpoint of the generation-set model in order to emphasize the cultural-historical continuity with the *gada* system of East Cushitic culture. Schlee (1989: 74) translates the *fahan* as a ritual generation. Beaman (1981: 416–22) translates *fahan* as an institutionalized generation with the power to curse, but her usage of generation is arbitrary.

The Rendille explain that there are three kinds of age-sets: the first-born age-set (*kholoti-teiyane*), the middle-born (*kholoti-dehet*), and the last-born (*kholoti-mande*). The first-born age-set is that of *teeria*; the next junior one is the middle-born, and the second junior one is the last-born. These three age-sets are regarded as 'brothers' and compose a stratum in the age-set sequence with a time span of forty-two years and defined as an 'age-set stratum' for the present. Any two consecutive strata are alternately called either *gaal-dahano* (white camel) or *gaal-daayo* (black camel). The period when any age-set of the former occupies the youth grade is thought to be the times of disturbance and disasters, and that of the latter to be a time of peace and prosperity. ( Beaman (1981) argues mistakenly that the sense of the times is expressed in conformity to the elderhood, but not to the youthhood.) Thus, good and bad times recur alternately every forty-two years. This sense of the times with an eighty-four-year cycle is represented by the historical concept of *daji* (Schlee, 1979: 89, Beaman, 1981: 253).

**211**

The *fahan* ceremony is performed every forty-two years soon after the three age-sets of an age-set stratum have shifted from youth to elderhood, and thus it makes a clear distinction between the two age-set strata. When an age-set of *teeria*, the first-born, is vested with *fahan*, it is in senior-elderhood, with the middle-born age-set in middle elderhood and the last-born age-set in junior elderhood. The timing of acquiring *fahan* differs from one age-set to another.

Beaman (1981: 416–22) regards *fahan* as a general term for generation-set which is equivalent to age-set stratum. This is not correct because a newly organized age-set stratum is not vested with *fahan* power unless it has shifted to elderhood. According to Schlee's interpretation, though he does not note the presence of *gaal-dahano* and *gaal-daayo*, the age-sets with *fahan* are integrated into a generation-set, whereas those without *fahan* are not. But any age-set is automatically classified into one or other of the two age-set strata on its formation, and any age-set stratum is vested with *fahan* as it shifts to elderhood. The *fahan* functions as an index which makes a clear distinction in the age-set strata. An age-set stratum is roughly equivalent to what Schlee and Beaman call a generation-set, and the senior generation-sets are vested with *fahan* power.

The discrepancy between the different views of the Rendille age system is derived from the two different models: age-set and generation-set. The age-set model emphasizes that an age system should be studied from the viewpoint of a practical institution, while the generation-set model maintains that it should be studied from the viewpoint of a cultural ideal. These two contrasting approaches can also be found in studies of age systems among other societies than the Rendille. However, I would like to argue that the two models are not mutually exclusive, because in reality as well as in principle the age-set system is quite inseparable from the generation-set system. The age-set system meshes in its value, as well as in its timing, with the generation-set system.

### Enrolment rules to age-set: the flexibility of generation principle

The order of boys to be circumcised and enrolled into an age-set is in principle determined by three considerations. The first is the biological age. It is thought that the boys are to be circumcised when they are over twelve years of age, after having extracted their teeth and become capable herders. The second is the seniority among brothers. A younger brother cannot be enrolled into an age-set senior to that of his elder brother. The third is the paternal linkage of age-sets between a father and his sons and between a grandfather and his grandsons.

If the rule of paternal linkage is applied strictly, all eldest sons are enrolled into the third junior age-set from that of the fathers, and their eldest sons, namely grandsons, into the sixth age-set from that of the grandfathers. This linkage is what we call the age-set line. In other words, ideally, the individual age-set line reflects patrilineal affiliation. Thus, an age-set stratum coincides with a biological generation. The generation-set model, on which Schlee (1989) and Beaman (1981) are based, is in conformity with this ideal model, which is also conceived of by the Rendille themselves.

However, these fundamental rules are applied flexibly to real situations. According to the two combined statistical analyses of 136 youths by Beaman (1981: 397) and 65 youths by Stewart (1977: 112), about 71 per cent of the total 201 youths join the third age-set and 23 per cent the fourth, while the remaining 6 per cent belong to the second, fifth and sixth age-sets. Exceptions to the rule therefore share 29 per cent; the rule of paternal linkage is not strictly applied. The above situation occurs because of the following practices. Although the eldest son normally belongs to the third age-set from that of his father, younger sons may belong to the third or more junior age-sets. So grandsons belong to the sixth or more junior age-sets from those of their grandfather. Moreover, in cases such as the death of a young man, his younger brother is hastily circumcised to join his age-set in order to cover the loss. If a man belongs to the fourth age-set from that of his father, his son is allowed to join the second age-set from the father's because of the paternal linkage between a grandfather and his grandsons. There can be a case, although it seems to be rare, when an elder without a brother is allowed to get his eldest son circumcised and to join the second junior age-set from his own.

The ideal model is therefore at variance with the real conditions. Such variance is brought about by the age criterion as well as by the circumstances of subsistence. Some younger sons have delayed being circumcised and joining an age-set because the father needs to be sure of having capable herders to take care of his herds. Soon after they have finally joined an age-set, most of them marry earlier than their other age-mates, and move up into the adjacent senior age-set. Within a household, a father makes his sons join an age-set with due regard not only to paternal linkage, but also to both biological age and subsistence conditions.

## Descent Groups and the Age System

*Descent groups and settlements*

The Rendille are patrilineally organized into nine exogamous clans. The five clans (Dupsai, Nahagan, Matarba, Rengumo and Uiyam) constitute

**213**

the western moiety (*belesi bahai*) and the remaining four (Salle, Urwen, Galdielen and Tupcha) the eastern moiety (*belesi*-beri). The coherence of the moieties is expressed in ritual contexts such as the sacrificial feasts (*sorio*) and the pan-Rendille ceremonies of the age-set cycle.

A clan is compared to a family and the clansmen have exclusively affectionate feelings for one another. Clansmen of the same generation regard one another as brothers or sisters and keep faith with one another, and those of adjacent generations are compared to parents and children. A clan is sub-divided into sub-clans, whose number ranges from two to six, and a sub-clan is further sub-divided into between five and thirty lineages. The genealogical depth of a lineage is usually two to three generations. The Rendille do not actually trace the genealogical relation to the apical ancestor of their clan or sub-clan.

The descent groups are ranked at various levels such as moiety, clan, sub-clan and lineage. Seniorities between moieties and clans are displayed at the pan-Rendille ceremonies of the age-set cycle and in terms of the dates for *sorio*-feasts. In the case of the age-set ceremonies, a gigantic ritual enclosure is constructed, inside which the clansmen build discrete clan enclosures clockwise, starting at the westernmost point. The clans of the western moiety occupy the northern half which is regarded as the senior position, whereas the clans of the eastern moiety occupy the southern and junior position. The *sorio* feasts are performed in each settlement four times a year ( in the first, second, sixth and seventh months ); each time every household sacrifices an animal. For clans of the western moiety, the *sorio* feast takes place on the ninth day after the new moon, and on the following day for the clans of the eastern moiety. Seniorities between sub-clans and lineages of the same clan are displayed in terms of the residential arrangement in a settlement. Every settlement has at its centre a praying place (*nabo*) with a fence of thorny branches, around which between two and 67 portable huts are arranged in a circle. The most senior household builds its hut at the westernmost point, and the remaining huts are built clockwise according to descent seniority. A settlement is named after the seniormost person who occupies the highest status in the descent seniority of the settlement.

Most of the residents of a settlement belong to a sub-clan, and live together with a small number of other sub-clansmen of the same clan and their affines. Usually a clan has two to five such settlements. The Rendille do not like to reside in a settlement of other clans and prefer to live in either their own or a wife's clan-settlement. Thus, the settlement, the co-residence of which largely overlaps with its clanship, functions as a communal unit for ritual and political activities. At the same time co-residents and clansmen work together in herding and share the culture of begging ( Sato, 1994a) as a means of mutual help.

*The Ritual Offices of Age System and Descent Groups*

As briefly mentioned above, a number of ritual offices for age-set ceremonies are attached to specific descent groups. It should also be noted that some ceremonies become the arena where inter-clan hostilities are openly manifested. Before the circumcision ceremony, the boys perform two preparatory ceremonies. The first one, which is called '*wahar-lagoraha* (the male goat to be sacrificed)', takes place in the bush away from the settlements and herding camps three years before the circumcision. In this ceremony, a male goat must be slaughtered by a member of the Nebei sub-clan of the Salle clan. The second one, '*her-laduro* (the ox-dance)', is performed in the bush in the year before the circumcision, when an ox, offered by the Logor family of the Samburu, is sacrificed. The circumcision itself is carried out by the elders of the Bolo family and those elders of the Tupcha clan who are authorized by them. The name-giving ceremony is performed under the leadership of the Wambire family of the Dupsai clan. The elders of the Mirkarkona family (Nahagan clan) and Gaalikidere family (Matarba clan) announce the name of the new age-set. The *fahan* ceremony takes place in the settlement where the seniormost elder of the Galale family, the Orbora sub-clan of the Tupcha clan, resides. He sacrifices an adolescent female sheep, and smears the foreheads of the participants with the fat. The participants then tie strips of sheepskin around their new sticks (*usi-fahan*).

For the marriage-opening ceremony, the youths of the Dupsai clan secretly choose four kinds of ritual actors from among their age-mates: the man-of-the-fire (*dab-lakabire*), the man-of-the-feather (*oeyabokhote*), the man-of-the-*gudur*, and the man-of-the-horn (*arap-lagate*). The man-of-the-fire and the man-of-the-horn are chosen from among the *wakhamur* class of sub-clans.[5] The man-of-the-feather is always a member of the Lekila family (the Nebei sub-clan of the Salle clan). The man-of-the-*gudur* is installed from either the Duroro family (the Galoleiyo sub-clan of the Salle clan), or the Kimogor family (the Gobanai sub-clan of the Salle clan).

The man-of-the-feather is seized and a feather is stuck upright into the ground in front of him. He must then pick it up. This role is regarded as one of only mild ridicule (Spencer, 1973: 50). The Wambire family has an ivory horn (*arap*) which some members of the family blow on and call out the name of the man-of-the-horn at the marriage-opening ceremony. Regardless of his presence or absence at the ceremony, he is the man-of-the-horn from the moment his name has been called out when the horn of the Wambire is blown (Spencer: 1973; 50). The man-of-the-horn is an unimportant role, and he feels insulted by his installation. The man-of-the-*gudur* is made ritually responsible for the fertility of his age-mates'

**215**

marriages. He must obey a number of ritual restrictions from the install-ment at this ceremony until that of the man-of-the-*gudur* for the next age-set (fourteen years later). He is given camels by all the clans (Beaman, 1981: 468-469; Schlee, 1979: 353; Spencer, 1973: 50).

Except for the man-of-the-*gudur*, the installation of the other three offices constitute an insult for the actors involved. This is particularly so for the man-of-the-fire. The four or five youths of the Rengumo clan catch the man-of-the-fire whom the Wambire family of the Dupsai clan has secretly installed. They approach him politely and seize him to knock him down. His right sandal is taken off and placed on his right knee. A small fire is kindled on the victim's shoes by firesticks; after removing the shoes from his lap, the live kindling is directly placed on them four times. His necklace is cut off and a necklace made of an elephant's tail is put around his neck in its place. The captors take away the victim's clothes and the ivory ear-ring from his right ear, and give him a white cloth instead.

The captors then take the victim to the praying place of the Wambire's settlement (*nabo-ti-Farah*), where he is promised to the girl whom he wants to marry. Therafter he is released. This role causes the most serious humiliation to the victim. It is generally held that he will suffer severe mis-fortune for the rest of his life. This custom is carried out in order to protect the other age-mates from a similar fate (Spencer, 1973: 49). It is clear that he has to be compelled to act as a scapegoat.

The man-of-the-fire does not always tolerate this humiliation, and may seek his revenge. Schlee (1979: 400-5) has given a detailed des-cription of such a disastrous incident for the Ikichiri age-set.[6] A certain Lekuti Eisingabana, who was a youth of the Deele sub-clan (the Tupcha clan), was installed as the man-of-the-fire, and violently insulted in the bush by the youths of both the Dupsai and Rengumo clans in April 1976. Thereafter Lekuti set out to seek his revenge, and eventually killed three people, including one of his attackers, a woman whose husband informed the youths of Lekuti's coming, and a girl whose brother attacked him. He then gave himself up to the police and was jailed at Marsabit. According to what I heard from some of the elders, the police authority decided to release him after a two-month examination. But he hanged himself in the jail on 24 July 1976 in order to defend his honour. One year after his suicide, his father also hanged himself from a tree near the settlement.

The Lekuti incident was not limited to his own affairs. Immediately after his capture, the chain of violence spread to inter-clan (Dupsai vs Tupcha), and then to inter-moiety, disputes. Most of the clans of the eastern moiety including the Tupcha therefore boycotted the marriage-opening ceremony which took place on 12 July 1976. Tupcha clansmen, who are empowered to circumcise Rendille boys, also said that they would refuse to circumcise all the boys of the western moiety. However, after extensive discussions, the circumcision of the Ikororo age-set took place as scheduled in 1979. In 1982 the inter-clan antagonism again intensified, triggered off by a personal fight when a youth of the Ikororo age-set of the Tupcha clan was slapped on the face by the Ikichiri elder of the Dupsai clan, who was his mother's brother. He was blamed for losing a heifer to a hyena. On hearing of this incident, Tupcha youths beat up the Dupsai elder on the ground that no youth should be beaten by an elder. In revenge, youths of the Dupsai clan attacked the camel camps of the Tupcha and seriously injured five youths, who were in turn taken to hospital. From 1982 to 1985, youths of both clans repeated this sort of conflict at least eight times, resulting in a number of casualties: ten seriously injured and four killed. Neither the elders nor the government administration were able to bring the situation under control. As the marriage-opening ceremony of the Ikororo youths was approaching, the District administration and most of the Rendille elders were anxious to suppress the installation of the man-of-the-fire by Dupsai youths, for fear of a recurrence of the Lekuti incident. None the less, Dupsai youths chose a youth of the Tupcha clan and severely harassed him. The District administration took decisive punitive measures by confiscating all the camels of the Dupsai. The Dupsai clan submitted themselves to the District administration and released him. The young people of both clans still manifested antagonistic feelings towards each other, and each moiety performed the marriage-opening ceremony separately.

As mentioned previously, the traditional Rendille political system is based on a precarious coalition of clans, each of which is autonomous and with a strong corporate sense. The Rendille lack a central institution to cover and control their society as a whole. Pan-Rendille ceremonies of the age-set cycle are the only occasions when all the clans get together. For these ceremonies, the ritual offices are allocated among descent groups such as sub-clans and lineages. The differences and complementarities between the diverse ritual offices enforce cooperation and unity among the different clans. However, as these ritual offices, that of the man-of-the-fire in particular, play the role of institutionalized scapegoat, it is very likely that the installation will manifest and intensify the antagonism between clans and moieties. Age-set ceremonies therefore integrate the society as a whole, on the one hand, and often engender internal fissions within the society, on the other. The fact that the elders could not control the inter-clan conflict among the youths of the Ikororo may indicate that such conflict could lead to a fission of Rendille society, in the absence of powerful state administration.

## The Developmental Cycle and Household Cooperation

In Rendille society, the age system strictly regulates sexual relations, married life, and the developmental cycle of the household. Unmarried girls are prohibited from having children. While young men are allowed to have sexual relations with lovers, they can become socially recognized fathers only after marriage. An elder is recognized as the father of the children to whom his wives have given birth, regardless of whether he is alive or dead. Married women may live a comparatively free sexual life within the regulations of the *dumassi* institution (open-lover institution). For a man, the word *dumassi* denotes in a narrow sense a kinship term for his elder brother's wife and his wife's sister; in a wider sense it is extended to refer to the wives of those clansmen who belong to the paternal alternation[7] of his own and his two adjacent senior age-sets. *Dumassi* partners are allowed to joke and dally with each other, and this often develops into sexual relations. When children are born to the *dumassi* pair, the *dumassi* man has no legitimate claim to them, and instead the husband of the *dumassi* woman, irrespective of whether he is alive or dead, is recognized as their legitimate father. The *dumassi* institution as well as polygynous marriage thus make for a wider variance in age between brothers, because it takes longer for all the brothers to complete their marriages.

There is also a wide variance in age between age-mates. If a youth marries immediately after the marriage-opening ceremony, which takes place in the eleventh year after circumcision, and begets his first son in the following year, the son will be two years old on the formation of the next age-set to his father's. He will be thirty when the circumcision ceremony is held for his own age-mates, as he is supposed to belong to the third junior age-set to that of his father. Thus, taking account of the general assumption of the appropriate biological age for circumcision (i.e. over twelve years of age), there may be a difference of eighteen years between age-mates. According to my statistical data (Sato, 1980), on average youths are circumcised at the age of twenty-three, and marry at thirty-four. The senior members of an age-set are called *nchokinibir*, and the junior members *gaaldano*. These two categories do not form sub-sets which have any significance in the ritual context, as is the case among the Samburu (Beaman, 1981: 424, Spencer, 1975: 88).[8] The former plays an active role in performing age-set ceremonies and herding livestock.

The actual work of herding livestock is done by boys and girls under the supervision of young men who are responsible for herding management and protecting livestock from raiders. The young men stay at the livestock camps for fourteen years until the next age-set is organized.[9] They then move up to the elderhood and live in the settlements in order to engage in community affairs.

A formal marriage should be arranged by the collective consent of the bride's clan elders and be legitimated by the payment of bridewealth. The middle elders take the initiative in talking with their clan elders about marriage affairs. The preferences of the bridegroom and bride are apt to be neglected by elders who prefer to marry their daughters to their own age-mates. On the other hand, young men want to marry 'their own girls', namely, the daughters of the second and third senior age-sets, and try to prevent men of other age-sets from marrying them. In other words, for the young men, senior and middle elders are potential fathers-in-law and rivals in competition for marriageable girls. In order to achieve their desire, the young men sometimes elope with their lovers with the assistance of age-mates. Girls can also visit their lovers to ask them to marry them. Although such irregular marriages do happen, they should be finally formalized by the payment of bridewealth.

The conflict between youths and elders over marriageable girls has been considered in the context of gerontocracy, which is allegedly maintained and manipulated by elders who try to marry as many girls as possible and to enhance their social influence through marriage alliances (Rey, 1979; Spencer, 1976: 165; Almagor, 1978b). However, if we examine the number of livestock per capita and the polygyny rate among different societies, we find that the prerequisites of gerontocracy do not always hold true. This is particularly the case among societies following the collectivity-centred adaptive strategy. Among the Rendille, Gabbra and Boran, for instance, the amount of bridewealth is fixed and is less than three times as much as the *per capita* number of camels or cattle, whereas among the Karimojong, Jie and Turkana which adopt the individuality-centred adaptive strategy, the amount of bridewealth is negotiated by the two parties concerned and is more than ten times as much as the *per capita* number of cattle. The polygyny rate is 1.1 for the Rendille as well as the Gabbra, which is much lower than that among the neighbouring peoples such as the Samburu, Turkana, Karimojong and Jie, which is from 1.5 to 2.3 (Sato, 1984a). These comparative figures would consequently indicate that the conflict between youths and elders over marriageable girls should be far less serious among the Rendille than among their neighbours.

A married couple build their hut and live their family life in the settlement. Admittedly, for a while after marriage young elders continue to herd their small stock until their children grow up, but they are never engaged full-time in herding camels or cattle. This division of labour by age-grade results in a different composition of residents between the settlements and the camps. My data on a particular clan population illustrate this situation (Sato,1986). The clan consisted of 551 persons, 338 of them living in five settlements and 213 in four small stock camps, three camel camps and one cattle camp. Married people and their small children made up 91 per cent of the total settlement population, and the unmarried were 85 per cent of the total camp population. The residents in the camel and cattle camps were all unmarried males.

*Table 10.2  Correlation of age-set with developmental cycle of the household (February 1983)*

| Age-set of household head | No. of households (huts) | No. of members per household (person) | No. of supporters* per household (person) | Effectives** (%) |
|---|---|---|---|---|
| Irbangudo | 1 | 1.0 | 0 | 0 |
| Difgudo | 4 | 2.3 | 0.8 | 34.8 |
| Irbales | 20 | 3.4 | 1.6 | 47.1 |
| Libale | 28 | 6.6 | 4.0 | 60.6 |
| Irbandif | 25 | 5.3 | 2.4 | 45.3 |
| Difgudo (Kichiri) | 49 | 3.7 | 0 | 0 |
| Average | | 4.5 | 1.6 | 36.1 |

*: subsistence supporter = unmarried persons over 7 years of age.
**: effectives = no. of supporters x 100 ÷ total no. household members

If a household is to be an independent herding unit, it should have at least two or three herders to take care of the camels and small stock which are essential for subsistence. However, most Rendille households are monogamous, and the average household size is 4.5 persons, 1.6 of them being subsistence supporters, who are defined as unmarried persons over seven years of age (see Table 10.2). As an average household cannot adequately cover the demand for herders, one household seeks out cooperation with another in the sphere of herding activities. By means of this sort of cooperation they can manage both camels and small stock. It is true that a polygynous household builds up a self-sufficient homestead in terms of labour, but this is the case for only 8 per cent of twenty-six homesteads of the Tupcha clan settlements. The remaining 92 per cent are homesteads formed by means of cooperation among households, whose heads are the same clansmen and close agnates (Sato: 1986).

The number of subsistence supporters and the subsistence rate (the ratio of subsistence supporters to total household members) change in accordance with the developmental cycle of the household. Junior elders have no subsistence supporters as their children are still small, and they have to take care of small stock themselves. Middle and senior elders have

2.4 and 4 supporters respectively. In terms of the subsistence rate, households of middle, senior and retired elders show 45, 61 and 47 per cent, respectively. Middle and senior elders can therefore provide enough labour to maintain their livestock independently, and are actively engaged in community affairs. The retired elders no longer commit themselves on community affairs, and leave the legal matters concerning family herds to their already married sons.

In terms of the social control of young men, middle elders have the greatest influence in the direction of their age-set ceremonies. Since they have wives some of whom are prospective *dumassi* of the young men, they are also in an intimate relationship with them. But such an alternate relationship between the two age-sets is not institutionalized like the firestick relationship of the Samburu (Spencer, 1973: 73–5) and Maasai (Spencer, 1988). Senior elders are those of the young men's fathers' generation. It is both the middle and the senior elders who entrust boys and young men with herding their camels. In return, these boys and young men have the right to claim some camels from the elders. This sort of livestock transaction is an important means of social control, as noted by Spencer (1973: 98; 1988) and Fratkin (1991: 71–2).

## Age System as a Provider of Camel Transactions

Like other pastoral peoples, the Rendille use their livestock in various ways, not only for subsistence but also for social exchange through which societal relations are bound and regulated, and for communicating with the spiritual world. Among the different kinds of livestock, camels are the most important animals for these purposes and are most highly valued.

In Rendille society, only males are vested with the legal ownership of camels. A father does not transfer the ownership of his camels to his eldest son during his lifetime. Instead, the eldest son may be given some livestock by his mother's eldest brother. At his father's death, he succeeds to the patrimony and inherits most of his legacy of camels. The larger part of household camels are successively retained by eldest sons from generation to generation. In this way, the primogeniture system is maintained. This does not necessarily mean, however, that an eldest son monopolizes his father's camels. Upon inheritance, he is obliged to redistribute a female camel to each younger brother and a male camel to his eldest married sister (Sato: 1994b).

Besides inheritance, camels are transferred by means of four forms of transaction: gift, exchange, loan and trust, defined as follows. Gift means transferring one's personal camel to another for no direct return, whereas exchange is for a direct return. Loan means transferring a camel to another on condition that the transferred camel itself is returned in the future according to a prescribed convention, and trust means transferring female camels in accordance with the rules of the trust system (Sato: 1992a).

In any camel transaction, there is a clear distinction between the personal camel (*alal*) and the trust camel (*maal*) and this is confirmed by the persons concerned. Personal camels are valued more highly than trust camels. A man who keeps his own personal camel can dispose of it as he pleases. All male camels are categorized as personal camels, whereas female camels can be either personal or trust camels. The trustee has no ownership of the trust camels, but holds usufruct rights to their milk, blood, and male offspring. He has to return the camel to his trustor at his request. As long as any trust camel, including the one originally entrusted and its female offspring, is alive, the eldest sons of both parties inherit the credits and debts of their fathers over generations.

The trustee can sublease either the entrusted camel itself or its female offspring to a third person of his choice. A chain of trust relations is then formed on the basis of the dyadic interpersonal relation between the trustor and his immediate trustee. The first trustor (the owner of the original personal camel) retains the ultimate credit, so he is regarded as the owner of all the trust camels transferred through the chain of trust relations.

The first trustee never subleases the trust camel to the close agnates of his trustor if he belongs to the same clan as the trustor; nor does he sublease it to the clansmen of his trustor if he belongs to a different clan. In the whole chain of trust relations, the close agnates and clansmen demarcate a double boundary, which functions like a semi-permeable membrane. It means that those trust camels which have been once put beyond their boundary cannot be brought back in again through subleasing. In other words, the solidarity among the close agnates and clansmen becomes obvious in the trust system (Sato, 1992).

On some occasions and in some social relations a man is obliged to donate his personal camels to another. Such occasions include the death of parents, circumcision, the killing of an enemy, and marriage. If an eldest son is circumcised or kills an enemy, he is entitled to at least one female camel from his mother's eldest brother, whereas on the same occasion the other sons are entitled to at least one female camel from his father. Upon marriage, the bridegroom has to pay eight personal camels (four male and four female) as bridewealth to the bride's elementary kin, such as her mother, brothers and mother's eldest brother. Moreover, the bride's eldest brother is expected to give one female camel out of his sister's bridewealth to his father's brother's son. Since the bride's father has no share in the bridewealth camels of his daughter, he cannot divert them to his own marriage.

The above-mentioned occasions are landmarks in the developmental cycle of the household as well as in the age-set cycle. The eldest son is obliged to donate personal camels to his own and his wife's elementary kin, his father's brother's eldest son, and his sister's eldest son, and conversely he can receive personal camels from his sister's husband, his sister's daughter's husband, and his mother's eldest brother. I call the category of these persons effective kindred. The relationships among the effective kindred are maintained and reinforced by the reciprocal donation of personal camels, and are structured not only by the unity of a father with his eldest son, but also by the relationship of a mother's eldest brother to a sister's eldest son, and by the relationship among the eldest sons within close agnates.

*Table 10.3 Camel transfers by three sons of the same family in reference to the age-sets of the partners (as of 1988)*

| Age-set[a] of the partner | Eldest son (As-11t) | | Second son (As-11t) | | Third son[b] (As-11t) | | Total | |
|---|---|---|---|---|---|---|---|---|
| As-8t (Irbales) | 7 (+ 1)[c] | 11% | 14 (+ 6) | 25% | 7 (+ 3) | 25% | 28 (+10) | 19% |
| As-9 (Libale) | 14 (+ 4) | 22 | 11 (+ 7) | 20 | 1 (+ 1) | 3 | 26 (+ 12) | 17 |
| As-10 (Irbandif) | 5 (− 1) | 8 | 5 (+ 1) | 9 | 1 (+ 1) | 3 | 11 (+ 1) | 78 |
| As-11t (Difgudo) | 20 ( 0) | 31 | 21 (+ 5) | 38 | 18 (+ 4) | 62 | 59 (+ 9) | 40 |
| As-12 (Irbandgudo) | 18 (− 11) | 28 | 5 (− 3) | 9 | 2 (− 2) | 7 | 25 (− 15) | 17 |
| Total | 64 (− 7) | 100% | 56 (+ 16) | 101% | 29 (+ 7) | 100% | 149 (+ 17) | 100% |

a): Refer to Table 10.1
b): This man moved up to the Difgudo age-set from Irbangudo.
c): The figure '7 (+ 1)' means that the camel transfers amount to 7 times and that the balance shows an excess of one camel gained.

I have analyzed elsewhere (Sato, 1994b) the actual camel transfers made by three sons from one household (Table 10.3). The total number of transfers amounted to 149 cases, of which donations of female and male personal camels (44 and 41 cases respectively) made up 58 per cent and trusts 39 per cent (58 cases), making 97 per cent of the total transfers. The remaining 3 per cent is repayment and exchange of camels. In terms of social relations between the partners of the transfers, 99 per cent of all the 85 donations were carried out among effective kindred, 90 per cent of them family members, wife's elementary kin and sister's family members. On the other hand, 31 per cent of the 58 trust camels were transferred to patrilineal clansmen, 28 per cent to classificatory clansmen and 19 per cent to family members. Trust camels are transferred to a wider circle of people than other transfer camels, based on ego-centred dyadic relations.

In terms of occasions of transfers, marriage and circumcision represent respectively 40 and 13 per cent of the total. Those for pledges of bond-partnership formed at age-set ceremonies, represent 10 per cent. As a whole 63 per cent are transferred on occasions related to the age-set cycle. Other points shown in Table 10.3 are that 40 per cent of all transfers are carried out between age-mates, and that the members of the senior age-set tend to give camels to those of the junior age-set. In this way, the age system serves as an important provider of camel transfers.

## Conclusion

As a result of the rapid and far-reaching encroachment of the government administration and the market economy, the Rendille as well as other pastoral societies in East Africa have undergone drastic changes and been reduced to a marginalized state. Hogg (1986) noted with regard to Isiolo Boran society that economic differentiation was increasingly polarizing it and that the communal ties hitherto based on the ethos of equality were being weakened. He regards this phenomenon as a new pastoralism, namely, the wealthy are able to take advantage of socio-economic standing to elevate their status, while the poor cannot avoid either being employed as wage herders or dropping out of the pastoral economy. The same phenomenon of economic and social polarization is also reported with respect to the Chamus (Little: 1985).

However, Rendille camel pastoralism still persists. Although they are indeed involved in the market economy, they never sell female camels for cash, and instead keep them close at hand. When they need cash or commercial commodities, they first exchange camels for cattle with their relatives and friends, and then supply these cattle to the market. Camels are treated as livestock symbolic of their well-being. Camels are also their essential means of production, and at the same time important property for social exchange through which the solidarity of kindred is enforced and the network of favourable friends expanded. Such camel transactions are collectively activated through the age-set cycle as well as the kindred network.

It can be assumed that a man with more livestock is able to marry more wives; he can then build up a bigger and independent household so that he can have more favourable opportunities for making reliable relatives and friends. This is the individuality-centred strategy, which the Rendille do not follow. In Rendille society with its collectivity-centred strategy, private accumulation of camels is restrained by two fundamental institutions, quite apart from the slower growth of the camel population (Sato: 1980).

One is the age system which ensures that all young men should be engaged in herding management, on the one hand, and that all elders should be engaged in both legal management of camels and community affairs, on the other. Elders should be dependent on boys and youths for herding labour, while the latter should be dependent on the elders for acquiring camels. The flow of camels from elders to youngsters is activated by the developmental household cycle which is regulated by the age system. The other is the structural stability and corporate nature of patrilineal clanship and the household. A clan intensifies social, political and economic solidarity and functions as the corporate group. A household is based on the primogeniture system within whose framework camels are legally managed by the unity of a father with his eldest son. As camel-givers both the father and his eldest son dominate younger sons and/or brothers.

Thus, in Rendille society, the age system and the patrilineal clan system play an important role in organizing the division of labour by age-grades within a clan, whereby young men and elders depend on each other for mutual help. Moreover, the Rendille age system, which is intricately interwoven with clanship, functions to ensure full-time herders of livestock, in particular camels. The formation of an age-set every fourteen years and the closing of enrolment to it within a year stabilize the recruitment of full-time camel herders.

The Rendille age system is an eclectic type between the age-set and the generation-set systems. We can assume that it is modified by two elements. One is the practical flexibility-of-generation principle, in that a man's age-set affiliation is not strictly determined by the paternal linkage. The second is the mobility of age-set affiliation, in that young men are permitted to move up to the adjacent senior age-set above the initial one. These two elements are relevant to the same problem which underlies Rendille subsistence. They have to cope with the problem that they ought to secure full-time camel herders and at the same time make youngsters build their own households in order to maintain families. Analysis of the enrolment of sons to age-sets reveals that fathers try to get their eldest sons enrolled into an age-set as early as possible, while they tend to delay the enrolment of younger sons in order to secure full-time herders for their camels. However, such younger sons are apt to marry earlier than other age-mates, and they then move up to the senior age-set adjacent to that to which their eldest brothers may belong. Thus, it can be concluded that the eclectic feature of the Rendille age system is derived from the process of adaptation to the socio-ecological setting.

**225**

# Notes

1 I carried out intermittent fieldwork among the Rendille between 1975 and 1996. My research was supported financially by the Wenner-Gren Foundation for Anthropological Research, the Little World Museum of Man, and the Grant-in-Aid for Scientific Research of the Japanese Ministry of Education, Science, Sports and Culture.

2 The Rendille have twelve lunar months in a year. Each year is called by the names of the seven days of the week. Thus the same name of the day of the week is repeated every seven years. They also make a sense of propitiousness or unpropitiousness for the day of the week and the month. The prognostic calendar controls not only the treatment and transaction of livestock but also the date for settlement movements and ritual activities (Sato, 1992: 39–43; Spencer, 1973: 65–8; Beaman, 1981: 286–349). Schlee (1989, 91) regards the calendrical system of the Rendille as an important cultural element of the Proto-Rendille-Somali complex (PRS complex).

3 The Rendille boys follow two ritual forms of circumcision. The boy whose family maintains a strong affiliation with the Samburu is circumcised inside his father's camel enclosure just before dusk in the late afternoon. The boy who follows the Rendille style is circumcised at dawn in front of a shady structure of branches which is built outside the settlement. Beaman (1981: 455–62) made a detailed description of Ikororo circumcision on the basis of her own observation.

4 The grave of *fahan* elders has a different style from that of others, with a stone cairn built on it.

5 The Rendille sub-clans are classified into either *iibir* people or *wakhamur*. Except for the Uiyam clan, all of whose clan are *wakhamur*, a clan is composed of a mixture of *wakhamur* and *iibir* sub-clans. The *iibir* people are believed to have the ability of making direct communication with God by being the most efficient at praying and possessing the most powerful curses. The *wakhamur* people have no such ability, and play the role of scapegoat or coordinator on the ritual scene. For further information, see Spencer (1973: 61–2), Beaman (1981: 262–6), Sato (1992a, 1994a ), and Schlee (1979: 181–93, 1989: 10–11).

6 Ikichiri and Ikororo, which are the Rendille versions of the Samburu name for age-set, are equivalent to Difgudo (As-11t ) and Irbangudo (As-12), respectively (see Table 10.1). Historically, it has happened that because of some misfortune the Rendille have abandoned their own names for certain age-sets and used the Samburu names instead (Spencer: 1973; 33, Beaman: 1981: 394–5). Nowadays, the Rendille prefer the Samburu age-set names to their own in daily life. Thus, in this paper, I use the Samburu age-set names rather than their own.

7 Men are classified into two paternal alternations: big alternation (*maradi-buure*) and small alternation (*maradi-richur*). Sons belong to the opposite alternation to that of their father and to the same one as that of their grandfather. The alternate alternations of the Rendille are not groups but simply social categories whose affiliation is determined by paternal affiliation.

8 The word 'nchokinibir' is derived from the Samburu, 'chong'onopir'. According to Spencer (1973: 90), a more significant division in the age-set is between those initiates who are fully grown (chong'onopir) and those who are not. The word 'nchokinibir' means senior youth, whereas the word 'gaaldano' means junior youth in Rendille usage.

9 The Rendille young men bear a heavy responsibility for the management of livestock herding. Youngsters are engaged in the daily herding of camels under the young men's direction. Even elders cannot intervene directly in the young men's camp management. Beaman (1981: 474) has noted that the cognates of both the camel camp (*hero* in Somali) ( Lewis: 1961; 32, 72) and the young men (*her* in Rendille) apply to groups of young men, one of whose primary functions is the tending of livestock in camps away from home. On the other hand, they are not qualified to participate in the elders' meeting at the praying place, where final decisions are taken concerning community affairs.

# 11 Two Extinct Age Systems Among the Iteso

## NOBUHIRO NAGASHIMA

There is a sharp contrast in modern history between the Iteso of Uganda and Kenya and other Eastern Nilotes. The age systems of these peoples are a case in point. While ethnographic studies of the Eastern Nilotic peoples have presented us with a variety of age systems, which are yet related, ethnographic data on the same topic among the Iteso are scarce and fragmented, and it is difficult to reconstruct original forms. From the scanty literary sources available and from my own field data,[1] it seems probable that there were two distinct age systems developed among different dialect groups; one is the Eigworone system, an age-set system found among the Iseera and Ingoratok groups, and the other the Asapan system, a generation system among the Usuku Iteso. The former became defunct under the oppression of Baganda rule (1899–1904) and the last initiation took place around 1900. The latter seems to have survived till the 1950s, but the last initiation in which I participated in 1969 was merely an individual but vain attempt to revive the system.

In this paper I shall first describe the general situation at the beginning of the modern history of the Iteso and suggest factors which possibly accelerated the demise of their age system. The main features of the two age systems will then be presented, followed by detailed accounts of the Asapan initiation. Basic ritual groupings of *etem* and *airiget* which sustain the Asapan system will then be analyzed, together with passing comments on the relationship between the clan and age systems. Finally, I shall discuss the non-military nature of the two age systems, in contrast to many of the papers in this volume which emphasize the persistence of their unifying politico-military role. In a sense, therefore, this paper presents evidence contrary to the general theme of the book, but I trust that it is an aspect which should not be overlooked in considering East African age systems.

**227**

*Map 6  The Teso District*

## People Called Iteso and the Age System in Demise

According to their own definition, the Iteso are people who speak a language called Ateso, an Eastern Nilotic language, affiliated to those languages spoken by peoples of the 'Karimojong cluster', such as the Karimojong, Turkana, Jie, etc. The Iteso are spatially divided into two groups, which have conventionally been called 'the Northern Iteso' and 'the Southern Iteso'. The Northern Iteso live in and around the former Teso District of Uganda; there are also a considerable number of them living in Kampala. In the late 1960s they numbered almost 600,000 but the civil wars during the past two decades seem to have reduced them. They comprise several dialect groups (*eineresinei*, 'speech'), the Iteso, Iseera and Ingoratok being the major ones.

It is confusing that both the ethnic name as a whole and that of one of their dialect groups is Iteso. This situation was created in 1912 by the British administration when it named the newly founded District as Teso. Until then the area was divided into five autonomous counties, the boundaries of which more or less reflected those of dialect groups as recognized by the Kakunguru's Buganda forces (see below), and administered from Mbale as parts of Bukedi District (Lawrance, 1957:29). The name was, however, selected by local elders representing the main dialect groups, who agreed that all their people used to be called Iteso and that Teso was therefore the only reasonable name for the District (Teso District Annual Report, 1912/13). Without this external intervention unifying the name of the people and that of the District, the unity of the Iteso might have been much weaker and the main dialect groups would probably have become related but separate ethnic groups. The two different age systems which existed in the past should be considered in the context of this diversity.

To avoid confusion, I shall call the Iteso dialect group 'Usuku Iteso' after the place name Usuku where they are mostly concentrated. The Usuku Iteso are relative late-comers to Tesoland in the lengthy processes of migration from the east and northeast, and they are often abused as *Iloke* (a nickname for the Karimojong) by the rest of the Northern Iteso. Indeed, their linguistic and socio-cultural features differ considerably from those of the other dialect groups.

The Southern Iteso live on both sides of the Uganda-Kenya border in the Malaba-Busia area. Historians differ as to the possible date of their arrival from the north. According to historical traditions which I collected, they appear to have settled in the Tororo area of Uganda during the early part of the nineteenth century. They were cut off from their northern brothers by the Bagisu offensive in the latter half of the century. They number about 250,000, half of whom reside in Uganda. In terms of population, the Iteso as a whole in Uganda are second to the Baganda, while they are a minority in Kenya.

Unlike other Eastern Nilotes such as the Karimojong, Turkana, Toposa and Maasai, who resisted the encroachment of government administration and Western culture and sustained their predominantly pastoral way of life, the way of life of the Iteso underwent drastic changes. During the colonial era, they quickly adopted cash crops, school education, Christianity, Western clothing, and other new elements.

Several factors appear to have cumulatively contributed to these irreversible changes. The first, and very significant, factor was the subjugation of the Iteso by a Muganda general, Semei Kakunguru (Kakungulu) and his private army. Kakunguru occupied a high position in the Buganda kingdom, coming third after the *Kabaka* and the *Katikiro* (prime minister). He helped the British forces during the Bunyoro campaign of 1893–4 and proved himself an outstanding strategist and commander. He was then involved in the power struggle at court, and resigned to turn his attention to Lango and Teso with the ambition of establishing his own kingdom, while maintaining a relationship of mutual assistance with British officers. After pacifying southern Lango, he subjugated most of Teso in the five years from 1899 (Lawrance, 1957: 19–25). Only the Usuku Iteso managed to stage any organized resistance until they were finally defeated. It is noteworthy that, according to my field data on the oral traditions, the fighting unit of the Usuku Iteso was not based upon an age organization but on a territorial unit mobilized by a war leader. Kakunguru introduced a Buganda system of administration which was later inherited by the British. Even after Kakunguru was forced to leave by the British, many Baganda remained as administrative agents, and thus a dual indirect rule was practised in Teso. The most important feature of Kakunguru's rule in the context of this study was his suppression of the age organization to the extent of its destruction, which the Baganda carried out so thoroughly that none of the early European observers mentioned it (Lawrance, 1957: 72; for more details on Kakunguru's legacy, see Thomas, 1939; Waswa, 1950).

A second significant factor was the introduction of cotton cultivation by the Church Missionary Society in 1907 or earlier, which was 'followed up with an all-out effort by Government with spectacular results' (Lawrance, 1957: 27). This accelerated expansion in communications, on the one hand, and in education and technical training, on the other, both of which demanded increased administrative services. Socio-cultural and economic changes were thus set spirally in motion. In 1929, the railway reached Soroti, the centre of Teso District, which was to bring about more changes.

A third factor, whose influence is difficult to assess was the people's experience of government employment in straightforward work and forced labour, especially during the First World War. Demand for native labour came from different sources. One was to construct the road system and buildings within the District. A second was the essential porterage for the transport of cotton, as its production increased in the early war years. Then came the operations of the King's African Rifles against the Turkana and in 1918. More than 32,000 Iteso were recruited as porters to transport supplies to Moroto in Karamoja (Lawrance, 1957: 31). This was a historical irony, in that two formerly closely related ethnic groups had now taken opposite sides. Meanwhile, about 4,000 Iteso were sent in 1917 to German East Africa recruited into the Carrier Corps. Many of them were later absorbed into the chiefs' police. These cumulative individual experiences of contacts with new external elements had undoubtedly extended the general understanding of the Iteso about the new situation imposed upon them and contributed to their quick adaptation to it.

A fourth factor was the school education facilitated by both Protestant and Catholic missionaries. The Iteso seemed relatively quick to be attracted to it, and enthusiasm for sending children to school and for higher education was shared by many parents. The attitude towards education is another contrasting feature with other Eastern Nilotes. At the time of my fieldwork during 1968–70, there were more than 200 Iteso undergraduates at Makerere University.

A fifth factor was the introduction of the cash economy, combined with the poll tax and cotton cultivation. Cattle markets and small shops mainly managed by Indians, who appeared in Teso as early as 1908, contributed to its penetration. These and other factors accelerated the change in the way of life of the Iteso, and daily life in Teso, where people wore Western dress. It became in visible contrast with that in neighbouring Karamoja District where people maintained their indigenous culture.

*Two age systems recorded and observed*

It was A. C. A. Wright, District Commissioner of Teso District in 1935–6, who published the first account of the Iteso age system (Wright, 1942). He suggested the co-existence of two different age systems. The first, whose initiation was called *eigworone* and which I shall call the Eigworone system, appeared to be common among the Northern Iteso apart from the Usuku Iteso, and became extinct around 1900. The other is a generation-set system, although Wright does not use this term. It will be called the Asapan system, according to the name of its initiation, *asapan*. This system was still functioning, although weakly, among the Usuku Iteso at the time of my fieldwork. Wright reported its existence in Bukedea and at Tororo (1942: 66), the latter being the old concentration area of the southern Iteso. If this was the case, neither Ivan Karp nor I could find any old men among the Kenyan Southern Iteso who remembered the word *asapan* or any age system for that matter. We may have been too late. Only a song about the retirement of an aged couple was collected by either of us (Karp, personal communication).

This system was basically a generation-set system combined with a male group called *etem* and its component units called *airiget*. The available literature varies as to the number and names of the generation-set and as to whether it was cyclical or non-repetitive. This may be partly due to regional differences, since no comprehensive age organization covering the whole dialect group existed. There are also socio-cultural differences between northern Usuku (Usuku sub-county) and southern Usuku. The largest political unit was called *ebuku* (shield), which was adopted as the term for a sub-county by the colonial administration, and was also extended to mean 'country' or 'nation'. It is not certain that one unitary age organization prevailed. Another possible reason for the inconsistency is that, while one generation-set was open for fifteen to twenty years, *asapan* initiation took place every three years or so and was held by family or small descent groups, not by the regional group as a whole. Initiates of the same period might have been given a nickname as a group and this name might have been inserted among the names of generation-sets.

In the core area of Usuku sub-county, where I collected most of the data concerned, generation-sets definitely numbered five and were cyclical with no named age-sets. The male groups of *etem* and *airige* were still functioning for rituals of death and for twins. *Asapan* initiation, however, was said to have not been held for many years and no young men were therefore recruited to the groups. In other words, the system was dying out. One old man, deploring the waning of the tradition, decided in 1969 to hold *asapan* for his and his relatives' children. I was also allowed to be initiated. Not all rituals were performed, such as painting initiates with the pattern of a zebra (the name of the generation-set which was opened by this *asapan*) for several weeks following the initiation, and no other elders followed this initiative. Successive civil wars have devastated the area and it is unlikely that the Asapan system will be revived.

Wright suggested that both the Eigworone and the Asapan systems were once component parts of one unitary system (1942: 66–7), drawing an inference based on comparative data from the Toposa and the Turkana. King reported that there were *amaget* (age classes) and *nyithapan* (bull classes) among the Toposa and 'the age classes are periodically "raised" to bull classes, entry into which gives the member warrior status' (King, 1937; Wright, 1942: 67). E. D. Emley, a missionary, distinguished

**232**

two types of initiation among the Turkana; entry into the special class of *Nagban* and entry into a 'decoration class' (*athapanu*), the latter obviously being the alternation of Rocks and Leopards (see below) (Emley, 1927; Wright, 1942: 72).

It should be noted that these reports are very preliminary in character, and at that time European understanding of age systems was also at an early stage. In any event, Wright was thus tempted to think that the Iteso system was very similar to those of the Toposa and the Turkana; age-sets which had been forgotten among the Usuku Iteso and generation-sets which had disappeared from among the rest of the Northern Iteso (1942: 72, fn.).

It is true that similar words with the root *sapan* (*thapan*) are common among the 'Karimojong cluster' of Eastern Nilotes, and it is also found among the Western Nilotic-speaking Langi in the form of *achapan* (John Tosh, personal communication). Whatever the English translation may be, there are certainly common features of meaning designated by these vernacular terms, such as initiation into manhood or warriorhood (see Tornay's paper in this volume for the Toposa and Nyangatom). The Eigworone system is, however, very different from the age systems of related peoples and it is difficult to find a similar term among them. Given the fact that the culture of the Usuku Iteso generally differs in many respects from that of the other Northern Iteso, and that most of them have oral traditions of migration of their own, although it is misleading to suggest that all of them have a common origin, I take a negative view of Wright's hypothesis; the Asapan and Eigworone systems could not have been parts of one unitary system. I am inclined to think that the Eigworone system can be presumed to be a new development, or an invention, by the Southern Iteso other than the Usuku Iteso.

*Eigworone system*

Two accounts of the systems are available, one by Wright and the other by J. C. D. Lawrance, District Commissioner of Teso District, who published the first monograph about the Iteso (1957). This monograph, *The Iteso*, is not very satisfactory from a professional point of view but it provides us with a useful lead. Lawrance encouraged Iteso elders to talk about their traditional customs and also made use of a memorandum produced in 1946 by the Iteso elders' group called *Amootoi ka Etesot* (Intestines of the Iteso), which made significant references to the Eigworone system. We find considerable differences between the two accounts. Both agree that the system comprised eight cyclical age-sets which were divided into the alternation of right and left according to the position of the set in the kraal during the initiation. Lawrance argues that the age-set names and the order were constant all over Tesoland (1957: 74) (Table 11.1), in spite of Wright's report that there were 'sectional' differences (1942: 72) and Lawrance's own remark that 'in South Teso, among the Ingoratok, Rhinoceroses replace Bushbucks' (1957:74) (Table 11.1). The word *eigworone* was derived from the verb *aigwor* ('to cry') and the word for an age-set was *ewoe* ('singing'). According to Lawrance, the period between initiations was about three years and the whole cycle was therefore about twenty-four years. 'It was therefore not unusual to have two age-sets of the same name, a senior and a junior, in existence at the same time' (Lawrance, 1957: 74). Wright states that initiation intervals varied from one to four years according to 'sections' of the tribe (1942: 68).

*Table 11.1 Cyclical age-sets of the Eigworone system*

| Right side | Left side |
| --- | --- |
| A. Ikaalen (floods) | |
| | B. Ikosobwan (Buffaloes) |
| C. Itomei (Elephants) | |
| | D. Imoru (Rocks) |
| E. Iputrio (Warthogs) | |
| | F. Igolei (Hawks) |
| G. Iderin (Bushbucks)[a] or Imosing (Rhinoceroses)[b] | |
| | H. Irisai (Leopards) |

a): Among the Iseera dialect group. b): Among the Ingoratok dialect group.

*Source:* Lawrance, 1957: 74

The youth were initiated at puberty, around fourteen years old. Initiation into an age-set was said to have been sponsored by the age-set next but one in seniority, and there was whip fighting between the two age-sets immediately senior to the initiates. Thus when age-set C was opened, age-set A was the sponsor and age-set B was the contender in whipping against A. Initiates were not involved in the fighting (Wright, 1942: 69–71; Lawrance, 1957: 75).

Lawrence denies the possible existence of 'age-generation' or age-grades consisting of age-sets (1957: 76), although he suggests their existence in Usuku, but in relation to the Asapan and not the Eigworone system (1957: 78). However, Wright notes the 'warrior grade' consisting of two age-sets, senior and junior. They are the ones who contested at the initiation ceremony (1942: 69–71). Apart from this, nothing is known about the elders' grade or about generational aspects of the Eigworone system.

Each of the eight age-sets was said to control a particular set of natural phenomena, animals and trees, and to be endowed with a certain capacity. The Floods set, for instance, controlled water and heavenly bodies: rain, hail, sun, moon, rainbows, crocodiles, mosquitoes, lake plants, etc. (Wright, 1942: 74–9; Lawrance, 1957: 79-80). The significance of this cosmological classification was not, however, fully explored.

The Eigworone system resembles the Aworon system among the Langi (Lawrance, 1957: 75–6). Although J. H. Driberg does not use the term 'age system', this is apparently an age-set system comprising four cyclical age-sets, i.e., Elephants, Leopards, Rhinoceroses, and Buffaloes, whose cycle is twenty-five years. The system is concerned with rain-making, just as each age-set of the Eigworone system is endowed with power to control specific natural phenomena (Driberg, 1923: 243–4). This is not surprising since they have many clans claiming Iteso and Jie origins although they now speak a Luo language. The alternate division of age-sets into right and left sides is also found among the Turkana, Maasai, Lotuho and Pari. Otherwise, the system seems to occupy a unique position in the East African age systems.

*Asapan system*

Various evidence indicates that the Asapan system was more persistent than the Eigworone system, although the area where it was practised was rather limited, mainly in Usuku County. Although Lawrance calls its units 'age-sets' (1957: 77–8), this system, as we have already noted, was basically a generation-set system combined with a male group called *etem* and its component units, *airiget*. Members of these groups were recruited through the *asapan* initiation; a son normally entered into his father's *etem*. The time span of one generation was said to have been fifteen to twenty years (Wright, 1942: 66). I learnt that the general term for a generation set was *asapanu*, but neither Wright nor Lawrance recorded this word.

There are variations in the available literature as to the number and names of the generation-set and as to whether they were cyclical or non-repetitive. Lawrance gives five names: Ikosobwan (Buffaloes), Itomei (Elephants), Ituko (Zebras), Irisai (Leopards) and Iputiro (Warthogs) (Lawrance, 1957: 78) and claims that there was no fixed order. I was told, however, by elders that there are five sets and that the order is fixed and cyclical, although there are differences between northern and southern Usuku (Table 11.2). The general principle of the order, they said, is from bigger animals to smaller ones. At the time of my fieldwork in northern Usuku, most initiated men were Leopards, only a few old men were Lions and there were no Warthogs.

Before discussing *asapan* initiation, let me present an overview of the

*Table 11.2 Names and order of generation-sets in Usuku*

| | Southern Usuku | Northern Usuku |
|---|---|---|
| 1 | Itomei (Elephants) | Itomei (Elephants) |
| 2 | Ekorio (Giraffes) | Ingatunyo (Lions) |
| 3 | Iputiro (Warthogs) | Irisai (Leopards) |
| 4 | Ingatunyo (Lions) | Itukoi (Zebras) |
| 5 | Irisai (Leopards) | Iputoro (Warthogs) |
| | | Ikulicak (Uninitiated) |

Source: Nagashima, 1972: 56–7; 1976: 58.

available reports on the Asapan system in general, in the hope of tracing the process of its decline as far as possible.

None of the early European observers of Iteso, such as Dundas (1913) on the Southern Iteso or Roscoe (1915) on the Northern Iteso, mentioned any age system. Father Kruyer and Father Shut who worked among the Northern Iteso left personal notes on their customs, which apparently referred to the Eigworone system but probably not to the Asapan system (Wright, 1942). Wright revisited Teso in 1940 and tried to collect information about Iteso culture, especially aspects of age systems past and present. He reports that in Usuku there were two kinds of feast for the Asapan (he spelled it Esapan), one for the individual entry and the other for collective 'handing over of power', and that the latter did not appear to have taken place in either Usuku or Tororo for many years (1942: 74). This indicates that the basic part of the Asapan system had started to decline before 1920.

Gulliver, the first anthropologist to visit the Iteso, stayed briefly among the Northern Iteso in 1951 and recorded a resolution of Akumu Sub-County of Usuku County making the *asapan* initiation illegal by ten votes to three on the grounds of its involving excessive violence (1953: 25). This suggests that the *asapan* initiation itself was still being held. Lawrance also records attitudes of the Iteso around the same time towards the *asapan* initiation, quoting discussions at the Usuku Sub-County Council;

> The members who were in favour of *asapan* said that *asapan* used to be a Teso custom and nobody was forced [to undergo it]. That whenever a boy went *asapan*, at the end he would be awarded with a cow or five goats.
>
> The members who were not in favour said that *asapan* hinders the development of a country, and that there is no profit in it. It is a waste to slaughter cows or goats or to brew beer; all this should be used to educate children. During *asapan* people were chased and beaten so much that in the end they might die. A youth who goes to *asapan* must act like a slave; i.e. carry

water, grind millet, collect firewood, herd cattle, be smeared with butter like a woman. We would recommend that anybody who is caught performing *asapan* should be imprisoned for six months (Lawrance, 1957: 78).

This is a good example of conflict between the traditionalists and the development-minded 'modernists'. In the case of age systems the latter seem to have been the winners. The modernists saw the feast as economically wasteful and the violence and maltreatment inflicted on initiates as intolerable and unjust.

Webster, Professor of History at Makerere at that time, organized a research team of Iteso undergraduates and the History Department published its results (Webster et al., 1973). The book contains a brief reference to the Asapan system and its relationship with *emuron* (prophets or diviners), in that a novice who wanted to become a prophet was sponsored by an established prophet for *asapan* initiation and trained by the latter during the period. The main work of a prophet was to advise war leaders but there was no direct relationship between *asapan* initiation and military organization before the colonial period or at an early stage of it (ibid.). As to the process of its decline, their findings do not differ from what has been suggested.

In brief, the Asapan system was still functioning in the late 1960s for holding certain rituals, but had lost its structural base in terms of recruiting younger generations through initiation.

## *Asapan* Initiation in the Literature and in the Field

### Asapan *initiation in the literature*

I shall first present summarized accounts of what has been recorded in the literature about the asapan initiation. The following description was given by Aesopol, an old man in Toroma, Southern Usuku, and quoted by Wright (1942: 73).

> When a boy wishes to be admitted into an age-set, he first has to find a sponsor, with whom he goes to live, calling him father and his wife mother. Here he works for a month or more doing the tiresome work of grinding millet, collecting firewood and water, and receiving instruction from the old man. This period was called *aitemio* (testing)[preparation may be a better translation]. At the end of it, the boy's people prepare a feast for the boy's return, which is called *inyamat lu bwataret asapanan* [food for the returnee from *asapan*]. The boy comes home running and bursts through a new gap in the homestead hedge which has been prepared for his entry. He goes into the hut where beer is ready and his sponsor says to him; 'Go and kill elephants, lions, rhinoceroses, leopards and buffaloes'. Then the sponsor

takes a mouthful of beer and spits on him and the boy's mother gives the shrill cry of triumph. After this, the boy takes a new name from the bull that has been killed and his sponsor may give him a goat.

After summarizing Wright's note quoted above, Lawrance adds the following information about the manner of naming (1957:77–8):

> … the boy squats under the udder of a cow and his sponsor calls out 'Ojakol, suck the milk'. If the youth does not wish to accept this name he shakes his head. The sponsor might then call out, 'Lemukol, suck the milk'. If this name pleases him, the youth sucks the cow's udder to signify assent.

Webster regards those people of Usuku who claimed to have come from Oropom in Karamoja as originally belonging to a different linguistic group from that which he calls Ateker people (Karimojong cluster of Eastern Nilotes), and he categorically calls the former 'Iworopom'. The evidence he presents is very scant. However, based on this unestablished hypothesis, he goes even further to attribute almost every socio-cultural feature of the Usuku Iteso (his Iworopom) of northern Usuku to non-Iteso origins. Although it is true that elements of non-Eastern Nilotes, such as the Sebei, Itepeth, Iminito and Suk, have been incorporated into the Usuku Iteso, the majority of them, according to the oral traditions which I collected, appear to have spoken an Eastern Nilotic language, or Ateso itself. My own hypothesis therefore is that the main body of the 'Iworopom' were a part of the Iteso who had remained longer in Karamoja than the rest of the Iteso, sharing many socio-cultural features with the Karimojong.

In any event, the following account by Webster is based on his own rather far-fetched interpretation (1973: 35–6).

> Among the Ateker there was initiation of young men into manhood. This initiation among the southern Iteso was called *aijaun ewoye*, and in Amuria *eigworone*. In northern Usuku it was called *abwaton* which probably comes from the Iworopom, but whether the actual ceremony was different between the Ateker and the Iworopom is as yet unclear. However before one could take one's abwaton initiation which was done in groups or age sets, a young man had to go through an individual initiation called asapan. In northern Usuku this was a general practice among almost all clans whether of Ateker or Iworopom origin. In other words the Iworopom practice appears to have become general. In southern Teso and Amuria asapan was very rare.

Some of Webster's interpretations are problematic, or at least contradictory to the data collected by myself. First of all, the nature of the ritual called by him *abwaton*, which he considered a 'group initiation', may not have been so. According to Wright, a similar word *bwataret* means 'return' from the initiation. At the *asapan* initiation I observed that the word *abwatar* was used to describe the return home. Secondly, the word *abwaton* (it should be spelled as either '*abwatar*', v. or '*abwatun*', n.) is a genuine

Ateso word, and not of foreign origin. In our personal discussion at Makerere in 1970, Professor Webster insisted that it is an Iworopom, and therefore a non-Ateso, word. I then pointed out that the word is commonly used among other dialect groups of the Northern Iteso, meaning in the ritual context a sprinkling of water on the returning person at the gate of his/her home. The word is also found in two Ateso-English dictionaries, both of which were based upon the dialect of the Ingoratok (Kiggen, 1953; Hilders and Lawrance, 1958). It is also frequently used as a ritual term among the Southern Iteso of Kenya.

Asapan *initiation in the field*

General accounts of *asapan* initiation given to me by elders were short but consistent, and I present here a version narrated by Mr Petoro Okwi of Ongatunyo, Aketa Parish, Usuku sub-county, in November 1968.

Both my grandfather and father were born in Oropom in Karamoja. My father migrated to Lale in south Usuku, and I was born there. I migrated to north Usuku with my family in 1934, and settled at the present place where there were many lions (*ingatunyo*) and no human beings, and the place became called Ongatunyo after the animal. Asapan initiation was held first by a certain family which was keen to hold it, and other families of the same *etem* and those of other *etems* followed it one by one. As a result, young men of the appropriate age were initiated in the same year. This happened every two to three years, depending upon the availability of food and beer.

A boy stayed at the home of an old man, who belonged to the same *etem* as that of the boy's father, and worked for him like a girl, fetching water and collecting firewood for about a month. He had to obey whatever he was told to do, but there were no severe trials. While he stayed there, the old man taught him many things about customs. Occasionally, more than one boy were initiated together.

At asapan, a bull (*emathenik*) was slaughtered and the boy was smeared with its stomach contents (*ikijit*) and given a new name and a spear. On his return, a lot of beer was drunk because many relatives and friends came to celebrate. There was no ritual of group initiation. I myself had been initiated before I came to north Usuku and joined the *asapanu* (set) of Lions. There are very few old men of the Lions alive today.

I understand that there was a difference in names between the place where I was initiated and here in Usuku Sub-County. There, Lions followed Wart Hogs but here Elephants preceded Lions. Perhaps, each *ebuku* took its own decision.

As stated above, asapan initiation had not taken place for many years in Usuku. But in the middle of December, 1969, I heard a rumour that *asapan* might take place somewhere in the north, perhaps at Christmas time. Unfortunately, I had to go to Kampala and when I returned in the afternoon of the 26th, I was told it was being held. I rushed to the place and was allowed to be initiated, but it was the last part of the ritual which was going on, as it had started on the previous day. Thus the new generation-set of Zebras was opened. Next day I interviewed Mr Peter Kide, one of the fathers of the initiated boys, in order to learn what had been done before I arrived. The following descriptions of the ritual are a summary of the interview and my own observations.

**1. Preparation.** It was Mr Serusi Ogwani of Aterai, Okolitok Parish, who first proposed *asapan*, because he was worried about the decrease in the number of the initiated, which had made it difficult to perform *apunya* (the ritual of ending mourning), and also about the loss of good tradition. Eventually sixteen young men of his *etem*, ranging from five years old to their late twenties, were to be initiated. His *etem* was Ikangaeda and his *alriget* was Ikarebwok. Eight elders of the Leopards set of the *etem* and eight families of *asapanak* (initiates) began preparations for the ritual a month earlier.

**2. First day.** Initiates spent the previous night at the *atuket* (ritual grove) of the Ikangaeda *etem*. They each wore a woman's loin cloth, strings of beads and an iron bracelet of the traditional type at an elder's home. At sunset they left home in procession led by a cow (neither a bull nor an ox) and an elder who provided it, followed by other elders carrying spears, and reached the homestead of the 'father', Mr Ogwani, who was standing at the gate and smeared the initiates with cow dung.

Inside the gate, a fire-place called *etem loipiera* (fire for warming up) was prepared and lit by the mother (Ogwani's wife). The initiates sat round it and strict silence was ordered. The initiates were then led into the hut and beer was served by the mother.

**3. Second day**. At dawn, the initiates were led off to herd the father's cattle for three hours, carrying a spear and apariko (a branch of the black eparis tree) and singing five songs. They then went to collect firewood which they carried back to the homestead, where a calabash containing cooked food called *edeki* was placed in the centre. The initiates sat around it. Then the father called out asapan names, which were called 'bull names', one by one. An initiate who wanted a particular name came to the centre, sat down and tasted the *edeki*.

They went to the homestead of another elder situated in the direction of *iyale* (roughly to the south-east); this direction was said to have been that from which their grandfathers came. They only stopped at the gate and then went to the *atuket*, where the elders sat in a circle (*airiget*) and the initiates sat behind them on the western side. The cow was tied to a tree, and a man was chosen to spear it in its right *amuro* (the thigh of the hind leg). No blood was supposed to be shed by this. The dead cow was carried by initiates into the centre of the circle. The elders skinned and cut it up, made a fire, roasted some meat and ate it.

While the elders were doing this, the initiates started running round the cow anti-clockwise three times and then threw the stomach contents to each other, and women joined in this running after the initiates. The initiates went back to the cow and started drinking its blood. The women did not do this. Then the initiates were made to sit on the ground between the elders, who sat each on his own small stool. The father came in and told them 'Loesapanikitos yesi' (You have completed *asapan*). They were then given roasted meat..

A big beer pot was placed in the centre and the elders and the mother drank from it helped by the initiates, who then drank one by one. The pot was replaced by two skin mats. All the initiates, the women and the elders mixed together, started running round the skin anti-clockwise, while the father blew a long wooden horn. Songs were sung, the men jumped and the women ululated. Then they went into the centre and each stamped once on the skin mats. The singing, shouting and running round to the rhythmical sound of the horn were repeated several times. They again sat in a circle and the mother brought in cooked food (*emuna*) which the father distributed to the initiates, who had to refuse it three times before accepting it. The song of the Zebras was sung, followed by other songs.

The bones of the cow were collected and burnt and the procession of returning home (*abwatar*) left the place singing, led by the elders. On their way, a mock fight broke out between the elders who carried spears and the initiates who carried sticks, shouting 'kwo, kwo, kwo', a war cry. The elders advanced and the initiates retreated. I was not able to follow them to their homes, so I do not know how they entered their homestead.

Next morning, the loin cloth, beads and bracelet were taken off and a feast followed for each family.

They said that the whole ritual process was a sort of simplified version. For instance, painting the bodies of the initiates with the pattern of the zebra several weeks after the initiation was not done, and the initiation remained an isolated case, as no other elders in the area followed this initiative. The *asapan* initiation of 1969 seems to be the last one held. In 1995 I revisited Tesoland briefly. After the devastation and displacement caused by successive civil wars from the late 1970s till the early 1990s, I could find no indication that the Asapan system had been or was likely to be revived.

*Main themes of the* asapan *initiation*

The main themes of the *asapan* initiation can be enumerated as follows. First, the transvestitism of the initiates becoming women and being treated as women is obvious. This point is well stressed both in the literature and by the elders I talked to. The reason for this is not so obvious, however, and in fact the explanations I was given were such as 'to make the young men feel ashamed', 'to insult them', 'to make them obey when they are ordered by real men', etc. I expected deeper psychological comments such as 'in order to become a real man, one should go through its extreme opposite, that is, to become a woman', but it never happened.

Secondly, and related to the first theme, the value of obedience to the seniors is repeatedly expressed. The relationship between the senior and the junior generations is also expressed as that between parents and children.

Thirdly, in contrast to the second theme, bullishness as the most manly and desirable quality of an initiated man, is expressed by acquiring a bull name at the initiation. I myself was given the bull name of *Oblyangor*, which means 'a man skilled in handling weapons'.

Fourthly, the third theme inevitably leads to that of violence and of a rebellious attitude on the part of young men towards the elders. This is an accepted, or expected, virtue associated with the ideal image of a young man. Among the Usuku Iteso, there was a custom that a son was allowed to challenge his father openly by attacking him with a spear, while the father used only a shield; if the son won, he would establish himself as a worthy man.

Both Gulliver and Lawrance referred to the discussion of violence at the *asapan* initiation at Sub-County Councils, but unfortunately neither identified at what stage of the initiation this violence broke out. The mock fighting I observed could not be a model case, because the ritual itself was irregular since its initiates were too many for a traditional initiation. If it is true that one initial initiation formerly triggered off a series of asapan initiations everywhere among different *etems,* there could have been an occasion at which young men already initiated in the same year gathered together to support the later initiates and thus inspired the collective confrontation against the senior generation-set. The ceremony of 'handing over power' mentioned by Wright could have been such a case (Wright, 1942: 72–4). But this is only a guess with no concrete evidence to support it. And what the available evidence does suggest is that the form of violence exercised was presumably not a kind of inter-generational confrontation but individual flogging and beating of intiates by seniors.

## Generation-sets, *Etem* and *Airiget*

I learnt that the general term for a generation-set was *asapanu*, but neither Wright nor Lawrance recorded this word. Lawrance used two words for age-sets, *aturi* and *ewoe*, and I was told by Usuku elders that the former means 'old generation' or 'ancestor' and that they did not know the latter word. Names of generation-sets and their order in southern and northern Usuku are listed in Table 11.2 (Nagashima, 1972: 56–7; 1976: 58).

Understanding the territorial groupings in relation to the *etem* and *airiget* is essential to understanding Iteso society as well as the age system. The issue is complicated partly because of the intricate nature of their migration and settlement history and also because the colonial administration picked up words such as *etem* and attached to them concrete and fixed territorial meanings in the hierarchy of the administrative structure.

In the pre-colonial period, there seems to have been a distinctive territorial area called *ebuku* (shield), which could have been a political and military entity with a war leader (*lokajoore*). The term was adopted by the colonial administration to mean a County. It is not certain whether or not one unitary age organization prevailed in one *ebuku*. Another term *eitela*, which means a place where people live close together and separated from other populated places by bush or other natural barriers, was adopted to designate a Parish as an administrative unit. For a sub-county, as already noted, the colonial administration chose the word *etem*. This was a misconception, as I argue below, as the *etem* is not a territorial unit, although it does have a connection with a certain place. The fixation of the term's image as a bounded territorial group had the unfortunate effect of misleading the interpretation of the Asapan system in particular, and of traditional Iteso society in general.

The word *etem* (pl. *itemwan*) is common among the Karimojong cluster. Its original meaning is a 'fire place' for men inside a homestead (*ere*), situated in the central part of an open space where men come together. The distinction between a male fire (for roasting and warming) and a female fire (for cooking or boiling) is important in Iteso rituals and cosmology. The word also generally means a particular place where elders sit and people come to see them to discuss important matters or simply to gossip. A popular place for this is under a big shady tree. In this sense it may be translated as an elders' club or court and may refer to a particular place. It may also refer to a place where people reside, as Gulliver translates the same Jie word as 'settlement' (1958). It is suggestive that in his dictionary Father Kiggen translates *etem* as 'age-group' (Kiggen, 1953: 399). He is correct in the sense that he does not recognize it as a territorial group, but the translation is nevertheless misleading.

**243**

Incessant migrations are a prominent feature of the history of the Iteso and most of the Usuku Iteso of Usuku Sub-County are descendants of those who came there from Karamoja only two to four generations ago. A part of them migrated again to northern Amuria County and settled in Achwa only two or three generations ago. In the process of migration, it was not the case that they moved from one *etem* to another. Both Wright (1942: 66) and Lawrance (1957: 69) suggested that migrations had been carried out on an age-set basis, with a 'new' *etem* being formed at the destination. However, most of my data on oral traditions concerning migrations indicate that this was not so, because there were no definite patterns as to who migrated with whom. Sometimes it was a matter of family, and in many cases a group larger than a family moved together with no specific characteristics as to who they were. There were cases of young men migrating on their own decision, but not as an age-set or generation-set group.

Membership of an *etem* is patrilineal in the sense that in principle a son joins his father's *etem* after initiation. Deviations from this rule were said to be impossible but there were in fact such cases. For example, a son whose father was a member of the Igetoma *etem* joined the Imalera *etem* because he was given an ox for the ritual by an elder of the Imalera. Since membership of an *etem* was not determined by birth but by initiation, this kind of case could have happened, especially at a time of destitution and for young men of poor family.

An *etem* as a social grouping, or rather as a social category like a 'clan' (*atekere*), is essentially a ritual group, comprising initiated men.[2] It is a basic unit for the age system, in that asapan initiation was in principle held under the name of a particular *etem*, although in reality it was held separately by much smaller groups within it. Although members of the same *etem* tended to live close together, it was definitely not a territorial group; it is usual that more than one *etem* group live in a fairly limited area and conversely members of the same *etem* are scattered in wider areas.

At the time of my fieldwork eight *etem* groups existed in Usuku Sub-County of Usuku County and adjacent Achwa Sub-County of Amuria County (Table 11.3). They shared a common Asapan system, as most of them shared a common origin and history and members of the same *etem* of either side could join, and actually did so, any ritual held in the other Sub-County. Each *etem* group had a ritual group called *atuket*[3] and cutting its trees was prohibited on penalty of mystical death. This does not necessarily mean that all the members of one *etem* group share a single *atuket*. If some of them migrated to a distant place, they would choose a place for their own ritual grove, but they would revisit the original one if there were appropriate occasions on which to do so.

Among the eight *etem* groups there was a special relationship called

*Table 11.3* Etems *and their component* airiget *in Usuku and Achwa Sub-Counties*

| | Etem | Airiget |
|---|---|---|
| 1 | Isuguro | Ikuruka |
| | | Ikicira |
| | | Ikwongolo |
| 2 | Imalera | Ikarikarot |
| | (Ingariama) | Ikorinyaga |
| | | Idocatok |
| | | Isupatok |
| 3 | Igetoma | Ikolituko |
| | | Irieta |
| 4 | Ikangaeda | Ikarebwok |
| | | ___a |
| | | ___ |
| | | ___ |
| 5 | Ilalei | Ikaleryo |
| | | Ikuruso |
| | | Ikibiyo |
| | | Itwala |
| | | Iminito |
| | | Itikokin |
| 6 | Iusuko | Atap |
| | | Iteso |
| | | Icerekul |
| 7 | Isureta | Imodoi |
| | | Imugenya |
| 8 | Ikelimo | Icoma |
| | | Ipakwi |

a) There are three other *airiget* whose names are unknown to me.

*amuro* ('thigh of hind legs') between two particular ones. Members of both were obliged to attend rituals concerned with death and twins held by either of them. The eight *etem*s thus formed four pairs of *amuro* relationships (1 and 2, 3 and 4, 5 and 6, and 7 and 8 in Table 11.3)

An *etem* comprises a number of *airigets* (Table 11.3). The word *airiget* is derived from the verb *airigaun* ('to sit in a circle'), and means both a named group of initiated people within an *etem* group and the act of sitting together in a circle at rituals. Members of one *airiget* group were said to be of the same *atekere* but this is not always the case; in fact one *airiget* group might comprise members of more than one *atekere*. Exogamy is the rule for an *airiget* group irrespective of its constituent *atekeres*.

I have deliberately avoided using the English term 'division' or 'sub-section' to designate the *airiget* group in its relation to the *etem* group, because it may give an impression that these 'divisions' are fixed and

**245**

exclusive. An *etem* may accept a new *airiget* as one of its components, and two or more *airiget*s of the same name may belong to different *etem*s. For instance, the Iminito *airiget* or the Ilalei *etem* has certainly originated from people of the same name, the Iminito, who, according to Mr Watson, a painter living in Karamoja and interested in ethnic history (personal discussion in 1970), disappeared from Southern Karamoja in the last century (they are said to have evil eyes). This may suggest the possibility that a group of the Iminito migrated and were incorporated into the *etem* as an *airiget*. The case of the Iteso *airiget* of the Iusuko *etem* seems to have some significance, but I could obtain no satisfactory account of why the *airiget* bears the same name as the dialect group. The activities of an *airiget* group were the same as those of an *etem* group, retaining its autonomy as a working unit for rituals; when an *etem* group gathered together, each of its component *airiget* groups acted separately.

Father Shut translated the word *etem* as 'clan' but Wright refuted this as a misunderstanding (Wright, 1942: 64). The Iteso themselves sometimes said to me, 'An *etem* is a male *atekere*', or 'An *etem* is male and an *atekere* is female'. This statement may seem peculiar, since a clan system and an age system have been taken among anthropologists as being diametrically opposed to each other in organizational principle, i.e., descent vs age. The native view of the Iteso may to some extent modify the general view, in so far as 'clans' of the Karimojong cluster are concerned. As I have discussed elsewhere similarities and contrasts between the two groupings (Nagashima, 1976), I shall only summarize them here. An *atekere* is a named patrilineal descent group, but it is mainly concerned with married-in women and their young children, and its main functions are the regulation of marriage and holding rituals called *etale* for young wives and their children. An *etem* is also in principle based upon patrilineality realized by an asapan initiation, and it is an exclusively male group. The contrast between the two in the ritual context is as follows: *atekere/etem*; *etale/asapan*; wives and children/initiated men; hearth (female fire)/ naked fire(male fire); boiling/roasting; birth ritual/funeral; east/west; *esasi* (female stick)/spear.

## Military Conquest, Modernization, and the Age Systems

I have argued that the age systems among the Iteso had already started to decline at the beginning of this century and that the Asapan system was mainly concerned with male rituals. This does not imply, however, that in the pre-colonial period the systems had more politico-military charac-teristics. Neither the Eigworone nor the Asapan system embodied the political unity of a dialect group, to say nothing of the Iteso as a whole. I was able to collect only negative evidence as to the relationship between military activities in the past for both the Asapan system among the Usuku Iteso and the Eigworone system among the other Northern Iteso.

The Northern Iteso as a whole had had long experience of interethnic and occasionally intraethnic conflicts, mainly in the form of cattle raiding. According to oral traditions among the Usuku Iteso, each *eitela* or some-times several *eitelas* had a war leader (*lokajoore*), who played a leading role in the actual fighting. The bringing together of warriors under one war leader, however, had nothing to do with the age system, which comprised men of different ages who were able and willing to join. Alliances of war leaders were often formed, especially when there was a serious threat of large-scale raiding by the Karimojong.

When I stayed in Usuku, raiding was undertaken by the Karimojong almost every night during the dry season. The Iteso had to organize their own defence force under the leadership of a veteran Parish Chief, and this was composed of able-bodied men of all ages with no reliance on the age system which still existed.

The role of prophets (*emuron*) was inseparable from military activities as they were consulted by war leaders about the possible result of their fighting plans. It must be noted, however, that a prophet was not bound by territorial loyalty or by any particular group whatsoever. He accepted anybody who trusted him, even outside ethnic boundaries. Okolimong, the most famous prophet of the region, is thus said to have advised even the Turkana warriors. A prophet seldom left his homestead, and let his hair and his beard grow and often dressed like a woman. Dreaming, or vision, was the only method he used to divine future events.

There is a story which has often been told to me about Okolimong in the context of *asapan*. He migrated from Karamoja while he was still young and was initiated at the home of eastern Usuku *emuron* where he learnt the skill of prophecy from the 'father' for three months at his home during the preparation period for asapan.

When Baganda forces commanded by General Karunguru embarked on the military invasion of Tesoland in 1899, the Iteso were unable to organize effective resistance. The Baganda forces consisted of platoons of infantry armed with firearms supplied by the British, and they defeated the Iteso forces, which were merely a mass of spearmen, one by one. The Usuku Iteso were the last to be conquered. When in 1907 the combined Baganda-Iteso forces launched an operation against them, Iteso men under their war leader Abaremong ambushed the enemy, and defeated the allied forces. But eventually the Usuku Iteso were conquered and came under Baganda rule in 1908 (Nagashima, 1972).[4]

The British-Baganda administration had profound effects on Iteso society, as discussed earlier. Let us list important changes which took place as early as the first decade of this century: the Baganda oppressed the Eigworone system and extinguished it; a couple of urban centres were established with shops run by Asians; both Anglican and Catholic missions opened churches, schools and clinics; the cultivation of cotton was introduced, alongside the imposition of a poll tax. Cotton cultivation combined with ox ploughing spread very rapidly and Tesoland soon became a centre of cotton production in Uganda. It should be noted that it was carried out by small-scale Iteso peasants, not by European settlers (Nagashima, 1972: 108 12).

Of course, these modernization processes did not fail to cause problems in the society. While the asapan initiation was suppressed because of the violence involved, the irony was that the murder rate in Teso District was one of the highest in Uganda. Colonial administrators like Wright showed concern about this issue and pointed to 'dislocation of social solidarity' as its cause (1942: 62).

In any event, the various factors mentioned above undoubtedly seem to have operated to cause the decline of the two age systems among the Iteso, but reconstructing the process in detail is not possible because of the scantiness of the available historical data. What is certain is that the traditional age systems, even if they had been left untouched, were incompatible with so-called modern life and that for the Iteso they were not something worth maintaining or preserving. Otherwise, efforts to revive them might have been made, as was the case with the *asapan* initiation I observed, and could have been successful. As it is, the demise of their age systems may be regarded as an inevitable outcome of history.

# Notes

1   My fieldwork was conducted for 19 months among the Usuku Iteso and for 4 months among the Ingoratok from September 1968 to July 1970. Later, I spent more than 26 months among the Southern Iteso on the Kenyan side during several visits since 1977.
2   Webster calls it *aigeresit* (Webster et al., 1973), but he appears to have taken *airiget* as a ritual grove where an *airiget* group sat in a circle.
3   In the *Ateso-English Dictionary* by Kiggen (1953), it is translated as 'to hunt out from a place'.
4   The role played by Okolimong in the process of conquest is worth mentioning. When he was consulted by Abaremong, he advised him not to fight, because the enemy had deadly tools. When the warriors insisted on going to fight, he gave them his blessing. After the conquest, Baganda soldiers were staying at Okolimong's homestead. At that time he would have been a very old man, almost one hundred years old. He warned them that they should not cut down the trees of the sacred grove behind his homestead, otherwise they would face a serious problem. They ignored this, cut down the trees, looted the cattle, and seduced the Iteso girls. Then an unknown epidemic broke out and the Baganda soldiers died in great numbers. Finally they had to abandon their headquarters in Usuku. The Usuku Iteso see these events as an effect of the prophet's powerful curse. He conquered the Baganda without fighting (Nagashima, 1972: 113–16).

# Bibliography

Abélès, Marc and Chantal Collard (1985) *Age, pouvoir et société en Afrique noire*. Paris: Karthala.

Abrahams, R.G. (1978) 'Aspects of Labwor Age and Generation Grouping and Related Systems' in Baxter and Almagor.

—— (1986) 'Dual Organisation in Labwor?', *Ethnos* (1-2): 88-103.

Almagor, U. (1978a) 'The Ethos of Equality among Dassanetch Age-peers' in Baxter and Almagor.

—— (1978b) 'Gerontocracy, Polygyny and Scarce Resources' in J.S. Lafontaine (ed.) *Sex and Age as Principles of Social Differentiation*. New York: Academic Press.

—— (1979) 'Raiders and Elders: A Confrontation of Generations among the Dassanetch' in Fukui and Turton.

—— (1983) 'Charisma Fatigue in an East African Generation-Set System', *American Ethnologist*, 635-48.

—— (1985) 'A Generation After *From Generation to Generation*: Coevals and Competitors in "Cattle Complex" Societies' in Cohen et al.

—— (1989) 'The Dialectic of Generation Moieties in an East African Society' in Maybury-Lewis and Almagor.

Anderson, D.M. (1981) *Some Thoughts on the Nineteenth Century History of the Il Chamus of Baringo District*. Paper No. 149. Nairobi: Institute of African Studies, University of Nairobi.

—— (1995) 'Visions of the Vanquished: Prophets and Colonialism in Kenya's Western Highlands' in D.M. Anderson and D.H. Johnson (eds) *Revealing Prophets: Prophecy in Eastern African History*. London: James Currey.

Arnesen, Odd Erik (1996) 'The Becoming of Place: a Tulama-Oromo Region of Northern Shoa' in Baxter et al.

Asad, T. (1979) 'Equality in Nomadic Social Systems? Notes Towards the

Dissolution of an Anthropological Category' in L'Equipe Ecologie et Anthropologie des Sociétés Pastorales (ed.) *Pastoral Production and Society*. Cambridge: Cambridge University Press.

Bartels, Lambert (1983) *Oromo Religion*. Berlin: Reimer.

Bassi, Marco (1994) 'Gada as an Integrative Factor of Political Organization' in D. Brokensha (ed.) *A River of Blessings. Essays in Honor of Paul Baxter*. Syracuse, NY: Syracuse University Press.

—— (1996) 'Power's Ambiguity or the Political Significance of *Gada*' in Baxter et al.

Bateson, G. (1958) *Naven*. Stanford, CA: Stanford University Press (second edition).

Baxter, P.T.W. (1978) 'Boran Age-Sets and Generation-Sets: *Gada*, a Puzzle or a Maze?' in Baxter and Almagor.

—— (1979) 'Boran Age-Sets and Warfare' in Fukui and Turton.

—— (1994) 'The Creation and Constitution of Oromo Nationality' in Fukui and Markakis.

—— and U. Almagor (eds) (1978) *Age, Generation and Time: Some Features of East African Age Organization*. London: C. Hurst & Co.

—— and Richard Hogg (eds) (1990) *Property, Poverty and People: Changing Rights in Property and Problems of Pastoral Development*. Department of Social Anthropology and International Development Centre, Manchester Univesity: University of Manchester Press.

—— , Jan Hultin and Allessandro Triulzi (eds) (1996) *Being and Becoming Oromo: Historical and Anthropological Enquiries*. Uppsala: Nordiska Afrika-institutet.

Beaman, A. (1981) 'The Rendille Age-set System in Ethnographic Context: Adaptation and Integration in a Nomadic Society', PhD thesis, Boston University.

Beaton, A.C. (1932) 'A Short History of Ngangala'. Juba District Files 1/1/2. (C.D./66-1-2-6 15/7/32, Juba). National Records Office, Khartoum.

—— (1936) 'The Bari: Clan and Age-Class Systems', *Sudan Notes and Records* 19 (1): 109-45.

Berman, Bruce and John Lonsdale (1992) *Unhappy Valley: Clan, Class and State in Colonial Kenya*. 2 vols. London: James Currey; Nairobi: Heinemann; Athens, OH: Ohio University Press.

Bernardi, Bernardo (1952) 'The Age Systems of the Nilo-Hamitic Peoples', *Africa* 22: 316-32.

—— (1985) *Age Class Systems: Social Institutions and Polities Based on Age*. Cambridge: Cambridge University Press.

Bernsten, John L. (1979) 'Maasai Age-Sets and Prophetic Leadership: 1850-1910', *Africa* 49 (2): 134-46.

Blackhurst, Hector (1996) 'Adopting an Ambiguous Position: Oromo Relationships with Strangers' in Baxter et al.

Bonte, Pierre (1975) 'Cattle for God: An Attempt at a Marxist Analysis of the Religion of East African Herdsmen', *Social Compass* 22 (3-4): 381-96.

—— (1991) 'To Increase Cows Gods Created the King' in Galaty and Bonte.

Broch-Due, Vigdis (1990) 'Livestock Speak Louder than Sweet Words' in Baxter and Hogg.

Barton, Juxton (1923) 'Notes on the Kipsikis or Lumbwa Tribe of Kenya Colony', *Journal of the Royal Anthropological Institute* 53: 42-78.

Buxton, J.C. (1963) *Chiefs and Strangers: A Study of Political Assimilation among the Mandari*. Oxford: Clarendon Press.

Charsley, S.R. (1968) *The Princes of Nyakyusa*. Nairobi: East African Publishing House.

Cohen, Erik, M. Lissak and U. Almagor (1985) *Comparative Social Dynamics*. Boulder, CO: Westview Press.

Croll, Elisabeth and David Parkin (eds) (1992) *Bush Base: Forest Farm. Culture, Environment and Development*. London: Routledge.

De Heusch, Luc (1986) *Le sacrifice dans les religions africaines*. Paris: NRF.

Deng, Francis Mading (1987) *Tradition and Modernization: A Challenge for Law among the Dinka of the Sudan*. New Haven, CT and London: Yale University Press (second edition).

Dobbs, C.M. (1921) 'The Lumbwa Circumcision Ages', *Journal of the East Africa and Uganda Natural History Society* 16: 55-7.

Driberg, J.H. (1923) *The Lango: A Nilotic Tribe of Uganda*. London: T. Fisher Unwin.

Dundas, K.R. (1913) 'Wawanga and Other Tribes of the Elgon District', *Journal of the Royal Anthropological Institute* 53: 62-3.

Dyson-Hudson, N. (1966) *Karimojong Politics*. Oxford: Clarendon Press.

Ehret, C. (1982) 'Population Movement and Culture Contact in the Southern Sudan, c.3000 BC to AD 1000: A Preliminary Linguistic Overview' in J. Mack and P. Robertshaw (eds) *Culture History in the Southern Sudan*. Nairobi: British Institute in Eastern Africa.

Eisenstadt, S.N. (1956) *From Generation to Generation*. New York: Free Press.

Emley, E.D. (1927) 'The Turkana of Kolosia District', *Journal of the Royal Anthropological Institute* 67: 157-201

Evans-Pritchard, E.E.(1936) 'The Nuer Age-Sets', *Sudan Notes and Records* 19 (2): 233-69.

—— (1939) 'Introduction' in Peristiany.

—— (1940a) *The Nuer: A Description of the Modes of Livelihood and Political Institutions of a Nilotic People*. Oxford: Clarendon Press.

—— (1940b) *The Political System of the Anuak of the Anglo- Egyptian Sudan*. London: Percy Lund, Humphreys & Co. (reprinted in 1977 by AMS Press, New York).

—— (1954) 'The Meaning of Sacrifice among the Nuer'. The Henry Myers Lecture. *The Journal of the Royal Anthropological Institute* 84 (I): 1-13.

—— (1960) 'The Sudan: An Ethnographic Survey' in S. Diamond (ed.) *Culture in History, Essays in Honour of Paul Radin*. New York: Columbia University Press.


Fardon, Richard and Graham Furniss (1994) *African Languages, Development and the State*. London: Routledge.

Fortes, Meyer (1956) 'Mind' in E.E. Evans-Pritchard et al. *The Institutions of Primitive Society*. New York: Free Press

Fosbrooke, H.A. (1948) 'An Administrative Survey of the Masai Social System', *Tanganyika Notes and Records* 26: 1-50.

Foster-Carter, Aidan (1978) 'Can We Articulate "Articulation"?' in J. Clammer (ed.) *The New Economic Anthropology*. London: Macmillan.

Fratkin, Elliot (1979) 'A Comparison of the Role of Prophets in Samburu and Maasai Warfare' in Fukui and Turton.

—— (1987) 'Age-sets, Households and the Organization of Pastoral Production: The Ariaal, Samburu and Rendille of Northern Kenya', *Research in Economic Anthropology* 8: 295-314.

—— (1991) *Surviving Drought and Development: Ariaal Pastoralists of Northern Kenya*. Boulder, CO: Westview Press.

Fukui, Katsuyoshi and John Markakis (eds) (1994) *Ethnicity and Conflict in the Horn of Africa*. London: James Currey.

Fukui, Katsuyoshi and David Turton (eds) (1979) *Warfare among East African Herders*. Senri Ethnological Studies No. 3. Osaka: National Museum of Ethnology.


Galaty, John G. (1987) 'Form and Intention in East African Strategies of Dominance and Aggression' in McGuinness.

—— (1991) 'Pastoral Orbits and Deadly Jousts: Factors in Maasai Expansion' in Galaty and Bonte.

—— (1993) 'Maasai Expansion and the New East African Pastoralism' in Spear and Waller.

Galaty, John G. and Pierre Bonte (eds) (1991) *Herders, Warriors and Traders*. Boulder, CO: Westview Press.

Galaty, John G., S. Aronson and P.C. Salzman (eds) (1981) *The Future of Pastoral Peoples*. Ottawa: International Development Research Centre.

Githige, D.M. (1978) 'The Religious Factor in Mau Mau with Particular Reference to Mau Mau Oaths'. MA thesis, University of Nairobi.

Glazier, Jack (1976) 'Generation Classes among the Mbeere of Central Kenya', *Africa* 46 (4): 313-26.

Goldschmidt, Walter (1976) *Culture and Behavior of the Sebei*. Berkeley and Los Angeles, CA: University of California Press.

Gough, K. (1971) 'Nuer Kinship: a Re-examination' in T.O. Beidelman (ed.) *The Translation of Culture*. London: Tavistock.

Gray, Robert F. (1963) *The Sonjo of Tanganyika: An Anthropological Study of an Irrigation-Based Society*. London: Oxford University Press.

Gregerson, E.H. (1977) *Language in Africa: An Introductory Survey*. New York: Gordon and Breach.

Grub, Andreas (1992) *The Lotuho of the Southern Sudan: An Ethnological Monograph*. Stuttgart: Franz Steiner Verlag.

Grum, A. (1976) 'Rendille Habitation 1: A Preliminary Report'. (Unpublished).

Guichard, Martine (1996) 'Les Fulbe du Borgou n'ont Vaincu Personne: de la Culture Politique d'une Minorité Ethnique Beninoise'. PhD thesis, Faculty of Sociology, Bielefeld University.

Gulliver, Pamela and P.H. Gulliver (1953) *The Central Nilo-Hamites*. (Ethnographic Survey of Africa). London: International African Institute.

Gulliver, P.H. (1951) *A Preliminary Survey of the Turkana*. Cape Town: Cape Town University Press.

—— (1953) 'The Age-Set Organization of the Jie Tribe', *Journal of the Royal Anthropological Institute* LXXXIII (2): 147-68.

—— (1958a) 'Turkana Age Organization', *American Anthropologist* 60 (5): 900-22.

—— (1958b) *The Family Herds*. London: Routledge & Kegan Paul.

—— (1963) *Social Control in an African Society: A Study of the Arusha: Agricultural Masai of Northern Tanganyika*. London: Routledge & Kegan Paul.

—— (1979) 'Review of *Fundamentals of Age-Group Systems* by Frank Henderson Stewart', *American Anthropologist* 81 (3): 693-4.

Haberland, Eike (1963) *Galla Sudethiopiens*. Stuttgart: Kohlhammer.

Hallpike, C.R. (1986) *The Principles of Social Evolution*. Oxford: Clarendon Press.

Harako, R. (1982) 'The Role of Abela in the Gabra Society: A Case Study of Gerontocratic Society of the Pastoralists', *African Study Monographs*, Supplementary Issue (1): 63-9.

Harrison, Simon (1993) *The Masks of War: Violence, Ritual and the Self in Melanesia*. Manchester: Manchester University Press.

Herskovitz, M.J. (1926) 'The Cattle Complex in East Africa', *American Anthropologist* 28: 230-72, 361-88, 494-528, 633-64.

Hilders, J.H. and J.C.D. Lawrance (1958) *English-Ateso and Ateso-English Vocabulary*. Nairobi: East African Literature Bureau.

Hinnant, John (1978) 'The *Gujii Gada* as a Ritual System' in Baxter and Almagor.

Hino, A.O. (1980) 'A History of Plains-Otuho, 1800-1920'. MA dissertation, Institute of African and Asian Studies, University of Khartoum.

His Majesty's Stationery Office (ed.) (1931) *Kenya Colony and Protectorate, Native Affairs Department Annual Report*. London: HMSO.

Hogg, R.S. (1986) 'The New Pastoralism: Poverty and Dependency in Northern Kenya', *Africa* 56: 319-33.

Hosken, P. (1982) *The Hosken Report: General and Sexual Mutilation of Females*. Lexington, MA: Women's International Network News.

Howell, P.P. (1941) 'The Shilluk Settlement', *Sudan Notes and Records* 24: 47-68.

Hultin, J. (1979) 'Political Structure and the Development of Inequality among the Macha Oromo', *L'Equipe Ecologie*: 283-93.

Human Rights Watch/Africa Watch (1993) *Divide and Rule: State-Sponsored Ethnic Violence in Kenya*. New York, Washington, Los Angeles and London: Human Rights Watch.

Huntingford, G.W.B. (1953a) *The Nandi of Kenya: Tribal Control in a Pastoral Society*. London: Routledge & Kegan Paul.

—— (1953b) *The Southern Nilo-Hamites*. London: International African Institute.

Hutchinson, Sharon E. (1996) *Nuer Dilemmas, Coping with Money, War and the State*. Berkeley, CA: University of California Press.

Jacobs, Alan (1965) 'The Traditional Political Organization of the Maasai'. DPhil. dissertation, University of Oxford.

—— (1979) 'Maasai Inter-Tribal Relations: Belligerent Herdsmen or Peaceable Pastoralists?' in Fukui and Turton.

Jay, Nancy (1992) *Throughout Your Generations Forever. Sacrifice, Religion and Paternity*. Chicago and London: University of Chicago Press.

Jensen, Adolf Ellegard (1936) *Im Lande des Gada*. Stuttgart: Strecker and Schroder.

Jurey, D.A. (1981) *Agriculture among the Lopit Latuka in Eastern Equatoria*. Ithaca, NY: Department of Agricultural Economics, Cornell University.

Kawai, K. (1990) 'What Does Marriage Mean to Each Gender of the Il-Chamus? Husband-Wife Relationships of an East African Agro-pastoral People', *African Study Monographs*, Supplementary Issue 12: 35-49.

—— (1994a) 'The Folk-interpretation of Human Reproduction and Sexual Behavious among the Agro-pastoral Chamus in Kenya' in Y. Takahata (ed.) *Anthropological Studies on Sexuality: Bridging the Gap between*

*Primates and Human Beings*. Kyoto: Sekaishissha (in Japanese).

—— (1994b) 'Anthropological Study of the Ethno-Medical Treatment Systems of the Agro-pastoral Il Chamus in Kenya'. Doctoral dissertation, Faculty of Science, Kyoto University (in Japanese).

Keegan, John (1993) *A History of Warfare*. New York: Hutchinson.

Kenyatta, Jomo (1978, 1938) *Facing Mount Kenya: The Traditional Life of the Gikuyu*. Nairobi: Kenway Publications.

Kertzer, David and Oker B.B. Madison (1980) 'African Age-set Systems and Political Organization: The Latuka of Southern Sudan', *L'Uomo* IV: 84-109.

—— (1981) 'Women's Age-set Systems in Africa: the Latuka of Southern Sudan' in C.L. Fry (ed.) *Dimensions: Aging, Culture and Health*. New York: Bergin.

Kiggen, J. (1953) *Ateso-English Dictionary*. Ngora: Tanganika Mission Press.

King, G.R. (1937) 'The Topotha' in Nalder.

Kipkorir, B.E. (1973) *The Marakwet of Kenya: A Preliminary Study*. Nairobi: East African Literature Bureau.

Kipuri, Naomi N. Ole (1989) 'Diviners and the Transformation of Descent, Age and Gender'. Paper presented at conference 'Seers, Prophets and Prophecy in East African History', School of Oriental and African Studies, University of London, December.

Kituyi, M. (1990) *Becoming Kenyans*. Nairobi: Acts Press.

Komma, Toru (1991) 'Wisdom (*ng'omnotet*) and Riddle (*tangoita*): Adulthood and Childhood in Kipsigisland, Southwestern Kenya', *Social Anthropology Annual* (Tokyo Metropolitan University) 17: 19-50.

Korir, K.M.arap (1974) 'An Outline Biography of Simeon Kiplang'at arap Baliachi, a "Colonial African Chief" from Kipsigis', *Kenya Historical Review* 2 (2): 163-73.

Kurimoto, Eisei (1986) 'The Rain and Disputes: A Case Study of the Nilotic Pari', *Bulletin of the National Museum of Ethnology* 11 (1): 103-61 (in Japanese).

—— (1992a) 'Area, Inter-Ethnic Relations and Ethnography', *Minpaku-tsushin* 65: 93-102 (in Japanese).

—— (1992b) ;An Ethnography of "Bitterness": Cucumber and Sacrifice Reconsidered', *Journal of Religion in Africa* XXII (1): 47-65.

—— (1994) 'Civil War and Regional Conflicts: The Pari and their Neighbours in South-Eastern Sudan' in Fukui and Markakis.

—— (1995a) 'Coping with Enemies: Graded Age System among the Pari of Southeastern Sudan', *Bulletin of the National Museum of Ethnology* 20 (2): 261-311.

—— (1995b) 'Trade Relations between Western Ethiopia and the Nile Valley during the Nineteenth Century', *Journal of Ethiopian Studies* 28 (1): 53-68.

—— (1997) 'Primitive War, Modern War' in T. Aoki et al. (eds) *Conflict and Movement* (Cultural Anthropology Series Vol.3). Tokyo: Iwanami-shoten (in Japanese).

—— (n.d.) 'A Short History of the Pari'. Unpublished paper.

Lado, Eluzai Mogga (ed.) (1981) 'Lulubo in Perspective'. University of Juba (mimeo).

Lamphear, John (1976) *The Traditional History of the Jie of Uganda*. Oxford: Clarendon Press.

—— (1988) 'The People of the Grey Bull: The Origin and Expansion of the Turkana', *Journal of African History* 29: 27-39.

—— (1992) *The Scattering Time: Turkana Responses to the Imposition of Colonial Rule*. Oxford: Oxford University Press.

—— (1994) 'The Evolution of Ateker "New Model" Armies' in Fukui and Markakis.

Lamprey, Richard and Richard Waller (1990) 'The Loita-mara Region in Historical Times' in Robertshaw.

Lang'at, S.C. (1969) 'Some Aspects of Kipsigis History before 1914' in B.G. McIntosh (ed.) *Ngano*. Nairobi: East African Publishing House.

Laughlin, Charles D. Jr and Elizabeth R. Laughlin (1974) 'Age Generations and Political Process in So', *Africa* 44 (3): 266-79.

Lawrance, J.C.D. (1957) *The Iteso*. London: Oxford University Press.

Leach, E.R. (1961) *Rethinking Anthropology*. London; Athlone Press.

—— (1981/1954) *Political Systems of Highland Burma*. London: Athlone Press.

Leakey, L.S.B. (1977) *The Southern Kikuyu before 1903*. London and New York: Academic Press.

Legesse, Asmarom (1973) *Gada, Three Approaches to the Study of African Society*. New York: Free Press.

Lehmann, Arthur C. and Louis J. Mihalyi (1982) 'Aggression, Bravery, Endurance and Drugs: A Radical Re-evaluation and Analysis of the Maasai Warrior Complex', *Ethnology* 21 (4): 335-47.

LeVine, Robert A. and Walter H. Sangree (1962) 'The Diffusion of Age-Group Organization in East Africa', *Africa* 32 (2): 97-110.

Lewis, B.A. (1972) *The Murle: Red Chiefs and Black Commoners*. Oxford: Clarendon Press.

Lewis, H.S. (1965) *A Galla Monarchy: Jimma Aba Jifar, Ethiopia, 1830-1932*. Madison, WI: University of Wisconsin Press.

Lewis, I.M. (1960) 'The Somali Conquest of the Horn of Africa', *Journal of African History* 1: 213-29.

—— (1961) *A Pastoral Democracy: A Study of Pastoralism and Politics among the Northern Somali of the Horn of Africa*. London: Oxford University Press.

—— (1975) 'The Dynamics of Nomadism: Prospects for Sedentarization and Social Change' in T. Monod (ed.) *Pastoralism in Tropical Africa.* London: Oxford University Press.

Lienhardt, Godfrey (1958) 'The Western Dinka' in J. Middleton and D. Tait (eds) *Tribes without Rulers: Studies in African Segmentary Systems.* London: Routledge & Kegan Paul.

Little, D.P. (1983) 'From Household to Region: The Marketing/ Production Interface among the Il Chamus of Northern Kenya'. Doctoral dissertation, Indiana University, Bloomington, IN.

—— (1985) 'Absentee Herd Owners and Part-time Pastoralists: the Political Economy of Resource Use in Northern Kenya', *Human Ecology* 13 (2): 131-51.

—— (1987) 'Woman as Ol Payian (Elder): The Status of Widows among the Il Chamus (Njemps) of Kenya', *Ethnos* 52: 81-102.

—— (1992) *The Elusive Granary: Herder Farmer and State in Northern Kenya.* Cambridge: Cambridge University Press.

Llewelyn-Davies, M. (1981) 'Women, Warriors and Patriarchs' in B.S. Ortner and H. Whitehead (eds) *Sexual Meanings.* Cambridge: Cambridge University Press.

Lomodong Lako, Philip (1995) *Lokoya of Sudan, Culture and Ethnic Government.* Nairobi: Act Print Ltd.

Lonsdale, John (1987) 'La Pensée politique kikuyu et les idéologies du mouvement mau-mau', *Cahier d'Etudes Africaines* XXVII (3-4):309-57.

—— (1992) 'The Moral Economy of the Mau Mau, Wealth, Poverty and Civic Virtue in Kikuyu Political Thought' in Berman and Lonsdale, Vol. II.

Low, Donald Anthony (1975) 'Warbands and Ground-Level Imperialism in Uganda', *Historical Studies* 16 (65).

Lowie, Robert H. (1927) *The Origin of the State.* New York: Harcourt, Brace & Co.

Luttwak, Edward N. (1976) *The Grand Strategy of the Roman Empire.* Baltimore, MD: Johns Hopkins University Press.

Maconi, Vittorio (1973) 'L'iniziazione ai gruppi di etá femminili presso i Karimojong' in Kurt Tauchmann (ed.) *Festschrift zum 65 Geburtstag von Helmut Petri.* Cologne and Vienna: Bohlau Verlag.

Magut, P.K.arap (1969) 'The Rise and Fall of the Nandi Orkoiyot c.1850-1957' in B.G. McIntosh (ed.) *Ngano.* Nairobi: East African Publishing House.

Majima, Ichiro (1997) 'Historical Study on the "Central West Atlantic Region" and the Poro', *Journal of Asian and African Studies* (Tokyo) 53: 1-81.

Manners, R.A. (1962) 'The New Tribalism in Kenya', *Africa Today* 9 (8): 8-14.

—— (1967) 'The Kipsigis of Kenya: Cultural Change in a "Model" East African Tribe' in J.H. Steward (ed.) *Contemporary Changes in Traditional Societies* I. Urbana, IL: University of Illinois Press.

Markakis, J. (ed.) *Conflict and the Decline of Pastoralism in the Horn of Africa.* London: Macmillan.

Matsuda, Hiroshi (1992) 'Dance among the Koegu of Ethiopia: Identity and Interethnic Relations of the Forager', *Bulletin of the National Museum of Ethnology* 17 (1): 35-96 (in Japanese).

—— (1994) 'Annexation and Assimilation: Koegu and their Neighbours' in Fukui and Markakis.

Matsuzono, M. (1994) *The Gusii: Morals and Life among a Peasant Society in Kenya.* Tokyo: Koubund (in Japanese).

Mauss, Marcel (1931) 'La cohésion sociale dans les sociétés polysegmentaires', *Bulletin de l'Institut francais de sociologie* 1. (Reprinted in *Essais de sociologie.* Paris: Editions de Minuit, 1968.)

Maybury-Lewis, D. and U. Almagor (eds) (1989) *The Attraction of Opposites.* Ann Arbor, MI: University of Michigan Press.

McGuinness, Diane (ed.) (1987) *Dominance, Aggression and War.* New York: Paragon.

Meeker, Michael E. (1989) *The Pastoral Son and the Spirit of Patriarchy.* Madison, WI: University of Wisconsin Press.

Mol, Fr. F. (1978) *Maa: a Dictionary of the Maasai Language and Folklore.* Nairobi: Marketing and Publishing Ltd.

Molinaro, R.P.L. (1940/41) 'Appunti circa gli usi, costumi e idee religiose dei Lotuko dell 'Uganda', *Anthropos* XXXV-XXXVI: 166-201.

Molloy, Peter (1957) *The Cry of the Fish Eagle.* London.

Müller-Dempf, Harald K. (1989) *Changing Generations: Dynamics of Generation and Age-Sets in Southeastern Sudan (Toposa) and Northwestern Kenya (Turkana).* Saarbrucken and Fort Lauderdale: Breitenbach (Spectrum).

—— (1991) 'Generation-Sets: Stability and Change, with Special Reference to Toposa and Turkana Societies', *Bulletin of the School of Oriental and African Studies* 54 (3): 554-67.

Mungeam, G.H. (1966) *British Rule in Kenya 1895-1912.* Oxford: Clarendon Press.

Muratori, C. (ed.) (1948) *English Bari-Lotuho-Acoli Vocabulary.* Okaru: Catholic Mission Printing Press.

Nagashima, N. (1972) *Teso Minzokushi: An Ethnography of the Iteso of Uganda.* Tokyo: Chuokorunsha (in Japanese).

—— (1974) 'Age Grade Systems' in *The Encyclopedia Britannica* 15: 728-32. Tokyo: TBS Britannic (in Japanese).

—— (1976) 'Boiling and Roasting', *Hitotsubashi Journal of Social Studies* 8 (1): 42-62.

—— (1987) *Shi to Yamai no Minzokushi (An Ethnography of Death and Sickness: The Ideology of Misfortune among the Kenyan Iteso)*. Tokyo: Iwanami-Shoten.

Nalder, L.F. (ed.) (1937) *A Tribal Survey of Mongalla Province*. London: Oxford University Press.

Newbury, David (1991) *Kings and Clans*. Madison, WI: University of Wisconsin Press.

Novelli, B. (1970) 'Ergologia ed Etnosociologia Lotuho'. PhD thesis, Universita Cattolica del S. Cuore, Milan.

Oda, Makoto (1994) *Fieldwork in Structuralism*. Kyoto: Sekai- shiso-sha (in Japanese).

Orchardson, I.Q. (1961) *The Kipsigis* (abridged, edited and partly rewritten by A.E. Matson from the original manuscripts, 1929-37, Kericho, Kenya). Nairobi: East African Publishing House.

Paolucci, T. (1970) 'Animologia Lotuho'. PhD thesis, Universita Cattolica del S. Cuore, Milan.

Peatrik, Anne-Marie (1995) 'La règle et le nombre: les systèmes d'age et de génération d'Afrique orientale', *L'Homme* 134 (April-June): 13-49.

Peristiany, J.G. (1939) *The Social Institutions of the Kipsigis*. London: Routledge & Kegan Paul.

—— (1951) 'The Age-Set System of the Pastoral Pokot', *Africa* 21: 188-206 and 279-302.

Prins, A.H.J. (1953) *East African Age-Class Systems: An Inquiry into the Social Order of Galla, Kipsigis and Kikuyu*. Groningen and Djakarta: J.B. Wolters.

Rey, P. Ph. (1979) 'Class Contradiction in Lineage Societies'. *Critique of Anthropology* 13 and 14: 41-60.

Robertshaw, Peter (1990) 'Early Pastoralists and Their Herds in the Loita-mara Region' in Robertshaw.

—— (ed.) (1990) *Early Pastoralists of South-Western Kenya*. Nairobi: British Institute in Eastern Africa.

Roscoe, John (1915) *The Northern Bantu*. Cambridge: Cambridge University Press.

Roth, E. (1986) 'The Demographic Study of Nomadic Peoples', *Nomadic Peoples* 20: 63-76.

—— (1993) 'Reexamination of Rendille Fertility Regulation', *American Anthropologist* 95: 597-612.

Ruel, Malcolm J. (1962) 'Kuria Generation Classes', *Africa* 32: 14-37.

Sahlins, M. (1961) 'The Segmentary Lineage: an Organization of Predatory Expansion', *American Anthropologist* 63: 332-45.

Sato, Shun (1980) 'Pastoral Movements and the Subsistence Unit of the Rendille of Northern Kenya: with Special Reference to Camel Ecology' in S. Wada and P.K. Eguchi (eds) *Africa* 2. Senri Ethnological Studies 6. Osaka: National Museum of Ethnology.

—— (1984a) 'Ecology and Societies of East Africa', *African Studies* 24: 54-79 (in Japanese).

—— (1984b) 'The Rendille Subsistence Groups Based on Age System', *African Study Monographs*, Supplementary Issue 3: 45-57.

—— (1986) 'Pastoral Nomadism of the Rendille' in J. Itani and J. Tanaka (eds) *Anthropology of Natural Society: African Way of Life*. Kyoto: Akademia-shuppankai (in Japanese).

—— (1987) 'Subsistence Activities and Dietary Habits' in K. Fukui and Y. Tani (eds *The Original Imagination of Pastoral Cultures: Ecology, Society and Culture*. Tokyo: Nihon-Hosou-Shuppan-Kyoukai (in Japanese).

—— (1988) 'Two Adaptive Strategies: a Socio-ecological Comparison between the Turkana and the Rendille Peoples' in Y. Kohara (ed.) *Anthropology: Adaptation* 9. Tokyo: Yuzankako-Shuppan (in Japanese).

—— (1992a) 'The Camel Trust System in the Rendille Society of Northern Kenya', *African Study Monographs* 13 (2): 69-89.

—— (1992b) *The Rendille: Camel Herders in Northern Kenya*. Tokyo: Kobundo (in Japanese).

—— (1994a) 'The Aspects of Begging Culture: a Way of Life with Livestock' in M. Kakeya (ed.) *The Global Life: Socialization of the Environments* 2. Tokyo: Yuzankaku-Shuppan (in Japanese).

—— (1994b) 'Stock Associate: Personal Relations through Livestock Transactions' in R. Otsuka (ed.) *The Global Life: Socialization of the Environments* 3. Tokyo: Yuzankaku-Shuppan (in Japanese).

Schlee, Günther (1979) *Das Glaubens- und Sozialsystem der Rendille: Kamel-nomaden Nordkenias*. Berlin: Reimer.

—— (1989) *Identities on the Move: Clanship and Pastoralism in Northern Kenya*. Manchester: Manchester University Press; New York: St Martin's Press; Nairobi: Gideon S.Were Press (paperback 1994).

—— (1990) 'Holy Grounds' in Baxter and Hogg.

—— (1992) 'Ritual Topography and Ecological Use: The Gabbra of the Kenyan/Ethiopian Borderlands' in Croll and Parkin.

—— (1994a) '*Gumi Gaayo*: Some Introductory Remarks', *Zeitschrift fur Ethnologie* 119: 17-25.

—— (1994b) 'Ethnicity Emblems, Diacritical Features, Identity Markers: Some East African Examples' in D. Brokensha (ed.) *A River of Blessings: Essays in Honor of Paul Baxter*. Syracuse, NY: Syracuse University Press.

—— (1994c) 'Der Islam und das Gada-System als Konfliktpragende Krafte in Nordost-Afrika', *Sociologus* 44 (2): 112-35.

—— (1994d) 'Loanwords in Oromo and Rendille as a Mirror of Past Inter-Ethnic Relations' in Fardon and Furniss.

—— (in preparation) *Heilige Berge und Pilgerfahrten in Sudethiopien und Nordkenia*.

—— and Abdullahi A. Shongolo (1995) 'Local War and its Impact on Ethnic and Religious Identification in Southern Ethiopia', *GeoJournal* 36 (1): 7-17.

Seligman, C.Z. and B.Z. Seligman (1926) 'The Social Organization of the Lotuko', *Sudan Notes and Records* 8: 1-45.

—— (1932) *Pagan Tribes of the Nilotic Sudan*. London: Routledge & Kegan Paul.

Shongolo, Abdullahi A. (1994) 'The *Gumi Gaayo* of the Boran: A Traditional Legislative Organ and its Relationship to the Ethiopian State and a Modernizing World', *Zeitschrift fur Ethnologie* 119: 27-58.

Simonse, Simon (1984) 'Principles of Lulubo Political Organization: A Preliminary Account of Field Work among the Lulubo of the Southern Sudan'. Juba (mimeo).

—— (1992) *Kings of Disaster: Dualism, Centralism and the Scapegoat King in Southeastern Sudan*. Leiden: E.J. Brill.

—— (1993) 'The Monyomiji Systems of the Southern Sudan', *Nilo-Ethiopian Newsletter* 1: 6-11.

Sobania, N.W. (1980) 'The Historical Tradition of the Peoples of the Eastern Lake Turkana Basin c.1840-1925', PhD thesis, University of London.

Spagnolo, L.M. (1932) 'Some Notes on the Initiation of Young Men and Girls in the Bari Tribe', *Africa* 5 (4): 393-403.

Spear, Thomas and Richard Waller (eds) (1993) *Being Maasai*. London: James Currey.

Spencer, Paul (1965) *The Samburu. A Study of Gerontocracy in a Nomadic Tribe*. London: Routledge & Kegan Paul.

—— (1973) *Nomads in Alliance: Symbiosis and Growth among the Rendille and Samburu of Kenya*. London: Oxford University Press.

—— (1976) 'Opposing Streams and the Gerontocratic Ladder: Two Models of Age Organisation in East Africa', *Man* 11 (2): 153-75.

—— (1978) 'The Jie Generation Paradox' in Baxter and Almagor.

—— (1988) *The Maasai of Matapato, A Study of Rituals of Rebellion*. Manchester: Manchester University Press; Bloomington, IN: Indiana University Press.

—— (1989) 'The Maasai Double Helix and the Theory of Dilemmas' in Maybury-Lewis and Almagor.

—— (1991) 'The Loonkidongi Prophets and the Maasai: Protection Racket or Incipient State?', *Africa* 61: 334-42.

—— (1993) 'Becoming Maasai, Being in Time' in Spear and Waller.

Sperling, L. (1987) 'Wage Employment among Samburu Pastoralists of North-central Kenya', *Research in Economic Anthropology* 9: 167-90.

Spring, Christopher (1993) *African Arms and Armour*. London: British Museum Press.

Stanley, S. and D. Karsten (1968) 'The Luwa System of the Garbicco Subtribe of the Sidama (Southern Ethiopia) as a Special Case of an Age Set System', *Paideuma* 14: 93-102.

Stewart, Frank Henderson (1977) *Fundamentals of Age-Group Systems*. New York: Academic Press.

Sutton, J.E.G. (1973) *The Archeology of the Western Highlands of Kenya*. Nairobi: British Institute in Eastern Africa.

Thom, René (1988) *Esquisse d'une Sémio-physique. Physique Aristotélicienne et Théorie des Catastrophes*. Paris: Interéditions.

Thomas, H.B. (1939) 'Capax Imperii: The Story of Semei Kakunguru', *Uganda Journal* 6 (2): 125-36.

Tomikawa, M. (1979) 'Migrations of the Pastoral Datoga', *Senri Ethnological Studies* 3: 15-31.

Tornay, Serge (1975) 'Générations, classes d'ages et superstructures à propos de l'étude d'une ethnie du cercle karimojong (Afrique orientale)' in Equipe écologie et anthropologie des sociétées pastorales (ed.) *Pastoral Production and Society*. Cambridge/Paris: Cambridge University Press/Editions de la Maison des Sciences de l'Homme.

—— (1979) 'Armed Conflict in the Lower Omo Valley, 1970-1976' in Fukui and Turton.

—— (1981) 'The Nyangatom: An Outline of their Ecology and Social Organization' in M.L. Bender (ed.) *Peoples and Cultures of the Ethio-Sudan Borderlands*. East Lansing, MI: Michigan State University.

—— (1989a) 'Un Système Générationnel: les Nyangatom du Sud-ouest de l/Ethiopie et les Peuples Apparentés'. These d'Etat, Université de Paris X Nanterre. Microfilm edition: Atelier National de Réproduction des theses, Université de Lille III, 1991.

—— (1989b) 'Status individuel et Emergence de l'homme Exemplaire dans une Société sans chef' in *Singularités, Textes pour Eric de Dampierre*. Paris: Plon.

—— (1993) 'More Chances on the Fringe of the State? The Growing Power of the Nyangatom, a Border People of the Lower Omo Valley (1970-1992)' in Tvedt.

—— (1995) 'Structure et Evènement: le Système Générationnel des Peuples du Cercle Karimojong', *L'Homme* 134: 51-80.

Torry, William (1978) 'Gabbra Age Organisation and Ecology' in Baxter and Almagor.

Tosh, J. (1978) *Clan Leaders and Colonial Chiefs in Lango*. Oxford: Clarendon Press.

Toweett, Taaitta (1979) *Oral (Traditional) History of the Kipsigis*. Nairobi: Kenya Literature Bureau.

Trimingham, J.S. (1968) *The Influence of Islam on Africa*. London: Longman.

Turney-High, Harry H. (1991/1949) *Primitive War: Its Practice and Concepts.* Columbia, SC: University of South Carolina Press.

Turton, David (1979) 'War, Peace and Mursi Identity' in Fukui and Turton.

—— (1989) 'Warfare, Vulnerability and Survival: A Case from Southwestern Ethiopia', *Cambridge Anthropology* 13 (2): 67-112.

—— (1993) '"We Must Teach Them to be Peaceful": Mursi Views on Being Human and Being Mursi' in Tvedt.

—— (1994) 'Mursi Political Identity and Warfare' in Fukui and Markakis.

Tvedt, Terje, (ed.) (1993) *Conflicts in the Horn of Africa: Human and Ecological Consequences of Warfare.* Uppsala: Epos, Department of Social and Economic Geography.

Van der Loo, Joseph (1991) *Guji Oromo Culture in Southern Ethiopia.* Berlin: Reimer.

Ville, Jean-Luc (1985) 'Age et succession générationnelle chez les Kikuyu', *Production Pastorale et Société* 17: 83–9.

Waller, Richard (1976) 'The Maasai and the British 1895–1903: The Origin of Alliance', *Journal of African History* 17 (4): 529–53.

Waswa, S. (1950) 'Kakunguru mu Bukedi'. Manuscript in Luganda.

Weatherby, J.M. (1962) 'Inter-Tribal Warfare on Mt. Elgon', *Uganda Journal* 26 (2).

Webster, J. B. et al. (1973) *The Iteso during the Asonya.* Nairobi: East African Publishing House.

Welch, Claude E. Jr (1975) 'Continuity and Discontinuity in African Military Organization', *Journal of Modern African Studies* 13 (2): 229–48.

Wilson, M. (1951) *Good Company. A Study of Nyakyusa.* London: Oxford University Press.

Wolf, J. J. de (1980) 'The Diffusion of Age-Group Organization in East Africa: A Reconsideration', *Africa* 50 (3): 305–10.

Wright, A.C.A. (1942) 'Notes on the Iteso Social Organizations', *Uganda Journal* 9 (2): 57-80.

Zitelman, Thomas (1994) *Nation der Oromo: Kollective Identitten, Nationale Konflikte, Wir-Gruppenbildungen.* Berlin: Das Arabische Buch.

# Index